WITHDRAWAL

D1285596

Confronting
School Bullying

Social Problems, Social Constructions

Joel Best and Scott R. Harris, series editors

Confronting School Bullying

Kids, Culture, and the Making of a Social Problem

Jeffrey W. Cohen
Robert A. Brooks

LYNNE
RIENNER
PUBLISHERS

BOULDER
LONDON

HARVARD UNIVERSITY
GRADUATE SCHOOL OF EDUCATION
MONROE C. GUTMAN LIBRARY

Published in the United States of America in 2014 by
Lynne Rienner Publishers, Inc.
1800 30th Street, Boulder, Colorado 80301
www.rienner.com

and in the United Kingdom by
Lynne Rienner Publishers, Inc.
3 Henrietta Street, Covent Garden, London WC2E 8LU

© 2014 by Lynne Rienner Publishers, Inc. All rights reserved

Library of Congress Cataloging-in-Publication Data
Cohen, Jeffrey W.
Confronting school bullying : kids, culture, and the making of a social
problem / Jeffrey W. Cohen and Robert A. Brooks.
    p. cm. — (Social problems, social constructions)
  Includes bibliographical references and index.
  ISBN 978-1-62637-152-1 (hc : alk. paper)
1. Bullying in schools. 2. Bullying in schools—Prevention.
I. Brooks, Robert Andrew. II. Title.
  LB3013.3.C537 2015
  371.7'82—dc23

                  2014014361

British Cataloguing in Publication Data
A Cataloguing in Publication record for this book
is available from the British Library.

Printed and bound in the United States of America

The paper used in this publication meets the requirements
of the American National Standard for Permanence of
Paper for Printed Library Materials Z39.48-1992.

5   4   3   2   1

Contents

Acknowledgments

T his book has been a collaborative project in every sense. What started as an exploration of disparate news media coverage of two tragic youth suicides in western Massachusetts turned into a three-year project culminating in this book. It has been a difficult and rewarding journey held together by a sense of shared purpose, intellectual curiosity, and mutual support. We both wish to thank Andrew Berzanskis for his initial interest in our project and sustained support as we attempted to make sense of the sometimes dizzying constructions of school bullying. We also thank the outside reviewers, as well as series editors Joel Best and Scott Harris, for their critical, well-informed, and constructive comments on earlier drafts.

Thank you Marilyn, Ron, Matthew, and Rebecca for your unwavering support and love. Thanks also to EY for your strength and creative energy—I am eternally grateful. Finally, thank you Robert for your guidance, mentorship, and above all, friendship.

—*Jeffrey W. Cohen*

Thank you to Worcester State University for granting the sabbatical that allowed me to work on this project and to Jeff for your support and your sense of humor and balance. To Max: May your life be filled with the joy of reading. —*Robert A. Brooks*

May we all find ways to confront the bully in ourselves

1

Bullying and the Shifting Construction of a Social Problem

According to media reports, on Thursday, January 10, 2013, a 16-year-old boy entered his California high school, shot one classmate, and attempted to shoot another before teacher Ryan Heber and school counselor Kim Fields stepped in and defused the situation. Within hours the news media were searching for information and answers. On CNN's *Anderson Cooper 360* (January 10, 2013), correspondent Kyung Lah reported: "According to numerous parents and friends and students we talked to here, this boy had a hit list of . . . people who he wanted to kill." When Cooper asked about the boy's motivation, Lah responded: "What we have learned, Anderson, is that he's a troubled boy. . . . They believe he was bullied because he was so odd." Other CNN programs and other news media broadcasts (for example, *CBS Morning News,* January 11, 2013) also made the connection between the bullying and the shooting. By 2013, the link between retaliatory violence and bullying had become so ingrained that the news media also made it a point to highlight instances in which bullying was not seen as a direct factor. For instance, in a story about a Colorado teen who shot and wounded a teacher and then killed himself, the *Boston Globe* (December 15, 2013) reported that the boy held politically unconventional views but had not been bullied for his beliefs.

In addition to the link between bullying and retaliatory violence, news media accounts also drew connections between bullying and youth suicide. On Thursday, April 4, 2013, just a few months after the previously mentioned California school shooting, 17-year-old Rehtaeh Parson from Nova Scotia, Canada, died by suicide after a photo of what the news media called her 2011 "gang rape" was posted online. Some

1

media commentators claimed Parsons had been "bullied to death" (e.g., Erin Burnett, on her CNN program *Outfront,* April 10, 2013). Just two days after coverage of Parson's suicide had begun, CNN and other news media outlets linked her death to the September 2012 suicide in California of 15-year-old Audrie Pott. Members of the news media reported that Pott had also been bullied after photos of her own gang rape were posted online, and that three teenage boys were charged with the assault. CNN's Don Lemon claimed these two suicides were part of a "disturbing trend among teenagers" that involved house parties and alcohol: "Boys allegedly rape the girl, . . . pictures of rape [are] posted online, the girl [is] blamed, and then bullied and commits suicide" (*Newsroom,* April 12, 2013).

These incidents are only a few of the thousands of stories about bullying we found in news media transcripts; they illustrate that the linking of school bullying to retaliatory violence (e.g., school shootings) and to suicide had by 2013 become a dominant discourse in mainstream news media. Emphasizing such extreme outcomes—and linking them together to suggest first a trend and then an epidemic—is an important factor contributing to how school bullying has come to be perceived as a serious social problem. This contrasts with the early 1990s, when the threat of bullying was usually constructed in rather mild terms. While few dismissed bullying entirely with a "kids will be kids" attitude, descriptions like the following 1993 excerpt from a *New York Times* (*NYT*) "Parent and Child" column were not uncommon: "A 10-year-old who is extorting milk money or threatening to chase a child home after school can loom large in the fears of an 8-year-old. Handing over a quarter a day to avoid possibly being beaten up seems a small price to pay" (October 28, 1993). By 2010, bullying had been elevated to a threat of catastrophic proportions; John Quiñones opened a segment of NBC's *Prime Time Live* by asking: "Harmless bullying? A simple part of growing up? Or a tragic epidemic that leaves entire schools heartbroken, parents childless and families torn apart?" (October 29, 2010).

Besides an elevation of the magnitude of harm, the bullying threat came to be expanded in four other ways. Bullying was defined *down* to include nonproblems like consensual teasing and was defined *up* to include serious criminal offenses within its ambit. Bullying also was defined *out* by taking in more and more students as potential bullies and victims, and by the end of our study period it was regularly being defined *across* many unrelated areas of social life, from the trivial to the tragic. How this expansion occurred, and its impact in shaping explanations for and responses to school bullying, is an important theme of this book. Also of central importance is how the focus on bullying's causes and social control responses shifted between micro and macro levels, at various times emphasizing individuals, families, school institutions, or the larger culture. All of this occurred in a news media environment that favors simplifying complex social problems such as school bullying while also actively engaging in the construction of those problems.

News Media and the Construction of Social Problems

The news does not simply act as a mirror of the culture, even if one could indeed ascertain what "the" culture actually is. Moreover, public understanding of events and issues is highly dependent upon news media representations. Thus the production of news represents a distortion of reality grounded in political, socioeconomic, ideological, and journalistic interests. News, from one point of view, is not a reflection of what's "out there" but only of characteristics of news production (Fishman, 1997, p. 211; Molotch and Lester, 1974, p. 110). For others, the production of news represents a process through which reality is constructed, separate from those kinds of interests. From this perspective, reality exists independent of news media constructions and thus there is some objective aspect to news, unrelated to news production. We see news media as both producing news *and* reflecting cultural phenomena; they act under influences that are both cultural (including political, economic, and ideological forces) and also unique to news production. In addition, we take the view that news media do not simply transmit messages; rather, readers of media decode those messages and construct their own meaning. Some of those meanings may be contrary or resistive to the intended message (see White, 2012, for a summary of media reception theory). Two brief case studies may help illustrate what we mean by these points.

Case Studies in News Media Constructions of School Bullying as a Social Problem

One way media produce news is by constructing particular events as *signal crimes:* "events that, in addition to affecting the immediate participants . . . impact in some way upon a wider audience . . . caus[ing] them to reconfigure their behaviors or beliefs in some way" (Innes, 2003, p. 52). Coverage of the 2010 suicides of Phoebe Prince and Tyler Clementi starkly illustrates how news media claimsmakers actively construct signal crimes. Prince was a 15-year-old living in South Hadley, Massachusetts, who died by suicide in January 2010 in response to what media reports described as months of bullying by so-called mean girls over her dating relationships with two boys at her high school. Clementi was an 18-year-old incoming student at Rutgers University who leapt to his death from the George Washington Bridge on September 22, 2010, shortly after his dorm mate, Dharun Ravi, had streamed images of Clementi engaging in sexual behavior with another man and tweeted about it.

As news media coverage of both suicides intensified, each was framed as the impetus for a national conversation about bullying. Two weeks after Prince's suicide, ABC's Yunji de Nies reported: "Advocates say the country needs to wake up to this 21st century problem" (January 28, 2010). News media responded in force. For example, NBC described her case as "the ultimate example of school bullying" (*NBC Nightly News,* September 5, 2010). Similarly, more than a year after Clementi's suicide, news media claimsmakers noted that it "sparked a chain reaction generating a media and cultural firestorm" (ABC's *20/20,* March 23, 2012) and "became an international symbol of the consequences of bullying and homophobia" (*CBS Evening News,* February 19, 2012). Both suicides were also implicated in the adoption of antibullying legislation at the state level. More than a year after Prince's suicide, CNN legal contributor Sunny Hostin claimed: "Anti-bullying laws have been passed in Massachusetts because of Phoebe Prince. We are all talking about this because of Phoebe Prince. This has set a precedent. Again, bullying will never be seen the same way again" (*Newsroom,* May 5, 2011). The *New York Times* reported that Clementi's suicide "prompted New Jersey lawmakers to adopt one of the nation's toughest civil antibullying laws" (February 25, 2012).

Like other aspects of news, the construction of signal crimes is influenced by factors specific to news production. For instance, contemporary news media operate in a highly competitive, around-the-clock news cycle and thus pay greater attention to events that have news values such as emotion, conflict, and visual impact (McGregor, 2002). The significance of news values has increased with the proliferation of "infotainment" and talk shows, the rise of the blogosphere, the political polarization of media, hyper-competitiveness, and greater delivery of news in video form, on television, and on the Internet. Because events with the highest news values are by definition unique, news media coverage tends to produce a "law of opposites" whereby the most unusual incidents and least-likely victims receive the most attention (Surette,

2007). Within this lopsided coverage—and related to it—arises a hierarchy of victimization with disproportionate focus determined by victims'
demographic characteristics (including class or "respectability," gender,
age, race, ethnicity, and sexuality).

At the top of this hierarchy are *ideal victims,* a group that "includes
those who are perceived as vulnerable, defenseless, innocent and worthy of sympathy and compassion," such as young children (Greer, 2007,
p. 22). Those who are perceived as not possessing these characteristics
may see their stories receive little, if any, coverage. For example, some
studies have shown that crimes involving nonwhite victims receive less
media attention than those involving white victims (Pritchard and
Hughes, 1997; Weiss and Chermak, 1998). Both Phoebe Prince and
Tyler Clementi—young, white, and seemingly naive—were actively
constructed as ideal victims in news media coverage of their suicides.

Prince and Clementi as ideal victims. Initial descriptions of Prince
focused on three main characteristics—her status as a recent immigrant,
her physical appearance, and her age: "By all accounts a lively girl,
newly arrived at school last fall with an Irish brogue, Ms. Prince soon
caught the eye of Sean Mulveyhill, a senior and a football star, and they
briefly dated" (*NYT,* April 2, 2010); "15-year-old Phoebe Prince was an
attractive high school freshman who'd moved to Massachusetts from
Ireland last year" (*CBS Evening News,* March 29, 2010). By focusing on
Prince's status as an immigrant and newcomer to her school, her physical appearance, and her youth, the news media crafted an image of
Prince as especially vulnerable. Constructions of Tyler Clementi as an
ideal victim highlighted similar aspects. Clementi was new to his
school, newly "out," and the "shy aspiring violinist from Ridgewood"
(*NYT,* May 24, 2011). ABC's Chris Cuomo described Clementi as "shy,
reserved, a self-described loner" and a "skilled violinist" (*20/20,* March
23, 2012).

Once constructions of a victim as ideal take hold, news media
claimsmakers tend to maintain them even when faced with more complex narratives. For instance, over time, information related to Prince's
behavioral and psychological history emerged. The eponymous host of
CNN's *The Joy Behar Show* told viewers that Prince had "written essays
about self-mutilation before she committed suicide," noting: "It seems
as though she was tormented for quite a time before" (April 21, 2010).
News media claimsmakers also began to explore Prince's childhood in
Ireland. Freelance journalist Donal Lynch appeared in a report by
NBC's Jeff Rossen on *Today* discussing his interviews with what he

referred to as "many of Phoebe's friends in Ireland," noting: "They told me that [she] had grown up basically as a very happy girl, but in recent years she had kind of undergone a bit of upheaval." Rossen added: "Her parents had separated and her mom had decided to take her to South Hadley. She missed her father very much. She was, you know, not that happy at that point. She had her own baggage at that time" (April 21, 2010). *Slate* magazine's Emily Bazelon noted: "For me, the most surprising thing involved her mental health history because that really hadn't been disclosed" (NBC's *Today,* July 21, 2010).

Additional facts about Tyler Clementi also had the potential to complicate the narrative of the ideal victim. The *New York Times* (August 13, 2011) reported that this new information, including Internet chat transcriptions, created "a more complex picture" of Clementi. According to this newspaper, the Internet chats "appeared to cloud the image of Mr. Clementi as a shy, violin-playing innocent." (Because no new information was cited that would "cloud" Clementi's musicianship, we have to assume that, for the media, playing the violin marked Clementi as a particularly sensitive person.) The *New York Times* claimed that the transcripts "do not portray a man fearful of having his sexual orientation disclosed" and that Clementi "played down [his roommate's] telling people" about his sexual encounter. The transcripts also included Clementi making "some raunchy sexual comments" on an Internet site and evaluating his roommate as being "sooo indian/first gen american-ish" that his parents were sure to own a Dunkin' Donuts. ABC's Chris Cuomo reported: "The reticent violinist had been in turmoil. . . . Lost in the media crush, Tyler had been writing about his own depression, his loneliness and the rejection he felt after coming out to his parents" (*20/20,* March 23, 2012). In both cases, however, these layers of complexity did not significantly alter preexisting news media constructions. In fact, reports such as these were relatively rare and short-lived.

The evil predator. In juxtaposition to the narrative of the ideal victim, news media constructions of signal crimes employ the image of the evil predator, whose behavior tends to be described in increasingly menacing tones. This was definitely the case of both Prince's and Clementi's alleged bullies, especially after the announcement of criminal charges. Ten weeks after Prince's suicide, district attorney Elizabeth D. Scheibel held a news conference in which she announced the filing of adult criminal charges against six students at South Hadley High School, where Prince had been a student. Three additional students were charged as juveniles, as reported in the *New York Times* (March 30, 2010) the day after the press conference. Up until this point, few commentators in the broadcast media and none of the *New York Times* articles had mentioned Prince's suicide, let alone the status of the case as a national example. It wasn't until the filing of charges that the importance of the Prince case took hold. While this was not the first time charges had been filed against an alleged bully, the seriousness of the offenses worked to situate the Prince case as unique. Prince's alleged bullies were charged with offenses including statutory rape, criminal harassment, stalking, and violation of civil rights. Scheibel, during her press conference, noted that the bullying that Prince endured on the day of her suicide was "the culmination of a nearly three-month campaign of verbally abusive and assaultive behavior and threats of physical harm" (CNN's *Campbell Brown,* March 30, 2010). Drawing on the initial description provided by Scheibel, news media and other claimsmakers began to emphasize the seriousness of the bullying as well as its prolonged nature. The bullying was referred to as consisting of "physical threats," "verbal abuse," "harassment," and even "torture." Terms such as "relentless" were used to articulate the fact that the bullying had begun long before Prince's suicide.

Criminal charges also seemed to be the impetus for wider coverage of the Tyler Clementi case and greater focus on the young man who was said to have caused Clementi's suicide. In response to Clementi's suicide, Dharun Ravi, his dorm mate, was charged with and eventually convicted of crimes that carried the potential of a ten-year sentence, although he was ultimately sentenced to only thirty days in jail by a trial judge. The initial charging documents and trial testimony alleged that Ravi had twice streamed video images from his webcam to his computer. However, the media described Ravi's actions in ways that were frequently ambiguous and incomplete. What was streamed, and to whom and where, was often left unanswered. The lack of details likely led the public to assume the worst. As Chris Cuomo reported on ABC's *20/20* (March 2, 2012), media reports may have led the public to incorrectly believe "that Ravi not only watched Tyler having sex with his male lover, but that he secretly recorded the act, posted the video online, and outed his roommate out of spite."

Cultural influences. As mentioned earlier, broader cultural factors, including political, economic, and ideological forces, also influence news production. Our two case studies provide some illustration of this as well. While there were relatively few instances in which the evil predator construction was challenged in the Prince case, there were frequent debates in news media about how to frame the behavior of Dharun Ravi in relation to Clementi, even as he himself was almost universally condemned. A frequent question was whether the behavior was—as the *New York Times* (October 1, 2010) put it—"a thoughtless prank or a crime." This question was increasingly likely to be posed as the trial verdict approached and also after the verdict, and was asked in a variety of ways: "Was this . . . a malicious homophobe . . . or . . . a stupid prankster? (CNN's *Newsroom,* February 21, 2012); "Was it homophobia? Was it adolescent stupidity?" (CNN's *Erin Burnett Outfront,* March 1, 2012). As we detail later, the broader discourse on sexuality within news media and US society served to limit the discursive resources available to those who attempted to construct Clementi as an ideal victim and Ravi as an evil predator. Prince's case, however, fit comfortably within existing constructions of gender within the broader cultural discourse.

Coverage of these two cases was also influenced by the existing discourse of bullying. For instance, not only did the filing of criminal charges situate these two cases as unique (and therefore newsworthy), but they also constituted a simplification of the bullying narrative by articulating a direct link between bullying and suicide. The day after the district attorney's press conference regarding Prince's "bullycide,"[1] CNN's Tony Harris claimed: "Hard to believe. Bullied to death, literally" (*Newsroom,* March 30, 2010). After Clementi took his own life, news media also articulated a direct link between bullying and suicide among lesbian, gay, bisexual, and transgender (LGBT) youth: "bullying related to sexual orientation or perceived sexual orientation [was] *the* cause of some of the recent suicides" (*NYT,* May 29, 2011).[2] Additionally, by situating these two cases as signal crimes within the broader discourse on bullying, news media and other claimsmakers were able to present bullycide as additional evidence of a growing epidemic of (school) bullying. There now existed a national news media platform from which claimsmakers could articulate the need to treat school bullying with increased seriousness and impose mechanisms of social control.

Theoretical and Methodological Orientation

It may already be evident that our analysis of news media discourse regarding school bullying is grounded in a constructionist lens. As such, we view social problems as emerging from and being sustained through concerted human action, particularly discourse (Berger and Luckmann, 1966; Blumer, 1971). Whether a phenomenon such as school bullying is widely acknowledged as a social problem depends more on the outcome of an often highly contentious process of claimsmaking activities than on an assessment of the problem as intrinsically harmful, unhealthy, or unnatural (Spector and Kitsuse, 1977). This process of claimsmaking is most publicly carried out in news media. Therefore, our analysis focuses on national news outlets across multiple formats. From television, we focused on the news divisions of ABC, CBS, CNN, Fox, and NBC. From radio, we selected National Public Radio (NPR). And from the print media, we selected the *New York Times*. We accessed transcripts using the Lexis-Nexis database, which provides textual transcripts for newspaper articles and television and radio shows. We analyzed transcripts from each media source from January 1, 1992, until June 30, 2013. Our analysis was grounded in a critical realist methodological framework. Those interested in a more detailed discussion of our methodology are encouraged to read the Appendix at the back of the book.

Traditionally, constructionist researchers have focused almost exclusively on *how* social problems are constructed, shying away from statements about the broader implications of those constructions. We adopt a more contextual approach that recognizes that it is neither desirable nor possible to ignore the broader contexts in which social problems are constructed. We must, therefore, not only consider *how* a social problem is constructed through discourse, but *what* it is that is being constructed and *why*. In terms of what is being constructed, we must address larger cultural and social contexts that serve to both provide and limit the kinds of discursive resources that are available (Gubrium and Holstein, 2008), as we suggested earlier in relation to Clementi's sexuality. In terms of the why, we must be able to explain the intentional and unintentional implications of the construction of a particular social problem (Bogard, 2003). In line with the view through our contextual constructionist lens, we not only describe the process through which school bullying came to be constructed as a serious social problem, but also put forth the argument that its construction has broad cultural and social implications.

The Construction of School Bullying

Understanding how any cultural phenomenon has been constructed requires that we pay close attention to both popular and academic discourse. Each has its own methods of constructing social problems. Contrary to predominant notions of social science, academic scholars and researchers are not simply reporting reality; rather, they are producing realities through their application of particular disciplinary, theoretical, and methodological practices (Law, 2004). Hacking (1999, pp. 33–34) suggests that research creates purported facts that can create looping effects by influencing the behavior that is the subject of study. Interestingly, the mass media work in similar ways, as we explore in Chapter 7. Thus, both news media claimsmakers and researchers work to construct particular realities of bullying. Sometimes these realities work to more deeply entrench one another; at other times these realities compete with one another for legitimacy. That which is held as a valid truth claim regarding school bullying in one context may be expanded, adapted, or ignored in another. Definitions of school bullying are continuously re-negotiated within and across these contexts. As we will see throughout this book, news media constructions of bullying overlap with, but also differ from, constructions of bullying within academic discourse, leading some to suggest that definitions of school bullying held by researchers may differ quite substantially from those held by the general public (Griffin and Gross, 2004). Situating our analysis of news media constructions of school bullying in relation to the academic literature is important because the popular press often references researchers as experts, who thus serve as trusted claimsmakers regarding school bullying, its impact, and potential strategies for intervention. In addition, the findings of researchers are touted as evidence, lending credibility to efforts to curb school bullying, whether or not these findings are grounded in an accurate interpretation of their research.

The convergence of news media and public attention to bullying is in fact implicated in the emergence of school bullying as an area of academic study. Researchers trace the beginnings of academic interest in school bullying to widespread media and public attention in Norway in response to two bullying-related suicides—regarded as the impetus for Dan Olweus's work in the late 1970s and early 1980s (Beaty and Alexeyev, 2008; Griffin and Gross, 2004; Hoover and Stenhjem, 2003; Kochenderfer-Ladd and Troop-Gordon, 2010; Schoen and Schoen, 2010; Smith, 2004; Stassen Berger, 2007). However, it took a few more decades for bullying to become a sustained focus of research in the United States. In an analysis of citations from peer-reviewed journals in several online databases, Stassen Berger (2007) noted that attention to bullying in academic literature in the United States seemed to increase dramatically during the beginning of the twenty-first century. In particular, the study by Nansel and colleagues (2001) of the prevalence of bullying in the United States seems to mark the beginnings of more focused attention to bullying in US contexts (Spivak, 2003), and continues to serve as a rallying point for those who frame bullying as an epidemic worthy of serious concern. Moreover, attention to bullying in the United States is also intimately tied to the link between bullying and retaliatory violence, as articulated in both academic and popular discourse in the 1990s, such as in claims in the wake of the Columbine school shootings. As illustrated in later chapters, attention to bullying in the United States is also linked to bullycides. While our analysis focuses on news media and academic constructions of bullying within the United States, it is important to note that the literature on school bullying had a long history in European countries and elsewhere (most significantly in Japan) prior to garnering attention in the United States.

Over time, researchers have worked to construct a more stable definition of bullying; however, there are competing claims regarding the extent to which they have succeeded. Definitions of bullying are often relatively vague and imprecise, and vary across methodology and study context (Carrera, DePalma, and Lameiras, 2011; Griffin and Gross, 2004; Horton, 2006; Stassen Berger, 2007). Carrera, DePalma, and Lameiras suggest that "it is not simply that we lack a universally accepted definition of what many refer to as 'bullying,' but that the terminology itself, as deployed across different national contexts and languages, is varied and imprecise" (2011, p. 481). Even while acknowledging the difficulty of constructing a universal definition of bullying, academic researchers seem to agree on some common elements: repetition, a power imbalance, and (serious) harm (see Carrera, DePalma, and Lameiras, 2011; Greene, 2000; Griffin and Gross, 2004; Stassen Berger, 2007). These three elements come from the work of Dan Olweus, whose definition of bullying—"intentional, repeated, negative (unpleasant or hurtful) behavior by one or more persons directed against a person who has difficulty defending himself or herself" (Olweus and Limber, 2010, p. 125)—is often cited. This definition, and the three elements associated with it, remain dominant in the bullying literature (see, for instance, Griffin and Gross, 2004; Horton, 2006; Schoen and Schoen, 2010; Volk et al., 2012).

However, Carrera, DePalma, and Lameiras caution that "the notions of intentionality, repetition, and power imbalance, while accepted and employed in the majority of bullying research, remain subject to a certain lack of consensus within the academic community" (2011, p. 486). The lack of consensus seems to be more an issue of measurement than of conceptual consistency. It isn't that researchers are unable to agree on these fundamental elements of bullying as much as they are unable to come to agreement regarding the ways in which they should be measured. As Stassen Berger suggests: "The triad cited earlier—harmful, repeated, unequal—is generally accepted but specifics are not. For example, how often, [and] within what time period, must incidents be repeated to cross the line from occasional unpleasantness to bonafide bullying" (2007, p. 100). As we will see, news media and other claims-makers have not come to consensus either.

Analytic Themes

Our analysis of news media constructions of school bullying led to three important analytic themes. First, bullying became subject to domain expansion, whereby its meaning grew in various directions. Second, the causes of and social control responses to bullying shifted unsteadily among different explanatory levels, from the individual to the cultural. Last, the media and its claimsmakers oversimplified bullying in numerous ways. Each of these three processes occurred in an interdependent fashion and within a competitive news media environment. Each also occurred in the context of a continuous expansion of harm that worked to construct school bullying as an ever-growing and ever-worsening epidemic, and had implications for which formal and informal social control responses were deemed most appropriate.

Analytic Theme 1: Domain Expansion

Domain expansion can happen in a number of ways. *Substantive* domain expansion occurs when areas not originally thought of as aspects of the problem become incorporated through claimsmaking activities. It "involves rendering more and more conduct and/or social conditions 'at issue'" (Jenness, 1995, p. 233) and is an expansion of the "substantive territory" of the problem (Grattet, Jenness, and Curry, 1998). For example, Weitzer (2007) demonstrated how the original social problem of sex trafficking first expanded to take in prostitution—even when legally sanctioned—and then pornography. Best (1990) delineated the process by which the rather narrow "battered child" typification was expanded first to "child abuse" and then further to "child abuse and neglect." This shift was accomplished through deliberate and coordinated claimsmaking activities. But Best (1990, pp. 75–77) also provided a number of examples of entities outside the movement applying the label "child abuse" to a wide variety of conditions and behaviors that were likely unforeseen by the primary claimsmakers, such as circumcision, violence in rock music, and inadequate social services. Coincidentally, we found an instance of the news media referring to bullying as "a disturbing form of child abuse" (ABC's *Good Morning America,* January 19, 1999).

In terms of substantive domain expansion, definitions and applications of school bullying have expanded in four ways. The first kind of substantive domain expansion involves defining school bullying *down,* and it has occurred in two ways: (1) inclusion of behaviors that are probably unproblematic, such as apparently consensual "teasing" and "horseplay"; and (2) inclusion of youth conflicts that lack a traditional element of bullying, such as a power differential or repeated behavior (e.g., arguments and "drama" could be recast as bullying).[3] Interestingly, concerns about defining down emerged at the same time that news media began to define bullying *up* by conflating it with behaviors between or among youth that they had previously constructed as solely criminal. We found many instances where news media claimsmakers labeled onetime aggravated assaults between people who had not previously met as "bullying." We also considered formal social control responses that criminalized "common" kinds of bullying as a type of defining up if there were claims that they contributed to an extreme outcome such as a youth suicide. For instance, it is extremely unlikely that those who bullied Phoebe Prince would have been criminally charged had she not taken her life. The same can be said of Dharun Ravi's charges after the death of Tyler Clementi.

News media also engaged in defining *out* to include a wider range of individuals as likely bullies and victims. This sometimes was accomplished through reporting on academic studies that purported to enlarge the scope of potential bullies and victims. For example, several media outlets featured the research of Robert Faris and Diane Felmlee, sociologists at the University of California–Davis, who claim that bullying is a widespread and normative practice among most students and constitutes a process by which they jockey for social power and status. In addition to academics, other claimsmakers defined bullying out. For instance, some claimed that everyone has been a bully or a victim (or both) at some point. The fourth substantive domain expansion uncovered in our analysis, defining *across,* occurred when school bullying was analogized to other kinds of matters, from the insignificant to the very serious. By the end of our study period, bullying was regularly being defined across many unrelated areas of social life; we found claims that both communism and the singing of religious Christmas carols constituted bullying. In other words, the term "bullying" had become a catchall for any perceived form of abuse of power, regardless of quality or quantity (see also Horton, 2006). As depicted in Figure 1.1, while instances of defining bullying down occurred in the late 1990s and early 2000s, it wasn't until around 2009 that news media constructions of school bullying began to articulate all four kinds of domain expansion in quick succession and ultimately simultaneously. As we point out later in this book, these four types of domain expansion served to further confuse the news media discourse.

A second type of domain expansion, *rationale* expansion, was also evident in our analysis. Rationale expansion involves adding justifications for why certain conditions are objectionable. Kunkel (1999) showed how animal rights movements originally relied on arguments against "cruelty to animals" in opposing vivisection and factory farming. When this claim did not create sufficient traction, the activists expanded their rhetoric to incorporate concerns more likely to connect with the public, such as threats to the environment and misuse of tax money. In an analysis of news media coverage of the Columbine school

Figure 1.1 Domain Expansion Across Time

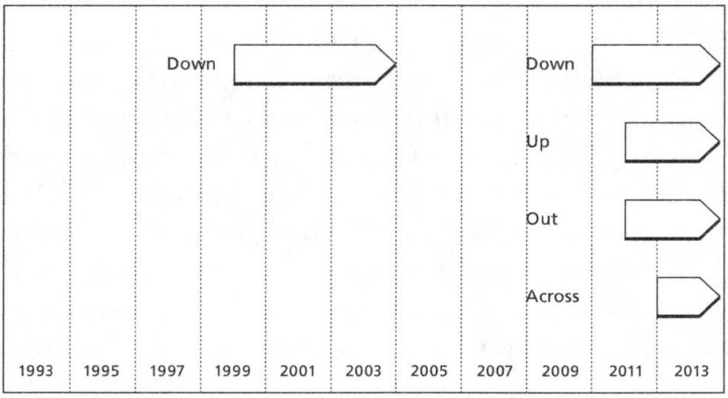

shootings, Muschert noted that the story was enlarged through an "expansion of the sphere of concern about Columbine-type crimes to include the wider national import of the crime" (2009, p. 169). In our analysis, we found that rationale expansion occurred when the media began to report on the homophobic *content* of bullying. Here, claims-makers asserted that bullying is "bad" because it reflects social intolerance. Both substantive and rationale expansion occurred simultaneously, but with different patterns of shifting focus.

Analytic Theme 2: Explanatory Shift

We found that the media's identification of the causes of bullying, and the suggested formal and informal social control responses thereto, shifted across various levels of explanation over time. In the broadcast media, we witnessed a general pattern (although not necessarily linear) over our study period (1992 to 2013). An individual focus was long favored, following which the attention turned to the larger society and culture then on to the familial and institutional (schools) level, and finally returned to the individual. At each stage, the prior causal explanations and social control responses were not completely abandoned. Thus, by the end of our study period there were several competing discourses that the news media made little attempt to reconcile or integrate, as illustrated in Figure 1.2.

Figure 1.2 Explanations for Bullying Across Time

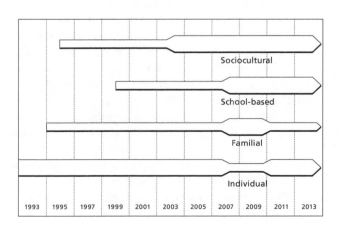

Analytic Theme 3: Oversimplification

School bullying is perhaps best understood as a complex constellation of processes that flow out of everyday behaviors and interactions, which themselves almost always involve some degree of conflict. Mishna (2012) exposes myriad contradictions and complexities, referring to the "phenomena" rather than the "phenomenon" of school bullying. As evidenced by the news media discourse, it is often difficult to determine exactly when "normal behavior" becomes problematic, which leads to bullying being identified with a wide range of behaviors that may in actuality require a wide range of responses.

Add to this the paradox of youth violence discussed later, and we begin to see just how difficult it is to balance the drive to help kids make better decisions and solve their own problems, with the drive to protect them from being harmed by their peers or themselves. Attempts to distill the complexity of school bullying down to a single phenomenon is inherently problematic and leads to the kinds of confusion that we suggest have plagued news media and popular discourse during the past two decades.

Implications

These three analytic themes are interrelated in ways that have serious implications for our understanding of and responses to school bullying. Through domain expansion, important distinctions are ignored. As playful and consensual teasing is conflated with serious violence, for instance, nuanced responses grounded in the inherent differences among these kinds of behaviors are jettisoned for mechanisms of control over individual students. Institutional and sociocultural responses—which could be both numerous and thorny—are dismissed or ignored in favor of increasingly punitive individual-level responses that mirror criminal justice practices. Responsibility for preventing school bullying, historically within the purview of schools and parents, shifts to the state through legislation, then to the federal level as policymakers take the stage to consider laws or regulations that mandate state requirements, and then down to the individual through the process of criminalization. Kids, of course, are easy targets, because they lack power to construct their own realities or define their own situations in ways that inform or problematize the public discourse. Thus they are the ultimate "docile bodies" in that they "can be subjected, used, transferred, and improved" (Foucault, 1977, p. 136) without the inconvenience of having to recognize their own lived experiences.

The end result is a distorted, confused, and conflicted discourse that fails to reconcile the complexity of school bullying with attempts to effectively address its root causes. It is clear to us that the term "bullying" has become so ubiquitous in popular discourse that its meaning has been blurred to the point that any and all problematic behavior on the part of today's youth can become emblematic of the growing epidemic of school bullying. Throughout this book, we explore the consequences of this ubiquity. More specifically, we explore the construction of school bullying as a social problem within news media discourse over the past two decades. In so doing, we trace the evolution of the discourse of school bullying, from its construction as a relatively innocuous part of adolescent development, to its construction as a serious social problem in need of widespread, large-scale policy remedies at the local, state, and national levels, with the ultimate effect of reestablishing informal and formal mechanisms for the social control of youth.

However, in line with the view through our contextual constructionist lens, it is not enough to simply describe the process through which school bullying came to be constructed as a serious social problem; we must also address "how broad cultural values, assumptions, expectations, and the like are employed and, in turn, given specific shape and meaning in this discourse" (Spencer, 2011, p. 13). Like Spencer's recognition of "broad cultural understandings of youth, gender, violence, and the city as a social place" as "interpretive resources" (p. 14) for understanding media constructions of youth violence, our analysis identifies broader cultural understandings of youth aggression, gender, and sexuality as resources for the construction of school bullying as a social problem.

Youth Aggression

It is our contention that responses to school bullying are grounded in long-standing attempts to control youth behavior. In addition, the discourse of school bullying taps into competing constructions of youth as both vulnerable and dangerous. For example, Daniel Scruggs was a 12-year-old boy who regularly was sent to school unbathed (*NYT,* September 27, 2003). Once there, he was mercilessly bullied and would defecate in his pants so that he would be sent home. In the months before his suicide, he missed forty-four days of school. Scruggs died by suicide in 2003 by hanging himself in the family home. Critics blamed his mother for Daniel's condition and his school for failure to act. More recently, in 2012, middle school students peppered their bus monitor,

Karen Klein, with insults that were shockingly heartless and obscene. The ten-minute video of the incident needs to be viewed in its entirety to understand the everyday depravity into which young people can sometimes sink.

The stories of Scruggs and Klein present the conundrum of how children can be simultaneously seen as both helpless, naive innocents in need of protection and also as violent predators in need of social control. As one newspaper put it: "We protect children from danger, from drugs, from disease. But how do we protect them from each other?" (*Berkshire Eagle,* February 26, 2011). Spencer (2011) terms this uneasy pairing the "paradox of youth violence." One common means of solving the paradox is to create a false binary that categorizes children as either "good" or "bad," with the goal being to protect the good ones and to punish or "fix" the bad ones, as seen in our case studies. Even if this construction were tenable, which it isn't, it would not address the question of how "bad" children come to be that way, or what to do about it. Differing answers to these questions direct differing social policies. The child savers of the Victorian age believed that "children are more sinned against than sinning" and thus "they are what they have been brought up to be" (*Our Sydney Letter,* 1911). In this formulation, the most compassionate response is to change the conditions under which children live. We find echoes of this sentiment as of this writing, but more common are "get tough" policies that focus on punishment rather than on addressing etiology.

The idea of treating schoolchildren like criminals may seem extreme. However, such an approach has gained considerable traction considering the rather bleak but rather common view expressed in news media that youth aggression simply comes from "the pitilessness of childhood . . . [and] is most likely a constant quantity" (*NYT,* March 3, 2013). News media and other claimsmakers constantly evoke a sense that youth violence is on the rise even as juvenile offense rates are dropping. The resulting "moral panic" of youth violence (Schissel, 1997) has led to an increase in the forms, methods, and severity of informal and formal social control directed at children. Casella (2001) calls this the "kid crackdown"; this is highly evident in US schools, which have become militarized through physical means (metal detectors and armed security officers) and through draconian policies such as "zero tolerance" (Robbins, 2008).

But schools have not acted in a vacuum. Agents of formal social control—lawmakers, law enforcers, courts, and the juvenile justice system—have enabled this increasing punitivity, some of which has surely "trickled down" from the adult justice system. Approximately 100,000 children are now arrested annually in US schools, a disciplinary response that appears to have been encouraged by the increasing number of armed school resource officers stationed in schools (see Justice Policy Institute, 2011). NBC's *20/20* questioned this mixture of "cops and kids" in a broadcast that featured a 12-year-old student who was arrested for doodling on her desk and a 5-year-old arrested for throwing a tantrum (September 28, 2012). Similarly, CNN reported that a 7-year-old was arrested for stealing another student's lunch money (*Newsroom,* January 31, 2013). The courts have also abetted the kid crackdown. For instance, in 2002 the US Supreme Court upheld random (suspicionless) drug testing of children as young as middle school age, finding that the policy's social purposes outweighed students' privacy interests under the Fourth Amendment.

Furthermore, federal and state legislators increasingly set local school policies. For instance, one early impetus for zero tolerance was the 1994 Gun Free Schools Act, which tied federal education aid to a requirement that schools institute a one-year expulsion policy for firearm possession. Three years later, 94 percent of US public schools had zero-tolerance policies for firearms, 91 percent for other weapons, 88 percent for drugs, and 87 percent for alcohol (Kaufman et al., 2000). The federal No Child Left Behind Act of 2001 and the Common Core standards adopted by most states have opened up more space for regulation at both the state and federal levels. Walton refers to "the great tide of accountability" that has swept schools, resulting in "cultures of authoritarianism and control, not only in codes of student conduct but in curriculum as well" (2005, p. 111). There is no shortage of book-length critiques of these policies, such as *Responding to School Violence* (Muschert et al. 2014), *Punishing Schools* (Lyons and Drew, 2006), *Lockdown High* (Fuentes, 2011), *Governing Through Crime* (Simon, 2007), and *Police in the Hallways* (Nolan, 2011). However, the policies remain widely prevalent.

Walton (2005) suggests that peer violence flows expectedly when hierarchical relations are combined with social oppression and a "might makes right" attitude. Although Walton doesn't mention it, this idea has a rather clear counterpart in cultural criminology, which theorizes criminal behavior and other deviance as resistance to authority. We could easily appropriate the following description by replacing "crime" with "bullying": Crime is a way for one to break free from "one's demeaning and restraining circumstances, to exercise control and take responsibility for one's own destiny. In a world in which individuals find themselves over-controlled and yet without control, crime offers the possibility of excitement *and* control" (Jewkes, 2011, p. 33, emphasis in original).

Adorno (1998) adopts a more sustained theoretical critique of educational practices. His theory is too complex to be explained fully here, but we can illustrate the relevance of his broad argument to the current discussion. Adorno believes that schools are in a unique place to combat barbarism and fascism. However, he finds that these institutions replicate what he terms the hyper-fascism of late capitalism through the qualities of hardness, coldness, and alienation. "Hardness" is attained by inoculating students from their own pain and from the guilt of feeling the pain of others. "Coldness" engenders an indifference to and isolation from others. These characteristics are achieved through methods of violence (physical and psychological), among others. Psychological violence includes an atmosphere of hyper-competitiveness in which students are reduced to objects. As to physical violence, Adorno finds "hyper-masculine bullying" to be one means by which hardness and coldness are embodied. He writes: "The child who in school experiences coldness, anxiety, [and] the pressure of the collective, psychologically saves himself by displacing it onto others, and groups form in order, as it were, to pass this burden of alienation onto others" (1998, p. 296). Thus, for youth who are experiencing the continued growth of educational militarism and its associated mechanisms of informal and formal social control, it is not too far a stretch to suggest that school bullying serves as a form of resistance. It is our contention that the very forms of control imposed *by* adults *on* youth are repurposed as a mechanism of informal social control employed *by youth* to enforce conformity in ways that mimic broader cultural discourses, especially around gender and sexuality.

Gender

Much of the mainstream academic and popular discourse of gender continues to be oriented around a fundamental distinction between sex as biologically determined and gender as a social construction. According to Beasley: "Gender in this setting was seen as a reference to 'social construction.' The word implied a radical critique of conservative views that asserted biological determinism" (2005, p. 13). Prior to the sex-gender split, purported biological dimorphism (i.e., the existence of two distinct sexes) both explained and justified gendered social structures.

There is no doubt that feminist and other scholars have done incredible work in weakening the hold of biological essentialism by situating gender as a social construction in contrast to biological sex. However, recent scholarship suggests that the sex-gender split suffers from its own limitations.

First, this split serves to further entrench the notion that biological sex is static and in no way impacted by social or cultural dynamics. In an attempt to challenge prevailing biological essentialism, the sex-gender dichotomy both opened the space for a discussion of the social construction of gender and, to some extent, closed the door on explorations of how biological sex is also in many ways socially constructed. Second, the sex-gender split has not wholly moved us away from sexual dimorphism. As Messerschmidt points out, scholars continue to assume "that there exist only two 'natural' sexes (male and female) and, therefore, but two genders (masculine and feminine)" (2006, p. 36). This leads to a third limitation—the continued conflation of sex and gender. If the categories of male and female represent innate biological realities, and two corresponding genders exist in ways that mirror those biological realities through social and cultural expressions, then what is the difference between sex and gender? Put differently, if all the things male-bodied individuals do, say, and think are viewed through the lens of masculinity and all the things female-bodied individuals do, say, and think are viewed through the lens of femininity, then what is articulated as the social construction of gender is actually just a different language through which we perpetuate sex and gender binaries.

What is perhaps most missing from the discourse of the sex-gender dichotomy is recognition that both are in fact social constructions. What many believe to be concrete biological traits that establish someone as either male or female are better understood as culturally embedded characteristics that work to reify gender (Messerschmidt, 2006). It is not that biology does not exist as physical reality. However, the degree to which biology is used to determine who is male and who is female is a choice made in particular social and cultural contexts and not in others (see also Cohen, 2008; Cohen and Martin, 2012).

Instead of eliminating biological essentialism, the sex-gender dichotomy has in many ways worked to make implicit what was previously explicit. While scholars, activists, and individuals work to fight the existence of gender stratification and discrimination across multiple arenas (e.g., work, politics, and family), many unwittingly reinforce established binaries. These dynamics have led some scholars to rethink the goal of feminist movements and call for what Lorber refers to as a "feminist degendering movement" in which we begin to "think beyond gender to the possibilities of a non-gendered social order" (2000, p. 81). As we will see in Chapter 5, such a social order is far from the current reality of the lived experience of youth.

The very fact that gendered norms and gendered bodies must be continually renegotiated and reinforced is itself an indication of gender as a social construction. In other words, if gender were indeed the result of innate biological differences between two distinct sexes, then there would be no need to continually police the boundaries of appropriate behavior along gendered lines. Building on Butler's work (2009), however, we posit that the use of bullying as a mechanism for the informal social control of gendered norms is part and parcel of gender and sex as social constructions, and, more to the point, as performance. Gender and sex are something that we *do,* not something that we *are.* As such, "there is no gender without [the] reproduction of norms that risks undoing or redoing the norm in unexpected ways, thus opening the possibility of a remaking of gendered reality along new lines" (Butler, 2009, p. i). Of course, those who violate gender norms are placed in a precarious position. As Butler suggests, "Those who do not live their genders in intelligible ways are at heightened risk for harassment and violence. Gender norms have everything to do with how and in what way we can appear in public space" (p. ii).

By understanding gender and sex as social constructions that require both performance and constant renegotiation, we open the space for three important insights. First, both sex and gender are more fluid than we often acknowledge. Second, both are confluences of distinct yet interrelated phenomena operating at micro (individual) and macro (sociocultural) levels. Third, and perhaps most relevant for our analysis of school bullying, gender and sex, like any other social construction, require persistent maintenance and monitoring, especially during adolescence, when individuals are exploring the boundaries of normativity and establishing more concrete identities. As we will explore in more detail in Chapter 5, school bullying serves as one mechanism through which the social construction of gender is monitored and maintained. In other words, school bullying serves as a form of informal social control employed by adolescents to police peer behavior and establish the boundaries of gender normativity. Violation of gender normativity is deeply implicated in bullying victimization in schools, especially for girls and young women who violate norms of appearance and sexual behavior. To put it more simply, bullying is one mechanism through which girls are taught what are acceptable female bodies and behaviors.

Sexuality

Similar to their views on gender, most contemporary scholars reject the essentialist notion that sexuality can be reduced to a biological drive that exists irrespective of culture or era. Rather, sexual life is subject to a "socio-cultural molding . . . surpassed by few other forms of human behavior" (Gagnon and Simon, 1973, p. 26), and thus sexuality can only be understood within its own time, place, and cultural and political context. For example, what is sexually appropriate or taboo is not fixed but highly contingent—it is not "deviant" until it has been labeled so (Greenberg, 1988). This is not to say that because sexuality is socially constructed that sexual identities are not real or significant (Vance, 1989). In fact, sexual attitudes and practices can have deep subjective meanings for individuals, but those meanings are inextricably bound up in the larger social and cultural context in which they take place. Even if the *etiology* of sexual desire were found to lie mostly in physiology, the *meanings* that are attached to sexuality would nevertheless vary over time, place, and culture.

One of the most important contributions of the constructionist perspective is the idea that the labeling of sexual behavior creates imbalances of power (e.g., Foucault, 1978). The kind of power envisioned here arises not from overt state action but from individuals' internalization of prevailing discourses and the resulting surveillance of self and others (see Foucault, 1977). We are our own (and each other's) policing agent. One of the most powerful sexual discourses involves hetero-normativity, which includes two related ideas: there are two "kinds" of people (heterosexuals and homosexuals), and heterosexuality is normal and homosexuality is deviant. These claims seem natural to most people only because they are deeply entrenched and continually enacted or performed. The locus of discourse condemning homosexuality as deviant was first based in religious notions of sin. Around the turn of the twentieth century, a medicalized model based in pathology gained ground, adding to but not replacing the religious model (see Greenberg, 1988). Each discourse is stigmatizing (and thus exerts control) in its own way. In the latter part of the twentieth century, the medical model began to erode but homosexuality was "repathologized" (at least among gay men) due to the HIV/AIDS epidemic (Conrad and Angell, 2004); what we now call "AIDS" was initially termed "GRID" (gay-related immune deficiency). In fact, homosexuality itself has sometimes been labeled a "contagion" that will infect young people if not stemmed (see Knauer, 2006). Thus, both religious and medical discourses continue to hold a great deal of power.

Hetero-normativity creates many incongruities. Heterosexuality is constructed as an innate and natural orientation, while homosexuality is sometimes claimed to be a choice. Indeed, even when homosexuality is acknowledged as shaped by biology, some nevertheless find it similar to harmful or deviant conditions or behaviors that also have a biological influence. Ken Buck, a Colorado candidate for US Senate, combined both of those constructions when he said, "Birth has an influence over [homosexuality] like alcoholism and some other things, but I think that basically you have a choice" (CNN's *Newsroom,* October 18, 2010). In an indication that countervailing discourses have developed, anchor Kyra Phillips asked rhetorically: "Mr. Buck, let me ask you a question. If sexual orientation is a choice, when did you choose to be straight?"

While the LGBT movement has had some success with establishing a counter-discourse that challenges homosexuality as sinful or psychologically disordered (the second component of hetero-normativity), it has expended less effort to challenge the first component of hetero-normativity—the essentialist idea that there are two "types" of sexual beings. The most obvious reason is that it is easier to build a movement when identity is not problematized. Notwithstanding this acquiescence by many LGBT activists, constructionists have convincingly demonstrated that the dualism of hetero- and homosexuality is deeply problematic, for several reasons. First, it is a false binary that ignores sexual fluidity. Longitudinal survey studies have shown that changes in sexual identity over the life course are not uncommon (e.g., Garofalo et al., 1999; Laumann et al., 1994), with greater fluidity of identity among women (e.g., Diamond, 2003). In addition, essentialism fails to take into account bisexuality and also that bisexuality itself can be more complicated than it may appear (e.g., Berkey, Perelman-Hall, and Kurdek [1990] propose a model with six types of bisexuality). The second problem with essentialism is that sexual orientation has at least three chief and distinct components: identity, desire, and behavior. The three are oftentimes conflated, even by researchers. For example, some surveys of sexuality ask about a respondent's identity while others inquire into behavior, but both surveys claim to measure the same concept. However, the three components do not always align in expected ways. Same-sex sexual behavior does not necessarily coincide with a gay or lesbian identity (Ellis, Robb, and Burke, 2005; Laumann et al., 1994). Contemporary examples include relatively high proportions of men in some Latino cultures whose behavior is bisexual but whose identity is heterosexual. This split of identity from behavior accommodates male-

male sexual relations while also serving an important cultural goal—creation and maintenance of a nuclear family (see Gonzalez and Espin, 1996; Rust, 2000).

Last, it is important to note that hetero-normativity also shapes a great deal of our behavior that is not at all sexual, largely because it is tied to gender ideologies. Sexuality and gender are inextricably interrelated; Schwartz and Rutter (2000) refer to this conflation as "the gender of sexuality." We use the term *hetero-masculinity,* as do Anderson, Adams, and Rivers (2010), to underscore that this conflation applies especially to men, for whom any behavior or identity considered as homosexual marks a man as feminine. Men are thus doubly stigmatized through a combination of "femphobia" and homophobia. Heteromasculinity imposes strict gender roles and causes heterosexual men to go to great lengths to avoid creating any perception that they are gay—thus, for example, they maintain physical and emotional distance from other men and display orthodox forms of masculinity. To maintain their dominance, then, heterosexual men must avoid any behavior, thought, or desire associated with homosexuality (see Butler, 1990), and remain "100% straight" (Messner, 2002, p. 42). Importantly, hetero-masculinity also has effects on the behavior of gay and bisexual men, who either remain closeted or, if they are "out," adopt some of the practices of normative masculinity, such as weightlifting. Research shows that hetero-masculine norms lead gay men to "defeminize" themselves during adolescence; if they show effeminate traits as adults, they risk marginalization, even from other gay men (see Taywaditep, 2002). In Chapter 6 we detail how these dynamics are also at play among boys. Like gender normativity, hetero-masculinity requires persistent maintenance and monitoring. As a result, bullying also serves as a form of informal social control employed by adolescents to police the boundaries of hetero-masculinity. Violation of hetero-normativity is deeply implicated in bullying victimization in schools, especially for boys and young men who violate or are perceived to violate norms of hetero-masculinity, whether or not they self-identify as gay (and even whether or not they are presumed to be gay) (e.g., McMaster et al., 2002; Timmerman, 2003). To put it more simply, bullying is a part of boys' gender and sexual socialization and is one mechanism through which they are taught what are acceptable straight male behaviors (see Pascoe, 2013).

It is vitally important to keep in mind that youth have not established these gender or hetero-masculine norms on their own. Quite to the contrary, these norms are learned through various cultural means, among them news media discourse. As we will see in Chapters 5 and 6, news media and other claimsmakers actively, if not intentionally, position some youth as more or less deserving of bullying based on real or perceived violations of gender and hetero-masculine norms. While it may be easy to blame young people for employing bullying as a mechanism of social control, the reality is that these messages are born out of a social and cultural milieu heavily influenced by adult discursive constructions. Schoolchildren learn gender and hetero-masculine norms in part through an internalization of adult discursive constructions, many of which are consistently and vociferously articulated in news media coverage of school bullying. Through this lens, school bullying is no longer viewed as a form of deviance, but rather as an implicitly and explicitly accepted mechanism of social control aimed at enforcement of gender and hetero-masculine norms.

Structure of the Book

In the remainder of this book we dig more deeply into news media constructions of school bullying as a social problem. In Chapter 2 we explore early constructions of school bullying as an individual-level problem. We examine how these early constructions situated school bullying as the result of individual pathology and worked to define bullying up, down, and out in ways that brought an ever-increasing number of individuals into its ambit. We also note the various ways in which victims, bullies, and victim-bullies have been constructed as deviant others. In Chapters 3 and 4 our focus turns to the shift from individual to sociocultural explanations for school bullying. In particular, in Chapter 3 we explore the construction of school bullying as a public health epidemic. In Chapter 4 we explore how this epidemic frame supported explanations for school bullying that included familial, institutional, and cultural failure. In Chapters 5 and 6 we turn our attention to contextualizing the construction of school bullying as a social problem by focusing on how it serves as an arena for the ongoing discourse of gender, sexuality, and social control. Relying on two case studies, we articulate how gender, sexuality, and social control serve both explicitly and implicitly as interpretive resources for news media constructions of school bullying. In Chapter 7 we switch gears to discuss the news media's active role in constructing school bullying as a social problem, through an analysis of the news production process. Included in this chapter is an analysis of the anti-bullying industry as seen through the lens of media waves. Finally, in Chapter 8 we return to our chronological account. We describe how the news media's re-individualization of school bullying has led to the imposition of mostly counterproductive forms of social control, such as zero-tolerance policies and criminalization. We end with suggestions for how we might begin to better define bullying through a more nuanced and complex framework grounded in the social-ecological approach, through which those most influenced by school bullying—youth—are more purposefully given a voice.

Notes

1. While the word "bullycide" was not widely adopted in the media and is also not technically grammatically appropriate (it actually suggests the killing of bullies), it is used here as a convenient shorthand. The earliest use of the term we know of was in Marr and Field's 2001 study. However, various other persons were credited with its invention in the media transcripts that we reviewed. The eponymous host of CNN's *Issues with Jane Velez-Mitchell* (April 8, 2010) referred to the death of Phoebe Prince as part of a "sick trend [that] has even coined a new term, bullycide." The next day on the same program. Velez-Mitchell credited the creation of the term to Sirdeaner Walker, the mother of an 11-year-old student, Carl Walker-Hoover Jr., who died by suicide in Massachusetts about nine months before Phoebe Prince took her own life, in a city about thirty miles from Prince's. (Interestingly, six months earlier on her program, on November 25, 2008, Velez-Mitchell said that she had "just learned" a new phrase: "cyber-bullycide.") In any event, the term was not new in 2010 nor was it coined by Walker. "Bullycide" appears for the first time in our transcripts in 2003 in an interview of Barbara Coloroso, author of *The Bully, the Bullied, and the Bystander,* on CBS's *Early Show* (March 3, 2003). Also that year, the *New York Times* (October 2, 2003) quoted a prosecutor as saying the following to a jury: "You have heard the term suicide. . . . But you wonder if a more appropriate term was bullicide."

2. Unless otherwise indicated, any italicized words within quotes from news media transcripts represent our own emphasis.

3. We do not mean to say that these distinctions are easily made. As we argue in Chapter 8, any approach to understanding bullying requires a great deal of nuance and flexibility, including a recognition that bullying is on a continuum of behaviors and thus "bleeds into" behaviors that are of great concern as well as behaviors that are of little concern.

2

Bullying as an Individual Pathology

Anyone who breaks the pattern of the stereotypical kid is vulnerable.
— Family therapist Terry Real
(CNN's *The Joy Behar Show,* May 13, 2010)

Most of the time, a bad child is really a sad child.
— Child psychiatrist Anh Nga Nguyen
(*New York Times,* December 2, 1997)

From the early 1990s through about 2007, constructions of bullying in both academia and the news media were predominantly organized around individual-level explanations. Bullies and victims were constructed as different from other children, and also as different from each other; in fact, as binary opposites. Theories purporting to explain these differences rested on biological or psychological models, including genetic influences, disorders such as attention deficit hyperactivity disorder (ADHD), personality traits, and behavior acquired through social learning. During this time, bullying prevention was also constructed at the level of the individual and focused on changing students' behaviors through various methods such as building empathy. In hindsight, it is unclear to us whether effective methods of prevention could have been designed, given the competing constructions of bullies and victims proffered by experts and other media commentators. For instance, bullies were simultaneously depicted as low in self-esteem and high in self-esteem, as powerful elites and as abused children acting out their victimization. Victims were more uniformly depicted as the deviant "other"—weak and physically or psychologically damaged—but they

29

were also further typified in contradictory ways. Toward the end of our study period, domain expansion took hold, whereby bullying was defined out to include nearly every student as both a bully and a victim, whether acting out a vicious cycle of violence or engaging in everyday social jockeying for status. Defining bullying out to include every student as both victim and bully appears to solve the problem of etiological complexity, but presents additional problems, including smoothing out important differences about the contexts in which bullying occurs. We take up these issues in more detail in Chapter 8. Here, we begin our journey with an exploration of how early constructions of bullying worked to situate individual youth as pathological and therefore deviant.

Constructing Victims as the Deviant Other

Generally we found that victims of bullying were pathologized and constructed as the deviant other. But before discussing this construction further, we must address one significant exception, namely that bullycide victims were portrayed as *ideal victims* (see Christie, 1986). They were innocent and blameless, pushed to suicide by cruel tormentors. The media quoted family and friends who lionized the victims and spoke of their loss in emotionally wrenching terms. For example: "Jon was a wonderful child. He was a straight A student. He loved his family. He spent 90 percent of his time with his father and I; just doing things around the house, or going to the movies and to the parks and museums. And he was our heart and soul. He was my husband's best friend that he no—no longer has any more. He's not only our child, but our best friend" (mother of Jon Carmichael speaking on CNN's *Anderson Cooper 360,* March 31, 2010).

Besides being depicted as blameless, such ideal victims were also reported to have positive qualities only: they were intelligent, cheerful, talented, and very involved in family life. For instance, CNN's Randi Kaye described one bullycide victim in the following manner: "By all accounts, Carl Joseph Walker-Hoover was a good kid, a Boy Scout who went to church every Sunday with his mother and prayed every morning before school" (*Anderson Cooper 360,* April 14, 2009). Many stories also emphasized characteristics that suggested the vulnerability of victims. Stories commonly emphasized their tender age, which ranged from 7 to 17 years, with many being in the middle school years. Stories also reported whether the victims were small in stature, or were a freshman or new to their school. Describing Jaheem Herrera, CNN's Gary Tuchman stated, "He was only 11 years old and had just moved to Atlanta this school year" (*Anderson Cooper 360,* May 14, 2009). If a bullycide victim had other troubles, in most cases those troubles were also said to have been caused by the bullying; in other cases, the victim's story was intentionally edited to avoid "problematic" facts until long after the ideal victim construction had become well-established, as was the case for Phoebe Prince as discussed in Chapter 1.

However, there was another set of bullycide victims who possessed most of the characteristics of ideal victims but whom the media ignored or marginalized. One of these was 12-year-old Gabrielle Molina, who took her life after being cyberbullied. Coverage of Molina's suicide showed up only once in our search, in a story on CNN.com (May 23, 2013). A later Web search found that the suicide was covered by some New York newspapers and local television stations, but not by the *New York Times* and apparently not by national broadcast media. Similarly, the suicide of a 7-year-old African American boy who police said had been bullied was covered very sparsely (e.g., CNN's *Saturday Morning News,* May 26, 2012). During the purported epidemic of LGBT bullycide victims in 2010, five suicides of white boys who were gay or were called gay were reported. Bullycides of lesbians were infrequently featured. Thus there was a near absence of LGBT suicides by children of color, and by girls, in the media. This is consistent with prior research (see Paceley and Flynn, 2012; Pritchard, 2013) and with the hierarchy of victimization discussed in Chapter 1.

The ideal victim construction posited bullies and victims as a clear dichotomy—a morality tale of good versus evil. However, there were obvious tensions between descriptions of these ideal victims and those of the generic victim. While many specific victims (particularly youth who died by suicide) were described in idealized ways, victims in general were often pathologized as the other—different from and mostly "less than" other children and thus also fundamentally different from bullies. The media and their experts emphasized two main differences. The first was that victims were said to possess external characteristics or to have psychosocial issues that made them targets for bullies. Second, and sometimes related, victims were depicted as weak.

Physical and Psychosocial Difference

Psychiatrist David Shaffer said that bullying victims may be "physically distinct, you know, overweight or clumsy" (CBS's *This Morning,*

August 29, 1996). Kids apparently risked bullying if they were "emphatically obese" (*NYT,* April 25, 2012) or merely "a little over-weight" (*NYT,* May 27, 2001). Disabilities such as cerebral palsy also made children "easy targets," according to psychologist Michael Bradley (ABC's *Good Morning America,* September 18, 2010). We learned from several sources that 85 percent of disabled students had been bullied (e.g., *NBC Nightly News,* September 21, 2010). Stories portrayed particular students' experiences as well as generalities; two stories in the *New York Times* profiled bullying victims who had missing limbs (January 28, 2007; May 27, 2001). In other cases, there was an implication that victims were deformed because they had undergone (or were to undergo) cosmetic surgery in response to bullying; Katie Couric said of her guests that "these teens used plastic surgery to fit in" (NBC's *Today,* March 30, 2010). There were even reports of using cosmetic sur-gery as a prophylactic measure against potential bullying; Juju Chang reported on a mother with "worries about bullying" who was planning ear surgery for her daughter, who had "already been teased" about her ears (ABC's *Good Morning America,* April 14, 2011). The fact that nearly all of the teens featured in such stories were girls is taken up in Chapter 5.

However, commentators sometimes strained to discover the key dif-ference that made a victim a target when they were presented with chil-dren who had no obvious physical flaw and thus didn't fit the victim stereotype. For example, the eponymous host of *Issues with Jane Velez-Mitchell,* discussed Alye Pollock, a 13-year-old girl who had posted a video on YouTube in which she revealed that she was being bullied. Velez-Mitchell said: "She doesn't seem to be your *typical bullying tar-get.* . . . She seems to me attractive, in good shape, assertive, smart" (CNN, March 28, 2011).[1] Dr. Drew Pinsky interviewed the same Ms. Pollock and said to her: "It's hard to imagine someone bullying you. I mean, *not to say that there's somebody who should be bullied,* but I can't understand what they'd be bullying you about" (CNN, April 4, 2011). Even though Pinsky attempts to walk back the underlying assumption in his original statement, these kinds of assertions work to reinforce the notion that those who are perceived as living up to gender norms of appearance should be immune from bullying, while the bully-ing of those who fall short is somehow expected. As Juju Chang said of a different bully victim: "She isn't the kind of girl you'd expect to be bullied. She's a popular and active eighth grader" (ABC's *Nightline,* October 11, 2011). In another case, a community member wondered why anyone would pick on a student who was a "bright young girl, very pretty" (NBC's *Today,* September 25, 2012). These comments reveal an implication that there must be something visibly "wrong" with a victim for bullying to occur, and that being "pretty" or "beautiful" should provide some sort of anti-bullying armor. Perhaps unsurprisingly, such comments about appearances were rarely made of victims who were boys.

Only occasionally did a commentator suggest that a victim could be bullied for having positive traits that other children might envy. The director of an anti-bullying organization said that bullies target "kids who are different in *any* way," including kids who are "more attractive" as well as those who are "less attractive" (NPR's *Tell Me More,* April 5, 2010). Jane Velez-Mitchell suggested that "the smartest kids" get bullied because "they're thinking adult thoughts" and other children feel threatened (CNN, March 28, 2011). A psychiatrist said she wasn't surprised that Hollywood stars had been bullied as children, because "many creative people are highly sensitive and bullies tend to zero in on people who are sensitive" (NBC's *Today,* May 7, 2011). Another example can be seen in how Drew Pinsky strains to locate a bullyable difference in a middle school caller with whom he was speaking on his CNN program (May 24, 2012). The student said that he was being bullied and wanted to know how to prevent it. Pinsky asked how old the student was, and when he said he was 14, Pinsky gushed: "Wow. You sound 27. Allen, good for you." He then probed: "Are you a big kid?" Allen replied that he was "about 5 foot 3" (this height is actually somewhat under the mean). Pinsky continued: "I guess what I'm asking is, *are you unusual?*" He went on to explain that kids tend to "go on the attack" against others whom they find different, and asked: "So, is there anything about you other than you sounding like an adult male, anything else different about you?" Allen responded that he was "growing a lot of facial hair faster than usual." Pinsky concluded that other children must be jealous of Allen, and compared the boy's situation to being like "when women go on the attack" when other women are "coming into their body, so to speak." In the broadest claim we found, Alexandra Robbins, author of *And the Geeks Shall Inherit the Earth,* made the rounds of the news and talk shows (e.g., NPR's *Weekend Edition,* May 22, 2011) espousing the theory that the traits that alienate kids in school are the same ones that help make adults successful. However, such claims came from distinctly minority voices.

The second type of victim was constructed as psychosocially impaired. Bill Cosby claimed that children susceptible to bullying are depressed, have low self-esteem, and don't have anyone at home looking after them, such as by asking "how do you feel today"? (CNN's *Larry King Live,* April 13, 2010). A psychologist on the same program agreed with this assessment. Neither considered whether bullying was the cause or the result of the alleged depression and low self-esteem in such children. A feature in the *New York Times* raised this connection, saying a "feeling of aloneness" is both a consequence of bullying and, "in some ways, a cause of it since it is almost always socially isolated children (the new kid, the fat kid, the gay kid, the strange kid) who are singled out for mistreatment" (March 30, 2012). Constructing victims in these ways stigmatizes them as both identifiably different and psychologically maladjusted, and also implies that the victims' traits are, as the *New York Times* put it, "in some way" the cause of their bullying. This labeling process bypasses the question of how victims come to be labeled this way and suggests that victims' best response may be to conform to group norms.

Weakness

The second major difference was that victims were constructed as weak. One school psychologist said that victims are "seen as weaker and insecure and anxious" (CNN's *Saturday Morning News,* December 6, 1997). The idea that bullies "prey on someone weak" (NBC's *Today,* October 10, 2010) flows from the notion of the power differential aspect of bullying. However, the news media tended to frame the power difference in absolute rather than relative terms: because the bully is stronger, the victim thus must be "weak" (not weak*er*). Besides being faulty in logic, such a construction ignores the larger context of bullying. Bullies may have the express or implied support of many of their peers, the school culture may support certain kinds of bullying, and the bullying may be of a type that is enabled or condoned by discourses in the larger culture. Expressing the power differential as one that exists solely between the bully and the victim thus does not take into account how the *content* and the *context* of the bullying can tap into existing structural or cultural power differentials, including those around sexuality and gender. Like the news media, most researchers appear to be unconcerned with the power differential in general as well as with the specific discourse of the bullying. The Centers for Disease Control compiled bullying questionnaires and found that almost none addressed the power differential and that only one involved content (a measure that addressed homophobic bullying) (Hamburger, Basile, and Vivolo, 2011). In this light, Pascoe calls for a "sociology of bullying," noting that the differences over which kids get bullied are not neutral but "reflect larger structural inequalities" (2013, p. 95). Walton similarly takes note that most analysis "tends not to emphasize the ways in which markers of social difference . . . inform the nature and reflect the characteristics of bullying among children" (2005, p. 112). Thus, bullying is just a more extreme form of what is already accepted in schools (Payne and Smith, 2013). If this goes unrecognized, then one is left with the conclusion that all victims of anti-gay bullying and all girls who have been sexually assaulted and mocked for that assault, are "weak." If it's true that victims/survivors are often stigmatized (see Dunn, 2010), then it is unsurprising that the media and academic researchers don't take more account of social and cultural processes that influence the bully-victim power differential.

Constructing Victim Types

The media further typified victims beyond constructing them mostly as weak and damaged. We call these types *complex victims, provocative victims,* and *retaliatory victims.* The complex victims category refers mostly to instances in which a combination of facts emerged that (1) indicated the victim had a personality trait or a mental disorder that made them more susceptible to bullying; (2) obscured the link between the bullying and the youth's reaction to that bullying; and (3) made the youth appear less sympathetic. In several cases, these facts were not brought to light until well after the ideal victim narrative had been solidified. The leading example is perhaps that of Phoebe Prince, the 15-year-old who died by suicide after bullying from so-called mean girls. Initial stories cast Prince clearly in the role of the ideal victim; this status was challenged much later by defense attorneys in the criminal cases brought against the students who allegedly bullied her. Emily Bazelon, a writer for the online news magazine *Slate,* also raised questions. A similar defense strategy was employed in the criminal case involving Megan Meier, who died by suicide after her friend's mother posed as a teenage boy on MySpace and then "dumped" her. During the mother's criminal trial, the defense attorney "obviously put some holes in the government's case" by getting Megan's mother to admit that "Megan had thought about suicide sometime in the past and had maybe scratch marks on her arms which were covered up by a shirt and were discovered by a school counselor" (Scott Glover, *Los Angeles Times* staff writer, speaking on CNN's *Issues with Jane Velez-Mitchell,* November 20, 2008).

Another high-profile example, although not involving criminal charges, involves Tyler Long, who was said to have died by suicide after being bullied and whose parents brought a lawsuit against the school district for failing to protect him. Long's father acknowledged in interviews that his son had Asperger's syndrome; he "didn't like things to be touched" and "some kids allegedly took advantage of that" (NPR's *Talk of the Nation,* March 23, 2010). Long's father asserted that the bullying had gone on for years, and that in "the last couple of weeks" of his life "he was a hollow person"—the bullies "took his pride from him" (ABC's *20/20,* October 15, 2010). Long was one of the five children featured in the documentary *Bully.* This film also presented claims that Long's suicide was brought on by the bullying. Gayle King was one of the few media figures to challenge this narrative. After a judge dismissed the Longs' lawsuit against the school district, King interviewed Cynthia Lowen, a producer of *Bully,* on CBS's *This Morning* (May 24, 2012). King asked Lowen why *Bully* had omitted several seemingly important facts about Long, including his Asperger's diagnosis and a possible diagnosis of bipolar disorder "which can also be link[ed] to suicide." King also noted that Long had been in a serious accident that "wrecked his car," that there was a delay between the bullying and the suicide, and that Long's suicide note did not mention bullying. King said these facts added "another layer" to the story (she later said that the additional facts suggested "that bullying may not have been the only cause" of the suicide). Lowen responded only to the omission of the Asperger's diagnosis, saying that the diagnosis did not relieve the school district from responsibility to protect Long, and that the producers of the film did not want to suggest that because Long was "in some way different . . . he was bringing the bullying on himself." We agree that victim-blaming should not be the intention of pointing out these complexities, but we must also be willing to address the influence of these other factors on the purported link between bullying and suicide.

Provocative Victims

Provocative victims are youth whose innocence is seriously called into question, which is a rare construction. One example is Billy Wolfe of Fayetteville, Arkansas. The *New York Times* (March 24, 2008) ran a story about Wolfe that described the bullying directed at him and noted that "some teachers think he's a sweet kid; others think he is easily distracted, occasionally disruptive, even disrespectful." The story also said that a school official thought that Wolfe "contributes to the problems that swirl around him." As to the bullying, the story said: "It remains unclear why Billy became a target at age 12; schoolyard anthropology can be so nuanced. Maybe because he was so tall, or wore glasses then, or has a learning disability that affects his reading comprehension. Or maybe some kids were just bored. Or angry."

Two months later, a more clearly sympathetic story about Wolfe on NBC's *Today* (May 26, 2008) began: "You have heard of bullies, but you probably haven't seen anything as bad as this. A teenager harassed so unmercifully his parents are going to court to get it to stop." There was an interview with Wolfe's mother and his attorney in which details of the bullying were provided, including a beating captured on cell phone video. The *Today* story may have been more sympathetic to Wolfe because of the use of a video of the assault. As we discuss in Chapter 7, the presence of video tends to heighten emotion, including an increase of sympathy for victims and an increase of outrage toward perpetrators. The only sign of ambiguity was when Wolfe's mother said he was "not perfect" but noted that he'd "never been in trouble for bullying." Six months later, NBC's *Dateline* (September 19, 2008) aired a lengthy feature asking whether Wolfe was "truly an innocent victim." Elsewhere in the program, it was reported that "there was no hint in his records of any behavioral problems, though sometimes, said a teacher, he didn't seem to pick up on social clues very well." Wolfe's father acknowledged this last claim and that his son was therefore "ripe for teasing," "playable," and "easier to get a response out of." Other students claimed it was more than that—that Wolfe had started fights and otherwise antagonized students. Matt Lauer questioned Wolfe: "But are you doing anything, Billy? Are you a wise guy? Are you the kind of guy who makes comments to kids as they go by? Are you provoking this in any way?" A fellow student said rather incredibly that "90, 95 percent of the stuff that has happened to him he deserved . . . like getting hit in the face, getting stitches, he deserved that. . . . It's high school. Get a helmet." The story was cast as a sort of "he said, they said" situation that appeared to pit the entire town against Wolfe. The story concluded: "Billy, *for whatever reason,* is bullied, resented, belittled, fights back in court and resentment spreads. In the lessons of suspicion and dislike, straight As all around."

Although we are perhaps making somewhat fine points here, and although our terminology may be different than that used by bullying researchers, we nevertheless distinguish between youth who are said to be victimized because they *intentionally* antagonize other students (whom we term *provocative victims*) and those who possess characteristics that bullies tend to zero in on because such victims have an enhanced reaction to bullying. Victimization of the latter group is akin to that described in victim precipitation theory: victims are sometimes partly responsible (in a factual, not a moral, sense) for their victimization (Curtis, 1973; Wolfgang, 1958). Although the theory has been interpreted as "blaming the victim," it is intended by its proponents to be a "neutral, non-legal concept that can help to explain the occurrence of criminal acts" (van Dijk, 1999, p. 2). A good illustration of this in the context of bullying is when Julie Hertzog, then-director of the National Center for Bullying Prevention, said on *NBC Nightly News:* "Kids with disabilities are oftentimes targeted by bullying because of their vulnerable reaction to the behavior. Whether it's getting mad or getting scared or getting angry, they're providing a response that makes . . . the person bullying feel in power and in control" (September 21, 2010). When considering the coverage of Billy Wolfe's story, we can see how he was constructed in both of these ways. We also get an indication of the complexity of bullying, as even the same victim is constructed and reconstructed by the media over time.

Retaliatory Victims

The retaliatory victim was depicted as "more provocative or aggressive," a youth who might bring weapons to school (CNN's *Saturday Morning News,* December 6, 1997). This type of victim does not respond to bullying in kind, but with discrete and deadly acts of violence. The most extreme example of this type of victim is the individual we term the *time bomb,* who could erupt in mass violence, seemingly with little warning. The time bomb construction arose during the mid-1990s and contributed to the evolution of bullying being framed as a problem distinct from other types of peer aggression in the United States. This construction should be very familiar to readers and is discussed in Spencer's book *The Paradox of Youth Violence* (2011). The most obvious examples are the two assailants in the 1999 shootings at Columbine High School in Littleton, Colorado—Erik Harris and Dylan Klebold, who were widely reported to have been bullied. (Cullen [2010] effectively deconstructs this "myth" and finds that the shootings were driven by Harris's psychopathology.) However, there were many other school shooters both pre- and post-Columbine who were constructed as time bombs (although that specific term was only occasionally employed). This construction continued to be applied in various cases of mass violence even as bullycides became the main focus of bullying stories in the news media.

Retaliatory victims, including the time bomb type, were the most demonized and vilified, as might be expected. One story in the *New York Times* (July 20, 1995) reported on alleged bullying victim Brian Wright, who had shot another student. One boy said, "Brian had been known as a nerd," and added, "If you carry yourself like you're a nobody, you're going to get treated like a nobody." However, retaliatory victims were sometimes treated more sympathetically. For example, CNN anchor Bobbie Battista reported the following after the widely reported school shooting in West Paducah, Kentucky: "The school principal suggested that Michael Carneal, described as small for his age was lashing out after years of being teased and bullied. Many may find that an inadequate explanation, yet almost everyone can relate. Kids can be extremely cruel, and most of us have memories of being picked on as children" (*Saturday Morning News,* December 6, 1997). A caller (Gwen) on CNN's *Dr. Drew* (February 27, 2012) was more visceral. She said that her daughter who has autism was beaten up by a classmate and added: "So, I completely understand probably why these [school shooters] do the things they do."

Interestingly, some people (mostly relatives) clung to an ideal victim narrative even when victims were said to have acted extremely violently. A grandfather described his granddaughter as "a very well-behaved girl" even though, according to the *New York Times* (November 20, 1993), after having been bullied for a year she allegedly responded by spraying sulfuric acid in a hallway, "critically burning an assistant principal." The mother of T. J. Lane, accused of shooting and killing several students, said that although people were going to "think that he's some monster," Lane "actually was and is a good person" but the "bullying and people making fun of him . . . led to what he did." Just as the news media typified victims, they also built psychological profiles of bullies. The result was a contradictory set of explanations that rarely was grounded in a discussion of actual bullies.

Typifying the Bullies

Given the attention paid to bullying, it is surprising how little attention was paid to the bully. Outside of the two seminal bullying cases in 2010 involving Phoebe Prince and Tyler Clementi, where the alleged bullies were identified by name and described in some detail (because they were criminally prosecuted), there was almost never a "face" or a name put to the bullies. They were the missing link—mysterious, shrouded, almost always lurking on the periphery, even in cases where victims suffered serious harm (suicide or aggravated injuries). They were mostly just "the bullies," "the classmates," or "the mean girls." They almost never spoke on camera and were almost never interviewed for a newspaper story; if they were interviewed, they were almost exclusively identified (and also self-identified) as *ex*-bullies. It was also relatively rare for an article or broadcast piece to discuss the potential harm bullies posed to themselves by their behavior.

This is not to say that bullies as a group were not analyzed. Most such attention focused on diagnosing them to explain why they bullied. Here, there was a striking lack of consensus that also contributed to the mystery surrounding the bully identity. We found that news media constructed four competing bully types: the compensators, the elites, the predators, and the wounded. Interestingly, it appears that the compensators and the elites are opposing constructions, as are the wounded and the predators. Compensators were depicted as individuals with low self-esteem, a poor self-image, and feelings of powerlessness who lash out at other students to mask their insecurities. These explanations often came from medical professionals and psychologists. For instance, in 1992, "noted pediatrician" T. Berry Brazelton commented that "bullies are insecure people and they're trying to show their macho side because they . . . have a very poor self-image. And . . . I think they need help" (CBS's *This Morning,* March 30, 1992). Steve Perry, a school principal and education contributor to CNN, said to Dr. Drew Pinsky (January 4, 2012) that "children with the greatest level of bravado are typically the ones who have the lowest self-esteem" and claimed a week later (CNN's *Newsroom,* January 28, 2012) that for a bully to cause such harm to someone else the bully can't love itself. This construction was also found in the *New York Times:* Stanford University psychologist Philip Zimbardo was said to have "found childhood bullies who were shy and used their behavior to keep people away from them and to hide their vulnerability" (January 2, 1992). In the newspaper's "Personal Health" column Jane Brody wrote: "Bullying is often perpetrated by teens who are unsure of themselves" (*NYT,* August 29, 2006). Others used less diagnostic language. Barbara Coloroso, author of *The Bully, the Bullied, and the Bystander* and a frequent commentator for both print and television stories, was more direct, claiming that "bullies are cowards" (CNN's *Anderson Cooper 360,* April 1, 2010). A *New York Times* letter writer used the same words (July 28, 2010), and the newspaper quoted a student as saying: "Most of the bullies aren't strong; they just have a lot of friends who are" (October 22, 1995).

Elites

An opposing construction—bullies as powerful elites—was more commonly offered, sometimes as a direct rejoinder to the compensators construction. Jodee Blanco, a self-described "bullying survivor" and author of *Please Stop Laughing at Me,* called bullies "elite tormentors" (CNN's *Issues with Jane Velez-Mitchell,* April 2, 2010; CNN's *The Joy Behar Show,* April 5, 2010). Barbara Coloroso agreed: "Many [bullies] are high-status, elite kids" (CNN's *Issues with Jane Velez-Mitchell,* September 17, 2010). As noted earlier, Coloroso had also described bullies as cowards. Dr. Susan Lipkins said on *Today* that "the bullies are often jocks, they're athletic, they have that power and they use it" (NBC, October 27, 2010). "Dr. Phil" McGraw said on *Anderson Cooper 360* that bullies "generally perceive themselves to be powerful" (CNN, October 8, 2010) and said on *The Joy Behar Show* that "these kids are often precocious; they're often larger, stronger, and very self-confident" (CNN, February 1, 2011). The *New York Times* frequently constructed bullies as powerful and popular; in doing so, the newspaper was more likely than the broadcast media to rely on academic research for support. One early article (October 22, 1995) said that "the pioneer researcher, Dan Olweus . . . debunked myths like the one that bullies have low self-esteem." Another (May 20, 2001) also relied on a researcher (Laura Hess Olson) who noted "that the old stereotype of the bully as an antisocial and unpopular misfit is false," and that, in fact, bullies were the second most popular group in one study. This was echoed in another article almost a decade later (June 19, 2010) by another researcher (Mitchell J. Prinstein) who said that highly popular students "can be bullies or part of the mean-girl clique."

Predators

Bullies were sometimes constructed in the broadcast media as senseless, aggressive predators whose only motivation seemed to be to hurt others. As early as 1992, NPR's *Weekend Edition* (March 21) reported that teachers were "shocked at how unpredictable and vicious [angry children] can be." Janis Mohat, mother of Eric, a bullying victim who died by suicide, called Eric's bullies "little terrorists" (NBC's *Today,* October 11, 2010). And there were many examples of "mean girls" who were said to "really get into the brutality of how they treat others" (Dr. Drew Pinsky on CNN's *The Joy Behar Show,* August 25, 2010). The *New York Times,* in its "Parent and Child" column (October 28, 1993), offered a more nuanced, psychological version of the predator. A developmental psychologist (Deborah Capaldi) was quoted as believing that bullies are antisocial and aggressive, partly because they tend to "view the world as a more dangerous and hostile place than other children do." She did not explain why some children come to adopt this view.

The Wounded

The wounded constitute the last category of bullies. This group was sometimes constructed rather vaguely; for example, Kyra Phillips commented that "bullies have feelings, too, and sometimes if you dig really deep down you can see a good person who is just having a tough time" (CNN's *Newsroom*, April 13, 2010). Others offered a medical cause; psychologist Michael Oberschneider said that children with mental health problems such as ADHD and depression were "more vulnerable to acting out in different ways" (ABC's *Good Morning America*, November 6, 2010). However, the most common explanation was that the wounded were acting out the aggression they had been subjected to in the home; they had been "violentized," to use terminology coined by Athens (1989). For these children, bullying was employed as a strategy through which to cope with their victimization and (re)establish some sense of power. An ABC *20/20* report referenced "research [that] shows that bullies at school are often victims at home, and picking on other kids makes them feel more powerful" (April 28, 1995). This explanation persisted across the years in our sample. For instance, in 1999, Michael Thompson, psychologist and coauthor of *Raising Cain,* said, "We often find in the background of a bully some harsh discipline at home"; in fact, the bully may have been "hit around" (CNN's *Saturday Morning News,* May 1, 1999). More than a decade later, child psychologist Charles Sophy agreed, and suggested that parents "check the emotional temperature in your home" and ask whether children are "actually being bullied [at home], either verbally, physically or some other way that then translates itself down out into the schoolyard, where they find a weaker person to prey on" (NBC's *Today,* October 27, 2012).

Claimsmaking experts' estimates of the wounded as a share of overall bullies were highly variable. Psychologist Brenda Wade said that "a *huge percentage* of [bullies] are themselves being abused in the home" (CNN's *Issues with Jane Velez-Mitchell,* March 28, 2011). Joy Behar said that "*most* kids who are bullies were bullied themselves . . . probably by their own parents" (CNN, September 21, 2010). The one academic study that was referenced in our media sample reported that 20 percent of both bullies *and* victims had experienced violence in the home (CNN's *Newsroom,* March 22, 2011). Not surprisingly, there was a tendency to construct the wounded as the most sympathetic type of bully; psychologist Brenda Wade said: "There are no bad kids. I think there are just parents who need more training" (CNN's *Issues with Jane Velez-Mitchell,* March 28, 2011). The wounded constitute a category that links the psychological state of the bully to parental and family influences, something that we take up in Chapter 4.

Claimsmakers only sometimes acknowledged that typifying the bully was not a simple or obvious process. Dr. Susan Swearer admitted that there is no "bully profile" (CBS's *Sunday Morning News,* January 19, 2011). Dr. Susan Lipkins, identified as a hazing expert, initially said something similar on *Today*: "anyone can be a bully" and "there is no prototype" (NBC, October 27, 2010). However, she immediately went on to offer two competing constructions: bullies as popular, powerful jocks (part of the elites), and what we consider a subtype of the wounded, the bully-victim.

Complicating the Binary: The Bully-Victim

The media mostly affirmed the dichotomy between bully and victim and the moral discourse associated with it. However, the differing depictions of Billy Wolfe discussed earlier demonstrate the difficulty of maintaining the binary construction of bullies and victims. Thus there was occasionally some recognition, particularly in the later years of our analysis, of the bully-victim, a youth who was both bullied and bullier. (As was the case with bullies in our media sample, if a bully-victim acknowledged bullying behavior, it was always constructed as having happened in the past.) The media also sometimes explored the relational aspects between bullies and victims and the larger social context in which bullying takes place. Stories about bully-victims or the complexity of the bullying context directly or indirectly challenged stereotypes that victims and bullies are fundamentally different (victims are weak and passive, and bullies are aggressive) and that victims are targeted due to their possession of some external "difference." Sometimes these stereotypes were in conflict; for example, bullies were stereotyped as both popular jocks and aggressive outcasts.

The broadcast media did not begin to identify the bully-victim as a category until about 2010. They did, however, air several interviews in the 1990s that featured what would become known as bully-victims.

These were usually a part of larger stories that aired following school shootings and thus were focused on the potential time bomb effects of bullying. Given such massive potential harm, it was perhaps logical to focus on children who are bullied and then act out aggressively, even if their response was "only" bullying. In an interview in the wake of a school shooting in West Paducah, Kentucky, one student said that she had been bullied because of her weight and that it was "shocking" when someone pointed out to her that she bullied other students for the same reason (CNN's *Saturday Morning News,* December 6, 1997). Another story aired after a school shooting in Springfield, Oregon, in which a student disclosed: "I was bullied . . . and then I'd take it out on the younger kids to try to get my power back" (ABC's *Good Morning America,* June 22, 1998). In a piece after the Columbine shooting a student was asked whether she was "teased" or did the teasing, and she responded: "Both, I think. I think when I've been mean to people it's been either because they've been mean to me, or because somebody was mean to me earlier and I was just mad, and then they just came in my face, and so I was ready to be mean to somebody else and I took it out on them" (CNN's *Talkback Live,* April 23, 2008).

The *New York Times* did address the bully-victim construction in the 1990s and also addressed some actual examples. In late 1993, its "Parent and Child" column (September 28) read in part: "Many adults think that . . . chronic victims of bullies are passive, shy children, but researchers say that's not always the case. Highly aggressive children, including bullies themselves, are at least as likely as nonaggressive ones to be picked on repeatedly. One reason is that aggressive children tend to be rejected by their classmates." Several other articles followed. The *New York Times* reported that bully-victims had the worst of both worlds, experiencing poorer social outcomes than students who were only one or the other; they "were lonely and had trouble making friends" (April 25, 2001), had "weak social skills" (March 17, 2002), and "exhibited the highest level of school avoidance, conduct problems and school difficulties" (January 13, 2004). The last article also reported the results of research that showed that bully-victims "best fit the profiles of seriously violent offenders." The newspaper also addressed the bully-victim at least twice in the context of school shootings, suggesting that in the cases of both Columbine and West Paducah, the shooters were bully-victims. The *New York Times* also reported that, according to his friends, Kip Kinkel, the Springfield, Oregon, shooter "got bullied, and did his share of bullying" (March 24, 1998). The newspaper also relied on students' accounts of the relationship among students at Columbine High School in stating: "According to these descriptions, the jocks and the trench coat group could act as bullies, the jocks sometimes referring to members of the other group with derogatory homosexual terms and the outcast group sometimes invoking Nazi terminology and threatening to unleash violence at the school" (April 23, 1999).

Constructing youth as both bullies and victims appeared to have the effect of eliciting empathy from commentators and their guests, including experts. Anderson Cooper said that "some kids who get bullied turn around and bully others. . . . You know, no one is all evil or all, you know, a saint. It's a complex thing, especially when you're a kid" (October 7, 2010). Jodee Blanco said on *CBS Evening News*: "Bullying is about kids needing compassion. And my perspective is that the bully and the victim are flip sides of the same coin. They both need to be treated with compassion" (February 27, 2012).

Defining Bullying Out

Identifying the bully-victim was a significant step toward adopting the narrative that nearly every student could be both a bully and a victim. But before exploring this evolution further, let us first turn to another kind of defining out that added to the roster of victim types.

Defining Victims Out

The media were somewhat consistent over our study period in constructing three types of particularly vulnerable children: the overweight, the short, and the disabled. However, there was also expansion of victim types. There was an increase in stories starting in 2008 involving children who were Muslims or of Middle Eastern ethnicities, and Sikhs who were inaccurately perceived to be Muslim. Stories about particular victims appeared in both the *New York Times* and broadcast media; CNN reported that a child had been bullied "because of his middle name, 'Osama,' and because of his Middle Eastern heritage" (*Newsroom*, November 16, 2011). There were also reports that bullying of such students had increased overall. NBC's *Dateline* (May 6, 2012) reported that "Muslim children have become increasingly victims of harassment, bullying."

Other new victim types emerged. The media reported studies showing that students with food allergies were at higher risk of victimization (e.g., CNN's *American Morning*, March 24, 2011). There were also several stories that children with red hair had been targeted. These stories ranged from the very serious to the somewhat surreal. The media reported that Haylee Fentress, who died by suicide, was bullied about her red hair (e.g., NBC's *Today,* April 21, 2011). Regarding a different victim type, John Quiñones led a "What Would You Do?" segment about "ginger abuse" after receiving a letter from a 12-year-old boy, "one of three redheaded brothers [who] says he's constantly picked on at school" because of his hair color (ABC's *Primetime Live,* February 22, 2011). The *New York Times* (December 1, 2009) reported that three boys in Los Angeles were arrested and "booked on suspicion of bullying or kicking red-haired students at a middle school when a 'Kick a Ginger Day' prank inspired by a 'South Park' episode got out of hand."

Interestingly, even as more particularized categories of victims were added, the potential targets of bullying also were defined out through generalization. Anderson Cooper noted: "I mean, kids these days are bullied for all sorts of reasons: being overweight, having a speech impediment, the clothes they wear, a haircut—anything" (CNN, October 6, 2010). Juju Chang paraphrased a cosmetic surgeon as being "adamant that even the slightest abnormalities can bring on that teasing and bully-ing" (ABC's *Good Morning America,* April 14, 2011). Similarly, a letter to the editor in the *New York Times* (April 7, 2010) claimed that girls will seize on "the slightest difference" to "torment the chosen outsider." A guest on Joy Behar's show said: "Anybody who breaks the pattern of the stereotypical kid is vulnerable" (CNN, May 13, 2010). Such dis-course contributed to a sense that no child was safe; one can imagine frightened parents fretting over the many ways their children are not "stereotypical kids," whatever that is supposed to mean.

Defining Out to Everyone

In media coverage starting in about 2010, bullying was defined out to take in nearly all students as both bullies and victims; bullying was con-structed as a fundamental component of the social life of schoolchildren, a device by which students jockey for position on the social ladder. In this construction, bullying is not solely dyadic, victims and bullies are not mutually exclusive or even necessarily different from each other, and the social landscape in which bullying occurs is constantly shifting and "messy." This construction began to arise in its simplest form in claims that "most" bullies were also victims or that such a circumstance happened "very often." Usually a reason for this was not offered, but on CNN psychologist Susan Lipkins suggested a retaliatory bully cycle when discussing an allegation that singer Demi Lovato (who claimed to have endured school bullying) punched a girl while on tour (*The Joy Behar Show,* November 14, 2010). She, Columbia University professor Mark Lamont Hill, and host Joy Behar had the following exchange:

BEHAR: Does the bullied become the bully? It's like the abused becomes the abuser?
LIPKINS: Not always. But very often the victim does become a bully. They have had enough. They have lost themselves. It's gone over the top. And now they do unto others what has been done to them.
BEHAR: Right. I guess they would rather identify with the bully than the victim.
LIPKINS: You would rather be the bully than victimized.
HILL: Exactly.
BEHAR: Rather be the hammer than the nail as they say in the song.

Lipkins said something very similar on NBC's *Today* (March 22, 2011): "Very often we see that the victim becomes the bully when they have the chance to do it. It's like they do unto others what has been done to them. So we have a victim-bully cycle." The term "cycle" was also employed by Drew Pinsky on CNN (*The Joy Behar Show,* August 25, 2010) and Michel Martin on NPR (*Talk of the Nation,* March 15, 2011); we did not find the term used in the *New York Times.* This appears to be an extension of the previously mentioned social learning theory as applied to parents of bullies.

This idea was sometimes extended into a claim that *every* student is or has been a bully or a victim. This was most often put forth by nonexpert claimsmakers. Tina Meier, mother of Megan Meier, claimed on *Dr. Drew* (CNN, August 25, 2010) that "every child, every person, has bullied somebody at some point or been bullied." Drew Pinsky appeared to hedge his reply: "That's kind of an interesting statement to say that everybody may have been bullied or a bullier once." A student told Anderson Cooper: "Everyone is a bully and everyone is a victim. . . . like you've bullied. I've bullied. Whether you know it or not, you've bullied someone"; and another student told Cooper that "you can bully yourself" (*CNN Presents,* October 11 and October 9, 2011). However, Jodee Blanco went perhaps the furthest: "Bullying isn't just the mean things that you do, it's all the nice things that you never do" (*CBS Evening News,* February 27, 2012).

We found similar forms of defining out in the academic literature. For instance, Liepe-Levinson and Levinson wrote that "targets of bullies can be 'large,' 'small,' 'bright,' 'not so bright,' 'attractive,' 'not so attractive,' 'popular,' 'unpopular,' etc. What they all have in common is being the target of bullies" (2005, p. 7). The resultant tautology is that victims are those students whom bullies target. Robert Faris, a sociologist at the University of California–Davis, proposed a more sophisticated form of defining out. In partnership with CNN, Faris and colleague Diane Felmlee conducted a study of school bullying at the Wheatley School in Old Westbury, Long Island, New York. Their study was reported to have "found that popular but not the most popular kids are often the bullies. Kids who are social climbers, aggressively trying to be part of the in crowd are the ones who torment their peers" (CNN's *Newsroom,* February 12, 2011). The study received wide coverage on multiple CNN shows during October 2011—by then identified as bullying prevention month. It was discussed regularly and articulated as an important part of Anderson Cooper's CNN special *Bullying: It Stops Here* (October 9, 2011). In discussing the study's findings, Dr. Faris noted: "A lot of these aggressive behaviors are really rooted in the desire for status. It's about climbing these social hierarchies." Cooper confirmed that "it's actually a response to where they are in the social order. And they're trying to move up by putting somebody else down or by knocking somebody else down who's a little higher up than they are" (CNN's *Anderson Cooper 360,* October 10, 2011).

Coverage of this study situated it as a challenge to many of the explanatory frames previously articulated in the news media. In both the *New York Times* and broadcast media, the study's findings were constructed as signifying the emergence of a new lens through which to view bullying more broadly. Bullying was now viewed as functional in a school and cultural context that valued competition and getting ahead at the expense of others. Bullies were no longer maladaptive individuals with psychological problems, but healthy, adaptive beings using bullying behaviors as a means to an end. While this may indeed be true, we suggest that this new construction also further complicated the definition of bullying. In discussing his research with Anderson Cooper, Faris noted that "there's really kind of two types of patterns going on." One is where kids pile on and pick on "a vulnerable kid who's a little bit different in some way, who's kind of violated some of the unwritten codes of social life in a school." The other is where "kids are using [bullying] a little more tactically to climb these social hierarchies." It is the second pattern of aggression that is "more common" and "much more prevalent in all the schools that we've seen. And it seems to peak in the middle to upper ranges of the status hierarchy" (*CNN Presents,* October 9, 2011).

Rosalind Wiseman, author of *Queen Bees and Wannabees,* appeared to concur. She used the term "messy" at least three times in one interview to describe social relations among schoolchildren (e.g., CNN's *The Joy Behar Show,* August 25, 2010) and said in an interview a year later: "What we know is there's a small amount of kids who are targeted for being different and they are piled on by kids. But the vast majority of bullying is a competition, a social competition, where targets and bullies can be really fluid. And that makes it incredibly difficult for parents and for teachers to identify it. Because it looks like all of us" (CNN's *Your Bottom Line,* October 15, 2011).

As discussed in Chapter 1, however, definitions of bullying within academic discourse tend to organize around three common traits—repetition, power imbalance, and (serious) harm. The construction of bullying as "social combat" is focused on students in the middle of the school social hierarchy engaged in bullying those above them, a kind of behavior that would not fit the prevailing definitions articulated in the academic discourse. Defining bullying out in this way included just about every young person in school except those at the very top or bottom of the social hierarchy, and any "mean" thing they may have done, intentionally or not. As one young woman from the school where the research was conducted stated during Anderson Cooper's CNN special, "Everyone is a bully and everyone is a victim" (October 9, 2011). A young man who attended the same school was identified as being in the top 5 percent of both bullies and victims. When asked about this characterization, the young man stated: "I mean I can definitely see the victim part. I went through a lot of that. And—but the aggressive part, I don't really see because I'm not all that—I'm pretty quiet in school." This prompted Cooper to ask Faris, "Did you find it interesting—I mean a lot of kids didn't actually see themselves as aggressors." To which Faris responded: "Yes. And I think [they might] not realize that they've done something, you know, that was interpreted as mean, you know, to a peer. And so they're not—kids may not always be aware of it."

According to this construction, a majority of youth are involved in bullying in some way. As Anderson Cooper noted: "Fifty-six percent of Wheatley students surveyed said they were involved in either aggression, victimization or both" (October 9, 2011). As Faris and Felmlee note in their research report, their own rates are "somewhat higher than a national estimate of 19% annually [according to Nansel et al., 2001], but that study asked explicitly about 'bullying,' which research shows leads kids to underreport more subtle forms of harassment" (2011, p. 2). We agree that asking youth about bullying per se would likely result in underreporting of other forms of harassment and aggression. However, defining bullying down in ways that include onetime acts of meanness results in an exaggerated estimate of the prevalence of bullying in a news media discourse where terms such as "peer aggression" and "bullying" are used interchangeably with little attention to the ways in which they were measured within specific studies.

At first blush, the construction of school bullying as social combat suggests a kind of sociocultural explanation. One could argue, for instance, that youth are simply mimicking the adult world, in which getting ahead at all costs is valued to a greater extent than compassion, care, and cooperation. As one guest on CNN's *American Morning* suggested, "In a true sense bullies kind of rule the world to a large degree later on. I mean, large corporations, everybody knows, you know, a tough boss who yells at his employees to get productivity" (October 6, 2010). This narrative also seems to situate bullying as a process rather than the expression of problematic behavior on the part of individual evildoers. In this sense, the entire web of adolescent relationships is at play, suggesting a culture of bullying within schools. In fact, Faris himself expressed such an explanatory framework: "We need to direct more attention to how aggression is interwoven into the social fabric of these schools" (*NYT*, February 15, 2011). We agree with his assessment, and point out in detail in Chapter 8 the inadequacy of treating bullying as solely a psychological problem (or set of problems). However, while certainly adopting the language of institutional and sociocultural explanations, a more careful analysis suggests that this new construction continues to confuse the school bullying narrative in several ways, once again allowing blame to be laid solely at the feet of youth. Additionally, the construction of bullying as social combat does not address the content of the bullying or the ways that kids reenact larger cultural forces by employing bullying as a mechanism of informal social control. As we discuss in later chapters, bullying cannot be fully understood without attending to the broader contexts within which it arises (e.g., gender and hetero-masculine norms). By taking a narrower functionalist approach, the construction of bullying as social combat works to keep hidden these important sociocultural dynamics surrounding school bullying.

Such a construction also has the danger of collapsing in on itself. If the majority of youth are bullies and victims, can bully unconsciously and also through inaction, and can even bully themselves, then bullying has become everything and therefore means nothing. As we will see in Chapter 8, constructions of victims and bullies have implications for the types of prevention and intervention strategies that news media and other claimsmakers advocate. Proposed strategies would likely differ a great deal between someone who thought bullying was caused by bullies with low self-esteem versus another who saw the cause as everyday social combat. However, both such approaches would likely focus on the individual level, much the way that most systems of social control treat other forms of deviance. What is left behind in the construction of bullying as individual pathology are the ways in which bullying is linked to and can be partially explained by larger contexts, including the family, school, and sociocultural milieu. In the next two chapters we explore these very contexts as explanations propped up by the construction of school bullying as a public health crisis of epidemic proportions.

Note

1. Throughout the book, when a news media host is named, the reader can assume that the conversation took place on that host's self-named broadcast program unless otherwise indicated.

3

From Personal Pathology
to Collective Crisis

One of the biggest impediments to learning is bullying in school. It's
an epidemic.
                                        —Fox's Bill O'Reilly (January 27, 2011)

To me, it's an epidemic and it's a disease.
                                        —CNN's Dr. Drew (February 22, 2012)

In Chapter 2 we illustrated how the early dominant construction of
school bullying relied on a deeply individualized narrative in which
bullying represents a struggle between vulnerable victims in need of
protection and dangerous bullies in need of social control. However,
like other social problems, explanations for bullying expanded from
personal problems to cultural and social ills. In Chapter 4 we explore
the implications of constructing school bullying as stemming from a
culture of meanness. But here, let us first briefly touch on the process
through which this transition from micro- to macro-level explanations
took place. Specifically, the transition to cultural explanations of school
bullying relied on a series of expansions that situated school bullying as
a public health threat of epidemic proportions. As the construction of
bullying as an epidemic expanded in scope and depth, it motivated
action, attracted resources, and was implicated in new environments and
situations. This expansion, however, also created confusion, opposition,
resentment, and scorn. The shift from a focus on individual to cultural
problems through public health discourse fractured existing consensus
and threatened to collapse the construction of school bullying in on
itself. In this chapter, therefore, we focus on how the construction of

school bullying moved from a discourse of personal pathology to one of collective crisis. Over the course of our sample period, we found that the discourse on bullying expanded in many ways. News media were active participants in this expansion, reporting with increasing alarm on the so-called epidemic unfolding before their very eyes.

The Bullying Epidemic

In news media accounts, statistics were consistently presented in ways that supported a narrative of bullying as a growing national (and sometimes global) crisis and epidemic. This was more so the case in the broadcast media, which often uncritically reported social scientific evidence, and in many cases without any reference to the source of such evidence. The *New York Times* seemed to take a more measured approach, at times problematizing this framing to an extent.

From the early 1990s on, the news media framed bullying in terms that evoked a general sense of increasing seriousness. As early as 1995, the *New York Times* referred to bullying as a "life and death issue" (October 22), especially in relation to the increased use of dangerous weapons. Two years later, CNN anchor Bobbie Battista said to a guest, a school psychologist: "Ms. Peterson, some would say that bullying, I think, has reached epidemic proportions in this country. . . . Why are we . . . so hesitant to accept bullying and teasing as a serious problem?" (*Saturday Morning News*, December 6, 1997). Such alarmist coverage receded as the time bomb fears declined. However, in later years, and particularly in response to Phoebe Prince's 2010 bullycide, it was no longer a question of whether bullying was an epidemic, but whether the rest of the country was going to wake up to it. The media also supported the notion of this epidemic by references to other social problems that had already been identified as serious concerns in need of serious responses, such as mean girls and Internet threats. For instance, speaking on *Anderson Cooper 360* (March 30, 2010), Phil McGraw pointed to the "girl problem" and cyberbullying in ways that helped fuel the notion of a growing, more serious epidemic of bullying in the United States: "This is at epidemic proportions. It's happening on the Internet. It's happening on the schoolyards. It's happening more with girls."

The Numbers Don't Lie, Do They?

In a 2005 article, Best used coverage of the results of the study by Nansel and colleagues (2001) of the prevalence of bullying in the

United States as an example of how statistics can be presented in ways that construct particular kinds of narratives. Our analysis of news media constructions found a similar pattern. The process through which bullying became a nearly unquestioned epidemic involved consistent references to putative facts and statistics from various experts. These statistics and facts were often presented, especially in the broadcast media, with little reference to the limitations of the research that produced them and were used well past their methodological expiration date. They were also rarely challenged through the introduction of counterclaims. Again, this was not necessarily the case in the *New York Times,* where the frame of the bullying epidemic was a bit more muted and counterclaimants were given greater voice.

The most persistent statistic first appeared in our media sample in 1997, when it was noted that "160,000 children stay home from school every day because they're—they're fearful of going to school, either physically or—or scared that they'll be teased and tormented" (NBC's *Today,* April 16, 1997). The reasons for students' fear and the extent to which they stayed home as a result varied in specificity and magnitude across media reports. In 1997, the cause was "fear of intimidation" (*CBS Evening News,* December 14, 1997). In 2000, frequent expert claimsmaker Dr. William Pollack, an author and psychologist who specializes in the study of boys' lives, made the claim that "a hundred and sixty thousand children a year miss a day of school because they're bullied" (ABC's *Good Morning America,* June 7, 2000). Eight years later, Dr. Pollack claimed that "over 100,000 students every couple of days won't go to school because they've been bullied the day before" (CNN's *Newsroom,* April 14, 2008). Then in 2010, Anderson Cooper made a similar claim on his own CNN show: "And as many as 160,000 kids across the country say they've been so scared of their tormenters, of their bullies, they've actually stayed home from school" (March 30). George Stephanopoulos of ABC's *World News* was even more specific: "One startling number, 160,000 children missed school *today* because they were afraid of being bullied" (March 10, 2011).

The media rarely cited the source of the statistic, yet adopted it as an accepted and objective fact. From what we can tell, it appears that the statistic originated as an extrapolation from a single question on the US Centers for Disease Control's annual Youth Risk Behavior Surveillance Survey (YRBSS). This is a self-report survey administered to students in middle and high schools across the country. The specific question asks: "During the past 30 days, on how many days did you *not* go to school because you felt you would be unsafe at school or on your way to or from school?" (emphasis in original). In the 1993 wave of this survey, 4.4 percent of the respondents indicated that they had missed at least one day of school in the previous thirty days due to safety concerns. The state and local prevalence rates varied widely (Centers for Disease Control and Prevention, 1995). In 2011, the number was 5.9 percent, again with a wide range of state and local variability (Centers for Disease Control and Prevention, 2012).

The extrapolation of the prevalence rate among a study's sample to a population-specific number is certainly a common, albeit problematic, practice in the social scientific community, but this is not why we present this detailed discussion. Instead, we do so to illustrate the process through which putative facts are constructed by news media, expert, and advocacy-based claimsmakers. If repeated often enough, a statistic becomes part of the reality of a social problem, and as the source of the statistic becomes blurred or lost, claimsmakers are able to present it as an independently verified, valid truth. Even so, individuals in the broadcast media (experts included) reconstructed the basis of the statistic; it began to change based on the context and narrative and moved from "in the past 30 days" to "in a year" to "daily" to "today." The motivation for missing school also moved, from "fear" to "bullying" and even "torment." The statistic was also used as evidence of the worsening problem of bullying, which seemingly ignored all previous instances of the exact same statistic being presented for over ten years, as Chris Cuomo did on ABC's *20/20* (October 15, 2010). However, this claim contradicts the conclusion offered by the Centers for Disease Control: "Among students nationwide, the prevalence of having not gone to school because of safety concerns did not change significantly during 1993–2011" (Centers for Disease Control and Prevention, 2012, p. 9).

This, of course, was not the only evidence of the growing menace of school bullies offered in the broadcast media or of broadcast media claimsmakers' lack of attention to the origin or context of statistics. Not only were statistics presented in ways that implied increasing danger, but the inconsistency of findings also tended to muddy the waters. For instance, in 1997 it was claimed that 76 percent of students reported bullying victimization (NBC's *Today,* April 16). In 1999, ABC's *Good Morning America* reported that "at least 20 percent of our nation's school children" were victims of bullying (January 19), and little more than a week later the same show reported the statistic as one in four children, or 25 percent (April 26). A few months later, however, NBC's *Today* remained close to its previous assertion of 76 percent (September 1). In 2008, reported prevalence rates of victimization ranged from one in four middle school students (ABC's *Good Morning America,* April

10), to about half of the nation's children (CNN's *Anderson Cooper 360*, February 25), to 75 percent of middle school students (ABC's *Good Morning America*, May 2). As recently as 2012, estimates ranged from about one in six children being "regularly bullied in school" (NPR's *Tell Me More*, January 31), to one in five students (*NBC Nightly News*, June 7), to 25–30 percent of kids (CNN's *Newsroom*, March 17), to about a third of students between the ages of 12 and 18 (NPR's *Tell Me More*, January 16), to as many as 80 percent of kids (CNN's *Dr. Drew*, January 9). We found a similar pattern of inconsistency in statistics cited in the broadcast media as to the prevalence of bullies, bully-victims, and witnesses/bystanders. This dizzying array of statistics regarding the prevalence of bullying helped cement the notion of bullying as an epidemic and minimized the capacity for counterclaims to take hold, even though some counterclaims did emerge.

Counterclaims

So persistent was the framing of school bullying as a growing crisis and national epidemic that the few counterclaims that were presented in the broadcast news media tended to be ignored or modified to fit the dominant frame. This was illustrated in an exchange between two hosts of NBC's *Today* (March 23, 2010), Natalie Morales and Al Roker, and their guest, clinical psychologist Dr. Jeff Gardere. Morales said that teen violence had actually been dropping but added that "we are starting to see more" extreme cases. Gardere said: "Well, I think . . . that about 30 percent of teens have either bullied or been bullied. . . . So the statistics are still very high." According to this exchange, then, the problem is simultaneously shrinking, worsening, and remaining stable over time.

Some in the broadcast news media occasionally paused to question whether the increasing coverage of bullying reflected an actual epidemic. For instance, CNN's Kyra Philips noted: "School bullies [are] driving their victims to suicide. We've reported so many of these stories lately and [we're] not sure if it's an epidemic of cruelty or awareness, but in some cases, the bullies don't give their victims any outs" (*Newsroom*, May 14, 2010). In our sample, the *New York Times* clearly included more consistent counterclaims regarding the extent to which bullying constituted an epidemic and serious public health concern. It should be noted, however, that the newspaper also included references to the same studies and statistics included in the broadcast media. This makes sense, considering the relatively limited number of studies that have been conducted assessing national prevalence rates. Over time, however, the inclusion of counterclaims offered a more complex picture than the one constructed by the broadcast media.

Several articles in the *New York Times* challenged the notion of an increase in the prevalence of bullying. For instance, in 2007 in response to a report regarding an increase in harassment, intimidation, and bullying in New Jersey schools, the newspaper quoted education commissioner Lucille E. Davy, who "attributed much of the apparent increase to heightened public awareness of such misconduct and to more accurate reporting by school officials as the result of increased training and state oversight" as opposed to an increase in actual bullying behaviors (August 30). More specific frames were also challenged. For example, the *New York Times* took on the so-called girl problem in a 2010 opinion piece (April 2). There the authors first mentioned that the Phoebe Prince case had been presented by some "as evidence of a modern epidemic of 'mean girls' that adults simply fail to comprehend." However, they insisted that "this panic is a hoax" and that "every reliable measure shows that violence by girls has been plummeting for years." Another *New York Times* op-ed in 2010 challenged the notion that new forms of technology had somehow made kids meaner and more likely to bully: "It's important, first, to recognize that while cell phones and the Internet have made bullying more anonymous and unsupervised, there is little evidence that children are meaner than they used to be" (July 23). In a 2012 feature article, the *New York Times* reported on a recent analysis of data from the National Crime Victimization Survey that indicated that there had been a significant drop in youth exposure to violent crime: "The decrease corresponds with an overall drop in violent crime over the last two decades. But it also comes in tandem with substantial declines in other indicators of childhood distress, including teenage suicide, bullying, and physical and sexual abuse, [that] a number of studies have shown. Surveys indicate that children report feeling safer at school than they did in the past and are less likely to engage in risky sexual behaviors" (September 20).

We may even draw parallels between the construction of bullying as a growing epidemic and the dominant construction of the continuing "crime wave" in the United States. Some criminological scholars have long lamented the ever-present "tough on crime" discourse articulated by politicians and supported by the constant bombardment of television crime dramas and news media coverage. Of course, the reality in the United States is that crime rates, including for violent crime, have been declining for over two decades, since the early 1990s. For the most part, however, attempts to dislodge the hold of the crime wave construction, like those that challenge the bullying epidemic construction, often fall on deaf ears.

It is also important to note that we agree with Best's (2005) argument that these dynamics are less about deliberate lying about statistics than about a general lack of statistical literacy, together with an even greater lack of understanding of how statistics are also socially constructed. Our critique of the ways in which the so-called epidemic of school bullying is propped up by presentation of statistical data is also not intended to discount the very real problem that school bullying poses for individuals, schools, and the broader culture. We have no doubt that school bullying impacts the daily lives of hundreds of thousands of children. We also believe that expert claimsmakers are employing these statistics out of a genuine concern for the well-being of young people. However, the cacophony of claims espousing the growing epidemic of school bullying, grounded in putative facts, has not served this purpose. Instead, these dynamics have opened space for the continued discourse of bullying as an epidemic, elevated its status as a public health threat, and increased calls for poorly conceived responses that seem to further harm youth through the imposition of stricter mechanisms of social control (e.g., zero-tolerance policies).

Expansion of Bullying's Harms

The news media have not always depicted bullying as having serious and far-reaching consequences. In the beginning of our research period, bullying was constructed as harmful to only some children, sometimes. The *New York Times,* in its "Parent and Child" column (October 28, 1993), quoted a psychology professor as saying that "for some children [bullying] can be a traumatic and shaming experience" while "for others the effects may be minimal and transitory." Similarly, a journalist on ABC's *20/20* (April 28, 1995) said that "many children are bullied occasionally and are able to deal with it" and that only "one in 10 children is an extreme victim of bullying." In the late 1990s, the time bomb construction emerged, linking bullying to serious harm. Even so, bullying rhetoric did not cohere around a message of serious danger to all children, either because school shootings were exceedingly rare, because the time bomb risk of bullying was somewhat attenuated (the risk was to the victims of the bullies), or because the bullies' victims were not objects of our sympathy. However, during the last three years of our study period, the news media constructed a very clear and dramatic constellation of harms that included new victims and new injuries, and they also extended the temporality of harm well past one's school years. As depicted in Figure 3.1, while the time bomb narrative never fully dissipated, by around 2008 it was accompanied by additional harms linked to school bullying, including youth suicide.

The Risk of Bullycide

News media alarm over bullying-related youth suicides is quite recent. For many years the news media did not respond with widespread concern to reports of such suicides. When the news media did report them, they rarely linked them together as part of a trend (unless they occurred at the same school or in the same town). News media outlets were also unlikely to run multiple stories about a single suicide or even a string of them, although sometimes parental activism did catch the attention of the news media. Suicides due to bullying were also described as uncommon. A reporter on ABC's *20/20* said in 1995: "It is rare that a child commits suicide in response to being teased and harassed" (April 28). The link between bullying and suicide was also sometimes depicted as indirect. One story from 1993 said: "At least one expert says it's unlikely that bullying from classmates alone would lead to suicide" (NPR's *Morning Edition,* October 27).

Figure 3.1 Threat Level from Bullying Across Time

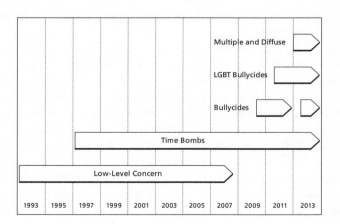

The earliest bullying-related suicide in our news media sample that received significant coverage was that of 11-year-old Daniel Scruggs, who died by suicide in 2002. Scruggs had been repeatedly bullied at school and subsequently hanged himself. Prosecutors brought charges against Scruggs's mother for her failure to care for him when it was alleged that the family lived in squalid conditions. She was tried and convicted in 2003, but the Connecticut Supreme Court overturned her conviction in 2006. Like later cases that received intense media attention, the press coverage focused more on the criminal charges against Mrs. Scruggs—which were very unusual—rather than on the boy's suicide. Thus, a clear narrative did not emerge from this case because of the ambiguity involved: Was it the bullies or living in a squalid home that led the boy to take his life? Five years after Scruggs's suicide, CNN reported on the suicides of several youth who had been bullied due to their perceived homosexuality, but other news media outlets did not echo this coverage.

As discussed in Chapter 1, the suicides of Phoebe Prince and Tyler Clementi in 2010 (and even more so the criminal prosecution of those said to have bullied them) received massive news media coverage and led to the establishment of a bullycide discourse. As a result, suicide from bullying was frequently invoked by an alarmed news media, some of which reported these bullycides to be an epidemic. The threat of suicide appeared to hang over many bullying discussions and was commonly invoked even if it was not the topic of the program or the article. This sometimes happened even if the subject was not originally related to bullying: in a program discussing an anti-obesity media campaign that featured overweight children, a media consultant said he was worried that the children in the ads would be bullied. He went on to say: "My biggest fear is that some child who isn't in those ads gets teased mercilessly and, God forbid, tries to attempt suicide or something like that based on that and it is tracked back to this" (CNN's *Newsroom,* January 5, 2012).

The bullycide discourse that arose in news media regularly constructed suicide as a direct and common (even expected) outcome from bullying; author and self-described bullying survivor Jodee Blanco said that bullying victims will carry their experience "their whole lives, if they survive it" (CNN's *The Joy Behar Show,* April 5, 2010). This narrative was also evoked frequently through commentators' tendency to frame bullying prevention as suicide prevention. Kevin Jennings, the federal "school safety czar," said on *NBC Nightly News* (April 3, 2010): "What keeps me up at night, and everyone in the US Department of

Education, is the idea that out there . . . are children who'd rather die than go to school."

Journalists sometimes only implied causality by simply claiming that children "killed themselves after being bullied" (CNN's *Newsroom,* May 22, 2010). A clearer, but still couched, narrative was told through journalists' reliance on another claimsmaker to make the link, such as when a journalist said that several youth "committed suicide after their families say they were bullied to death" (NBC's *Today,* January 11, 2011). However, it was not uncommon for journalists and others to declare the causation unambiguously, and sometimes highly emotionally. Anderson Cooper said that "kids are being bullied literally to death" (CNN, January 26, 2011). Occasionally an expert suggested that the link between bullying and suicide may be indirect, mediated by factors relating to the victim's psychological makeup or family dynamics. For example, Kenneth Trump, president of National School Safety and Security Services, said: "And we also have to look at the mental health issues of the kids who are committing suicide, because typically there's a lot of other things behind that, beyond just these incidents, that we have to wonder if there were other things that we could have done to build their foundation and self-respect as well" (CNN's *Rick's List,* March 31, 2011).

However, exploration of such nuances was not common, either theoretically or as applied to particular cases. While discussing the case of Amanda Cummings, who died after being struck by a bus, Dr. Drew Pinsky (CNN, January 9, 2012) strained to make an unambiguous connection between bullying and her apparent suicide. He first noted that police found a note in her pocket that mentioned a breakup with her boyfriend but apparently did not mention any bullying. He went on to say that Cummings was "bullied for years *and* heartbroken over a breakup." Pinsky concluded that Cummings was "*so tormented by bullying* that she felt compelled to throw herself in front of a bus" and then shortly afterward said Cummings "was so devastated *at least partially* as a result of a breakup, *but also* [because of] the relentless bullying at school." We discuss this example not to suggest that we know Cummings's motive (we don't), but to make the point that Pinsky couldn't have either. Through this unquestioning linkage, however, news media and other claimsmakers were able to target a single factor in order to simplify the explanation for what is often a complex phenomenon. News media coverage of the suicides of Haylee Fentress and Paige Moravetz in 2011 was quicker to provide complicating details about school expulsion, depression, and parental marital problems, and it also suggested that the two had become "more than friends," an insinuation that is discussed in more detail in Chapter 6.

In constructing the bullycide risk as an epidemic, news media and other claimsmakers first linked together several bullycides to construct the impression of a national epidemic. Then every subsequent bullycide "painfully highlighted" this "national problem" of bullycides, such as the suicide of Jamey Rodemeyer (CBS's *Early Show,* September 22, 2011). Thus, four to six rare events are agglomerated, and then each succeeding rare event is presented as evidence of what has been constructed as a national epidemic. During this process, news media emphasized three factors that added to a sense of alarm. The first was the emphasis on the ubiquity of the threat, a suggestion that *any* kind of bullying could give *any* child suicidal thoughts. Dr. Marc Lamont Hill, a Columbia University professor, said that "things that we think are minor that don't affect people in grand ways actually can end up causing suicide." He added that "heckling somebody over their weight, being too skinny, too small, making fun of the size of someone's head; I mean things that we might think of as ordinary childhood teasing can lead to suicide" (CNN's *The Joy Behar Show,* November 4, 2010).

The second factor was that suicide was a *hidden danger.* Many stories emphasized that bullied children are both embarrassed and disempowered, and that they don't want to report the bullying because they fear retribution or don't think that anyone can help them (e.g., CNN's *Issues with Jane Velez-Mitchell,* April 21, 2011). The third factor—inevitability—flows from the first two. A bullied child develops "a sense of worthlessness and the only way he [*sic*] can get away from his tormentors is by killing himself" (CNN's *Newsroom,* April 28, 2012). Krya Phillips evoked the following phrases during just a few sentences in one report: "bullies driving their victims to suicide," "the bullies don't give their victims any outs," "young bullies taunting their targets to the brink," "some of those victims seeing just one solution," "picked on, teased, taunted, harassed and threatened to a point of no return" (CNN's *Newsroom,* May 14, 2010). Thus, the following claustrophobic thought-spiral emerges: (1) just about *any* bullying could cause suicidal thoughts, (2) such thoughts won't be shared with anyone, and thus (3) the child's only option is suicide. Add to this the "constant threat" from cyberbullying, and it's no wonder that a CNN *Newsroom* correspondent said after reporting the suicides of two boys: "Experts say, everyone should be alarmed" (April 24, 2009). As we discuss at the end of this chapter, this kind of rhetoric has unintended consequences, including eventual disbelief and disengagement.

Longer-Term Damage

It is ironic that the media trumpeted the "It Gets Better" project (see Chapter 6) while simultaneously conveying an implicit message that *perhaps it doesn't*. Warnings of long-term, even life-long, harms from bullying emerged with greater frequency in the bullycide era, at least in the broadcast media. (Stories occasionally appeared in the *New York Times* over our entire study period, with no obvious pattern.) In the early years of our study period, there were a couple of examples in the broadcast media describing potentially serious harms, but these harms were described rather vaguely. Toward the end of our study period, it became common for the damage to be described in much more specific and frightening ways. Phil McGraw said on *Anderson Cooper 360* (April 9, 2010): "This stuff gets ugly. And even in cases where students, young people don't wind up killing themselves, they can be really scarred for the rest of their life [*sic*]."

Journalist Tony Cox claimed that "researchers are just beginning to understand how the effects of abuse stay with victims into young adulthood, middle age, and even retirement" (NPR's *Talk of the Nation,* December 2, 2010). Dr. Hill, the Columbia University professor who was quoted earlier, expanded on this idea with a dire claim that "some people never recover from bullying." He said that there are "people who can't have healthy relationships, who fail at marriage, who can't get a good job, who have low self-esteem and who may even do damage to themselves later in life because they never recovered from the trauma" (CNN's *The Joy Behar Show,* November 4, 2010). It was also common for those who called in to broadcast programs and wrote letters to the *New York Times* to disclose the lasting effects of their childhood bullying. A 42-year-old caller to NPR's *Talk of the Nation* (December 2, 2010) said he created "a website that started as sort of a cathartic way for me to tell my stories." A listener tweeted to Randi Kaye, host of CNN's *Sunday Morning* (April 1, 2012), that he had developed "PTSD [posttraumatic stress disorder], panic attacks, and depression" and asked: "Is there help and support for the adult survivors of bullying?" And there were many dozens of examples from our research that contained disclosures from famous persons about how bullying had scarred and shaped them in a variety of ways. Journalists also revealed their painful early experiences, something we take up in Chapter 7.

The media also gave some attention to long-term harm to bullies, although such coverage was spottier than for victims. For example, results of longitudinal research by Olweus (1992) on bullies' criminal careers were sometimes cited, although not always accurately so. Olweus had found that 60 percent of children who were classified as bullies in sixth through ninth grade had a criminal conviction by age 24, and 40 percent had three or more convictions. This compared to about 10 percent in the control group. This study was cited (or its findings appeared to be referenced) on NBC's *Dateline* (October 12, 1997), ABC's *Good Morning America* (April 10, 2008), and NPR's *Tell Me More* (March 15, 2011, January 16, 2012). It was also mentioned in the *New York Times* (March 27, 1996, April 25, 2001).

We note these reports not because they are hysterical or inaccurate. In fact, they highlight important research that indicates significant long-term effects of bullying across the life course, findings that continue to be supported in recent research (see, for instance, Ttofi et al., 2011). However, news media claimsmakers were citing research findings that in many cases had been published years or even decades prior. In these cases, academic research on bullying appeared to serve as a reservoir that the news media could draw on in augmenting and amplifying bullying's harms to suggest a growing threat. This was likely both frustrating and gratifying for academic researchers; gratifying because their research was finally getting sustained attention, but frustrating because the research was sometimes not well-described, and was largely wielded to generate fear. Besides deepening and temporally lengthening bullying's potential harms, the media also expanded the categories of persons potentially affected, well past the bully/victim dyad.

Secondary Victimization

The expansion of the bullying discourse to include secondary victimization echoes in some ways academic research that has increasingly looked at bullying in its "ecological" context, a trend we discuss in more detail in Chapter 4. The media constructed several categories of secondary victims, one of which consisted of witnesses to bullying, who are frequently termed "bystanders." Bullying was said to affect bystanders in several negative ways. They were "more likely to skip school or abuse alcohol," for example, according to research cited in a *New York Times* editorial (March 1, 2012). Bystanders who "witness their friends being bullied may also suffer from the same type of morbidity and potential mortality" as victims, according to a psychologist interviewed on NPR's *Talk of the Nation* (December 2, 2012). Psychologist and "hazing expert" Susan Lipkins claimed on CNN's *The Joy Behar Show* (November 4, 2010) that "even bystanders are affected when they watch a victim . . . [and] there is a trauma that they experience as well." Behar responded: "Second-hand bullying. . . . Like second-hand smoke," and Lipkins agreed with the metaphor. In a few cases the risk was broadened beyond the bystanders to the entire school. The *New York Times* (March 1, 2012) cited an academic study that found "that when a school has a climate of bullying, it's not just the targeted kids who suffer—the entire school lags academically." A journalist on *NBC Nightly News* (April 3, 2010) claimed: "Education officials are worried [that] bullying is causing a drop in the graduation rate," and linked this worry to the federal government's proposal for spending on bullying prevention.

The broadcast media in particular focused on a more intimate set of secondary victims—family members of the bullied. As can be imagined, such reporting was highly emotionally evocative, particularly in interviews of families of bullycide victims. Many interviews of parents opened with the interviewer asking how parents were coping. Sirdeaner Walker, mother of bullycide victim Carl Walker-Hoover Jr., said on ABC's *Good Morning America* (March 9, 2011): "Afternoons are hard because . . . when I see the kids walking home from school, you know, I expect Carl to . . . come home." Kirk Smalley, father of bullycide victim Ty, spoke of his heartbreak in a way perhaps only a parent could fully understand: "We haven't done his last load of laundry because it smells like him. We haven't washed his sheets because I can go in there and lay on his bed and smell my boy." He suggested a way to get at the heart of bullying: "You want to learn what bullying and suicide is all about? Talk to the people directly who it affects the most" (CNN's *Newsroom*, October 4, 2010). The media regularly heeded Smalley's advice to talk to the directly affected. Parents frequently were asked to recount the moment when they found their child dead; Cynthia Logan, mother of Jessica, said: "I walk into the room and I turn to the closet, and there is my baby hanging." She began to cry, and said: "I didn't know the magnitude of what was happening to her" (CBS's *48 Hours*, September 16, 2011). And when a parent was not available, a parental stand-in was sought. Jane Velez-Mitchell (CNN, April 21, 2011) spoke to an uncle of bullycide victim Paige Moravetz. Velez-Mitchell reported that the suicide occurred after Paige's parents had left for a vacation in Hawaii and continued: "I can't imagine what they are going through. It boggles my mind to end up in Hawaii and find out this horror happened to your own daughter. Can you tell us how they're faring?"

A final type of secondary victimization was constructed as affecting the larger community beyond the school; as in the prior example, this was clearest in cases of bullycide. When reporting occurred shortly after the event, the community was said to be "stunned" and "saddened." A double suicide was reported to have "left [a] rural community some three hours southwest of Minneapolis in shock" (NBC's *Today*, April 22, 2011), and in another case viewers were told that "a Detroit community is mourning the suicide of a seven-year-old boy, seven years old" (CNN's *Saturday Morning News*, May 26, 2012). Sometimes the community mood shifted to other stages of mourning; in the aftermath of the Phoebe Prince bullycide, the media reported that the community was outraged over perceptions that teachers and administrators had done little to stop Prince's victimization. This anger was also directed toward the several defendants who were charged after Prince's suicide and even "towards those parents . . . that are raising these monsters," in the words of one local resident (ABC's *Good Morning America*, January 28, 2010). Cynthia Lowen, a producer of the documentary *Bully*, said that "bullying affects 13 million kids every single year." She demonstrated an almost cosmic sense of bullying when she said: "If you extrapolate back generation after generation after generation, this is something that affected millions upon millions of people in this country and people around the world." She added: "And it doesn't end in high school, and the scars do not end once you graduate from high school" (CNN's *Sunday Morning News*, April 1, 2012). As expansion of the bullying discourse continued, arguments were put forth that bullying not only extended beyond the bounds of high school but also beyond previously perceived geographical boundaries.

Expansion of Bullying from Urban to Suburban Contexts

While not as consistent a topic in news media coverage of school bullying, the idea that youth violence and bullying were spreading from urban to suburban and rural contexts did spring up from time to time, even though academic research has long suggested that bullying is not limited to particular kinds of neighborhoods or contexts. Issues of class and race, as expressed through discussions of inner-city versus suburban schools, were more common in the *New York Times* compared to the broadcast news media. In both cases, however, challenges to the perceived safety of "good people" in "good neighborhoods" gave the sense that problems expected in urban, inner-city neighborhoods and schools (e.g., youth violence) were spreading to the quiet, white picket–fenced suburban and rural communities of the United States. This was especially the case when bullying was associated with more serious types of harm such as suicide and homicide. In line with the analysis of O'Grady, Parnaby, and Schikschneit (2010), an urban underclass framework is employed by news media to construct urban school violence as somehow different and, in the case of bullying, encroaching on the perceived serenity of suburban life.

In response to the 1993 bullying-related suicide of 15-year-old Megan Pauley in Goffstown, New Hampshire (the fifth suicide in two-and-a-half years in the town), an NPR reporter painted a picture of Goffstown as a "middle class, bedroom community" to which some "moved to escape urban bustle and crime." It was a town where residents "feel safe, not a place where [youth] should be driven to kill themselves" (*Morning Edition,* October 27). A 2008 ABC story about alleged bullying at an esteemed all-girls boarding school begins: "what you can't imagine, where you couldn't imagine it" (*Good Morning America,* December 12). Similarly, a 2009 ABC story (*Good Morning America,* June 8) in response to the killing of a young boy in a suburban Maryland community also implied the spreading of urban problems to suburban communities. The story reported that most people believe that gang violence "is in the inner cities [and] it's about drugs . . . [but] there is a whole world of violence out there that puts kids in suburbs at risk." The story went on to describe a mother from Maryland who "did everything she could to protect her son from bullies" but it "turned out they were gang members." It was "just a block from their home [that] her son met a fate that even his mother could never have imagined." The mother was quoted as saying that "he died on our street in suburbia, where we paid $350,000 for a townhouse in a neighborhood where our shutters have to match our doors." Elsewhere in the story, questions were raised as to whether the attackers were really gang members. In any event, the story cautions: "There is no such thing as fake gang members. When there's a group of kids bent on violence and there's a victim involved, that is a gang." Through this negotiation, what might be a common problem in all communities—schoolyard bullying—is framed as gang violence and articulated as the spreading of a traditionally urban problem to suburban communities. This story, taken as a whole, has the effect of maintaining the shock associated with bad things happening in good places, while simultaneously expanding potential locations for harm. It also conflates bullying with homicide, a form of defining up that we consider later.

A somewhat different framing took place in response to Megan Pauley's suicide. In articulating their outrage, parents (and the news media in its coverage of the story) worked to limit the challenge to perceived community safety to institutional failure within one particular high school. This resulted in diminished culpability on the part of the broader community, maintaining its status as a generally safe place to live, free of the crime and danger of urban contexts. When contrasted with the response to Chris Jones's "gang-related" killing, serious harm associated with school bullying remained expected in certain kinds of neighborhoods, while limited, hidden, and perhaps ignored in others. It may also be relevant to note that Megan Pauley's suicide took place before Columbine and other suburban school shootings that worked to further shatter the perceptions of immunity to violence associated with suburban contexts, although, as noted earlier, subsequent stories continued to illustrate the shock associated with the existence of bullying in suburban schools, at least when resulting in extreme outcomes.

In the *New York Times,* a similar notion of expected violence in inner-city/urban schools consistently emerged. A 2004 opinion piece was even titled "The Urbanization of Suburban Classrooms," suggesting that suburban schools may need more money "to offer anti-bullying and gang prevention programs" (July 25). The writer goes on to state that "huge demographic changes are not going to stop. Immigration and urban flight to the suburbs will continue. Our schools had better be ready," suggesting that bullying is creeping into "good" suburban schools due to the encroachment of people of color.

Other *New York Times* stories, like those in the broadcast media, were more implicit by discussing bullying in inner-city schools within the broader context of peer violence. In several articles from early in our study period, bullying was mentioned only briefly in the context of serious violence, including students' fears of being shot, stabbed, and assaulted at their dangerous urban schools. Additionally, the framing of urban and suburban bullying in different ways was quite common in both the broadcast media and the *New York Times*. In the latter in 2009, for instance, a feature article made the point that "many urban districts have found [that] empathy workshops and curriculums help curb fighting and misbehavior." This was contrasted with Scarsdale, "a wealthy, high-performing district with few discipline problems to start with." There, "educators see the lessons as grooming children to be better citizens and leaders by making them think twice before engaging in name-calling, gossip and other forms of social humiliation that usually go unpunished" (March 1).

Beyond class and place, race was also brought up in the context of school bullying from time to time. This was often implicit in the discussion of class and place. On rare occasions, however, an explicit reference to race was made. One radio show guest said that she and her husband were Caucasian and that her 11-year-old son "goes to a school that is pretty white, and they have a very clear, no bullying, no physical harassment" policy according to which "you can't touch or degrade any kid." The guest added that her son played basketball "in a mostly black league" where "there are different standards." She said that her son had been "shoved into the stands, he has scars and bruises all over his body from it, and it's not considered bullying. But then when he goes back to his white-dominated school he cannot be rough like that" (NPR's *Tell Me More,* July 8, 2008).

The notion that different communities, whether based on race or class or place, have different standards of what is or isn't bullying contributes to the expectation of bullying and other forms of youth violence in some communities and the shock that emerges when it is exposed in others. It also contributes to the construction of bullying as expanding from urban communities to suburban and rural communities in ways that put increasing numbers of "good people" and "good places" in danger. When bullying and violence in suburban, wealthy communities is exposed (e.g., because of bullycides or the violent acts of time bombs), the dominant framing is the spread of urban problems as opposed to causes that are shared by youth across social location. Similar to the use of bullying discourse to construct gender normativity (discussed in Chapter 5), the discourse described here works to construct race, class, and place-based norms that differentially situate individuals and communities in terms of expectations of violence and victimization. Serious bullying in urban, minority communities is seen as normative and expected, while such behavior in suburban, white communities is seen as aberrant and abhorrent.

This critique was sometimes articulated by news media claimsmakers. Some went so far as to accuse anti-bullying activists of middle-class and white bias. For instance, after showing a vicious "girl fight" in Detroit, Fox's Greg Gutfeld lamented the anti-bullying efforts of celebrities and journalists, saying: "but they have nothing to say about this because this bullying is not politically correct bullying. You have to have bullying against, you know, a young gay victim. But when it's black kids destroying each other, no one says anything" (*The Five,* December 2, 2011). While we are suspicious of Gutfeld's motives in making this critique, it does highlight a tendency for claimsmakers to construct particular victims as more or less worthy of attention. (We discuss Gutfeld's unique rhetorical style in some detail in Chapter 7.) What is clear, however, is that as these purported urban problems were constructed as spreading to suburban and rural communities, expanding concern regarding who were potential bullying victims also took hold.

Implications of the Epidemic Narrative

The expansion of the construction of school bullying from a problem of individual maladjusted kids to a public health crisis of epidemic proportions relied on several shifts in the news media discourse. No longer were only certain kids in certain schools at risk for the harms associated with bullying. School bullying was now a threat to every child, more harmful than previously thought and for a much longer period of time. Bullies not only victimized those they bullied, but also bystanders, families, and the community as a whole. Like a virus, bullying spread from community to community until no one was safe. Once the epidemic frame was conceded, parents and others saw the threat of bullying around every corner. A school required yoga, and parents responded with a lawsuit claiming that their children were being forced into a religious practice and would be bullied if they didn't comply (CNN's *Newsroom,* February 21, 2013). Those who were worried about their child becoming the victim of a bully because of their appearance were told to try cosmetic surgery (ABC's *Good Morning America,* August 9, 2012). Within the epidemic frame, tragic yet relatively rare instances of bullycide were now seen as common, if not expected. As Debbie Almontaser, founding principal of the Khalil Gibran International Academy, wrote in a letter to the editor in the *New York Times* (October 29, 2010), in response to the lack of attention paid to bullying on the basis of religion: "Do we have to wait for a Muslim-American youth to commit suicide or be killed by a bully?"

While the construction of bullying as an epidemic certainly works to focus attention, it also comes with unintended consequences. As the extent of bullying and its associated harms expands, claimsmakers run the risk of exaggerating fears. These exaggerated fears may lead to exaggerated responses, such as zero-tolerance policies and criminalization. A recognition that the sky is in fact not falling, however, could lead to a backlash, through which a discourse of disbelief is fostered and the public and policymakers disengage, something we discuss in Chapter 8.

However, the story of the social construction of school bullying does not end here. Concomitant with the framing of bullying as an epidemic, news media and other claimsmakers also worked to expand bullying in two directions. By expanding definitions of bullying down, claimsmakers enveloped minor, isolated forms of teasing into the discourse. Additionally, definitions of bullying were expanded up to include more serious felonies and single instances of violent behavior. In addition, explanations for bullying began to spread from individual pathology to parental and institutional failure and, finally, to sociocultural explanations that implicated everyone in the ongoing fight against the growing epidemic of school bullying. As noted by CNN's Rick Sanchez:

> You've heard the phrase it takes a village? Well, it takes a community to stop the epidemic of bullying. Parents, teachers, kids, until they all stand together and say we're not going to tolerate this any longer, until they say every person in our community must be respected and encouraged and loved, and until they say enough is enough, until they say these words and put them into action, their community will remain a breeding ground for bullies. (*Newsroom*, September 24, 2010)

In the next chapter we explore in more detail how the framing of school bullying as a public health crisis and epidemic opened the space for explanations that put us all on the hook.

4

From Collective Crisis to Collective Failure

Bullies do it because they can. They do it because their parents allow them, because the schools allow them, and because so many teachers and coaches are themselves bullies.
— Neal Conan (NPR's *Talk of the Nation,* March 23, 2010)

In the process of framing school bullying as an epidemic, a wider range of causal explanations and potential solutions began to take hold in news media discourse. As discussed previously, the dominant early construction of school bullying in the news media was one of individual pathology. The roots of victimization were said to lie in young people's physical and psychological traits and in their behaviors, mostly divorced from context. However, this focus on bullies and victims was never absolute. Parents were said to contribute in various ways to their children's bullying and victimization; for example, bullies were said to disproportionately experience violence in the home. In addition, media attention to the responsibilities of schools and school systems began to take hold toward the end of our study period, through the construction of a frame of institutional failure. A somewhat similar pattern emerged with regard to broader sociocultural explanations. Throughout our study period, news media claimsmakers occasionally presented the neoconservative argument that "society" encouraged overly permissive parenting (creating bullies) or allowed too much coddling (producing victims). Toward the end of our study period, news media increasingly featured the claims of progressives who suggested that a lot of bullying resulted from a hegemonic hetero-masculine/homophobic power structure that pervaded all social institutions, including K–12 schools. A different set

73

of cultural claims involved the putative effects of media. Beginning in the 1990s, claimsmakers blamed school shootings on heavy metal music and video games, much of which is consumed by teenage boys. Toward the end of our study period, more widely consumed media such as television and movies were implicated, and broader sociocultural explanations (such as adult hyper-competitiveness) were advanced.

Last, the narrative expanded into social media technologies, which were blamed for opening up a powerful and unregulated means for students to harass, exclude, and intimidate each other—a set of behaviors gathered under the umbrella term "cyberbullying." Cyberbullying and its attendant media tools were constructed in differing and sometimes contradictory ways, as has been the case with other threats to young people in the past. Journalists and experts simultaneously presented digital media as mystifying, malignant forces that seemed to independently act *upon* youth and as devices that youth *used* quite purposefully to magnify and extend their ability to act maliciously.

The emergence of the epidemic narrative described in Chapter 3 opened space for macro-level explanations. Such a progression seems logical because it is difficult to support an epidemic narrative solely by resorting to micro-level phenomena. To invoke a public health analogy: viruses and hosts are necessary but not sufficient elements of a flu pandemic. Such a pandemic could only be fully understood by analyzing how a multitude of interrelated factors—human and nonhuman, institutional, cultural, and political—occurring at and among different levels evolved over time. In this chapter, we show how the media framed the family, the school, and the culture as contributing, oftentimes simultaneously, to the bully problem.

The Discourse of Parental Failure

Family-based explanations for bullying behavior have been around for a long time, and we observed several of them during the entire span of our news media sample. Some theories focused on contemporary family lifestyles. Psychologist and attorney Dr. Bonny Forrest suggested that children of parents who are "too stressed" can become bullies because such parents lack time to help their children develop social skills (Fox's *The O'Reilly Factor,* March 21, 2013). Also, various "crises at home," such as a divorce or parental job loss, could trigger aggressive behavior, according to academic research cited in the *New York Times* (October 28, 1993). However, the dominant discourse related to family-based explanations for bullying focused on the parent-child relationship and most often purported to explain how bullies, and somewhat less frequently, victims, are "created." In a 1993 *New York Times* article, researcher and psychologist Leonard Eron was quoted as saying, "You first learn violence within the family" (August 11). This *cycle of violence* theory appeared throughout our study period. As an example of domain expansion, eventually the term "bullies" replaced the more generalized label of "aggressive children": "Part of how bullying gets started among young kids is they have observed it modeled in their own homes" (Linda Young, psychologist and spokesperson for Qwest Online's safety program, speaking on CNN's *Issues with Jane Velez-Mitchell,* November 25, 2008). Psychologist Jennifer Hartstein said it simplest: bullies "come from parents who are bullies" (NBC's *Today,* July 5, 2012). The suggestion that a child's behavior is influenced by his or her parents' actions and attitudes is certainly not new or controversial. Nor do we suggest that such research is necessarily misguided when applied to school bullying in particular. What is problematic in our view is that through the articulation of parental responsibility, parents were placed in a number of precarious and contradictory positions in ways that oversimplified and confused the problem of school bullying.

For instance, as early as 1993 the *New York Times* reported the results of academic studies linking particular types of discipline to aggressive children and bullying; harsh discipline such as hitting and spanking put children most at risk (October 28, August 11). Conversely, claimsmakers also laid blame on parenting styles that lacked sufficient discipline. In 1997, Ronna Romney, then a Republican candidate for the US Senate, said: "We have a society today where children are not taught the same discipline and respect for authority for elders, for teachers" (*CNN and Company,* December 15, 1997). Parents of a boy who was killed by a "bully" echoed this call for increased discipline when they asked the other boy's parents: "What were you thinking all these years when you were raising him . . . not giving the boy any consequences for his actions, what did you think you were going to end up with?" (*CNN and Time,* September 17, 2000). Sometimes the too-harsh and too-soft narratives were communicated simultaneously, as in this excerpt from a *New York Times* feature article: "Instead of working out issues themselves during free play outside, children are micromanaged by parents who step in to resolve conflicts for them. Debbie Rosenman, a teacher in her 31st year at a suburban Detroit school, said that helicopter parents simultaneously fail to provide adequate authority or appropriate forms of supervision" (October 10, 2010).

Others in the news media agreed. CNN's Don Lemon, speaking to his guest, child and school psychologist Rachel Scheinfield, suggested that some parents might feel that "we are coddling our kids way too much here" (*Newsroom,* June 17, 2013). "Yeah, that's absolutely the case," she replied, adding: "We really want to promote a way for them to resolve conflicts in a healthy manner, but we also want to teach them how to respectfully disagree." Journalist and author Emily Bazelon also noted the tension: "You know, I think the problem here is that we both have over-policing and under-policing at the same time. . . . Kids have to have some adversity in their lives in order to grow up" (NPR's *Morning Edition,* April 17, 2013).

Adding to the problem of bully-producing parents, according to many claimsmakers, was that such parents "don't like to hear [that their children] are the ones doing the bullying" (Eric Bolling, on Fox's *The Five,* April 3, 2012). Indeed, we saw relatively few examples of parents who acknowledged their child's bullying behaviors. Claims that parents produced their own children's bullying behaviors and also were in denial about it created a heightened sense of victimization risk, because this removed one form of potential informal social control.

Another persistent narrative regarding parental failure was the purported link between hours spent in day care and bullying. In 1994, psychologist and author Robert Cairn discussed research that suggested a link between early entry into full-time day care and bullying, noting that "children who are put in full time day care very early in the first year often end up with this condition known as insecure attachment" and that "they become more difficult in school, more defiant with adult authority, sometimes they become bullying [*sic*] with other kids, they definitely show more aggression" (NPR's *All Things Considered,* December 10). Nearly seven years later, in 2001, *NBC Nightly News* reported on "a major new study on child care in this country" that was said to "confirm the fears of working parents everywhere" when it was reported to show that "some preschoolers, who spend lots of time in day care, can be more aggressive than children cared for at home by their parents. Even to the point of becoming bullies" (April 19). This research was also reported on NBC's *Today* (April 20), several NPR shows (*Morning Edition,* April 20; *Talk of the Nation,* April 24), and CNN (*Live at Daybreak,* May 2). That same year a similar story was published in the *New York Times* (April 19, 2001), although the discussion was a bit more muted because researchers involved in the study were heavily quoted. For instance, one of the study's principal investigators, Dr. Jay Belsky, was quoted suggesting that "children who spent more than 30 hours a week in child care 'are more demanding, more noncompliant, and they are more aggressive. . . . They scored higher on things like gets in lots of fights, cruelty, bullying, meanness, as well as talking too much, [and having] demands [that] must be met immediately.'" The *New York Times* story followed this with the statement: "The researchers conducting the study did not have an explanation for why some children in child care might become more aggressive or disobedient." In quoting another one of the researchers, the story noted that "the children's behavior, while demanding and aggressive, was 'in the normal range,' not so severe it required medical attention." This, however, did not stop news media and other claimsmakers from drawing wider conclusions from the research. In 2007, the link between day care and bullying made its way back into the news media landscape, again in the *New York Times:* "A much-anticipated report from the largest and longest-running study of American child care has found that keeping a preschooler in a day care center for a year or more increased the likelihood that the child would become disruptive in class—and that the effect persisted through the sixth grade" (March 26).

Much of this discourse of parental failure was articulated in ways that either explicitly or implicitly implicated mothers more so than fathers. For instance, in line with traditional heterosexual and gender norms, the locus of responsibility for the increased use of day care was placed squarely on the shoulders of mothers: "Of course, day care is the norm now since almost 2/3 of mothers with children under the age of six are in the work force in some form" (*NBC Nightly News,* April 19, 2001). This framing of day care as dangerous also fit with the narrative of parents not knowing or caring about what their children were up to, which was further underscored by numerous alarming stories of deadly risks. News media also continued to report new bullycides and link them to parental failure. CNN's Dan Simon opened one such story by reporting the suicides of two girls who had been cyberbullied. He said the deaths begged the question: "Is there something more that parents can do to protect their kids?" (*Newsroom,* April 12, 2013). These kinds of calls for increased parental control were not uncommon in the bullycide era, an issue we take up in Chapter 8.

The Discourse of Institutional Failure

We use the term *institutional failure* to mark the construction of a "faulty system" frame (see Sasson, 1995) through which schools and school systems were seen as failing to protect innocent children from the harms associated with the epidemic of school bullying. A 2004 letter to the editor in the *New York Times* illustrates the articulation of an institutional failure frame. Responding to a story titled "For Parents, Courses on Remedial Bullying," Michael Greene[1] wrote that parents represent "only a small part of the problem" and that most of the responsibility lay with "teachers, school counselors and administrators" who fail to "set a tone and climate that [bullying] is unacceptable" (January 4). Greene's letter foreshadowed the shift away from parental explanations in favor of tasking the schools with bullying reduction and prevention.

News media claimsmakers also regularly featured parents who detailed their vigilant but fruitless efforts to enlist the aid of school personnel to protect their children. CNN reported that both a 14-year-old who was "brutally attacked" and her mother said that the school "knew about the bully, but didn't do anything to stop it" (*Starting Point with Soledad O'Brien,* March 14, 2013). Another parent told CNN that although she had gone to the school resource officer, and although the school had bullying incidents on video, "they did nothing, because the schools do not want to get involved at all" (*Dr. Drew,* September 13, 2012). Similar to the conflicting constructions of parental responsibility just discussed, the combined effect of these two narratives was to make the need to act both more urgent and more futile. The implicit message was: help protect *your* children by working with the school, but don't expect too much, because schools have consistently refused or failed to protect *other* children.

The overriding theme of institutional failure was indifference. The news media reported that teachers and administrators do not intervene in 85 percent of bullying cases.[2] The news media buttressed this claim through reports of students who didn't bother to report bullying because they knew it wouldn't be addressed. Nearly every bullycide involved a narrative of institutional failure, heightening the sense of alarm. During a report about Brian Head, a bullying victim who shot himself in front of his classmates at school, ABC's Beth Nissen noted: "Brian told his parents he was being bullied. They advised him to tell his teachers, who urged him to solve his own problems. Brian chose a horrifying solution" (*Good Morning America,* January 19, 1999). The failure of schools to protect innocent victims of bullying also quickly became a major focus of news coverage in Phoebe Prince's 2010 suicide, and the narrative continued years later. Kevin Cullen of the *Boston Globe* wrote several columns about Prince, and in 2012 said on NBC's *Dateline:* "I just find it hard to believe that no one in a position of authority, no adult in that school, knew that Phoebe was being persecuted because it was such common knowledge among the kids" (April 1). When placed within the context of zero-tolerance policies and increased criminalization, it is easy to see why students are unlikely to report bullying or other forms of problematic behavior to school officials.

One of the most nationally publicized narratives of school failure, although not involving a bullycide, involved Alex Libby. Libby was one of the victims on whom the documentary *Bully* focused; most of Alex's bullying occurred on a school bus. After the documentary's release, the Libby family was interviewed on numerous news programs, frequently along with the film's producers. Many programs aired a portion of the film that showed Jackie Libby, Alex's mother, meeting with Kim Lockwood, who was serving as assistant principal at the time of filming. Their conversation from the film was re-aired by many news programs (the following transcript is taken from CNN's *Anderson Cooper 360,* February 28, 2013) and offered as a prime example of the indifference of schools:

> LIBBY: I'm very upset. I'm going to be honest. I'm upset enough I don't want him to ride the bus [No. 54] anymore. . . . It's absolutely non-acceptable [*sic*]. I mean, they are stabbing him with pencils and choking him and—
>
> LOCKWOOD: Buses are notoriously bad places for lots of kids. You know, I wish I could make it stop on that, but I'm not going to lie to you, I can't. But what we can do is we can get him on another bus.
>
> LIBBY: So if I put him on another bus, I have, what, little to no guarantee that he'll be safe on that bus either?
>
> LOCKWOOD: I've ridden 54. I've been on that route. I've been on a couple of them. They are just as good as gold.
>
> LIBBY: You send your kid to school with the assumption that if they are out of your care they're in someone else's that's just as capable as you of keeping them safe, and I don't feel like that. He's not safe on that bus.
>
> LOCKWOOD: I don't either. We will take care of it.

Lockwood's rapid alternating between saying she can't stop the problem, denying there is a problem, and then saying she would take care of it, is likely what led Libby to tell Anderson Cooper that Lockwood "politicianed us." (The same program reported that after *Bully* was filmed, Lockwood was promoted to principal of Alex's school.)

The Libby-Lockwood exchange was also aired on *Good Morning America* (April 5, 2012), where Katie Couric suggested that perhaps the only reason that the buses were "good as gold" was because Lockwood happened to be riding on them at the time.

News media also featured parents who were angry that their children were punished when they chose to fight back against a bully, literally adding insult to injury. Rosalind Wiseman claimed that this was a common phenomenon in various kinds of peer aggression: "I always tell teachers you always see the second hit. You never see the first hit." Thus, the student "who reacts to aggression is . . . the one that gets in trouble by the teacher . . . [and] they actually aren't addressing the problem that started it" (NPR's *Tell Me More,* February 26, 2013). CNN reported on one Texas parent, Randy Duke, who claimed his 14-year-old son Max "finally fought back [against a bully] and wound up getting a suspension for it" (*Starting Point with Soledad O'Brien,* October 10, 2012). According to Randy, Max felt like no one at the school was listening to him; Max said that he "couldn't walk away because [the bully] just [follows] me and beats me up all the time." Randy decided to spend several hours a day outside his son's school wearing a sign that read: "Bullying victims are punished here." Indifferent schools and wrong-headed decisions are bad enough, but in about mid-2012 the media began to run stories about teachers, coaches, and administrators who bullied or assaulted students, or who encouraged other students to do so.

For example, in a fall 2012 program, CNN's Dr. Drew Pinsky announced: "We're going to kick off the discussion of the latest school scandal" (September 24). His introduction acknowledged that by then viewers had been treated to a litany of news stories that accused teachers and administrators of much more than indifference. (And there were more stories to come.) The particular scandal that Pinsky's program featured involved allegations that a boy's high school soccer coach "sort of winked and looked the other way" as older athletes sexually abused younger ones, allegedly by inserting a wooden pole into their rectums. And some guests freely speculated that the situation might have been even worse, or wider. Pinsky noted that some parents wondered whether incidents had occurred with the girls' soccer team. Reporter Jacqueline Hurtado responded: "Yes. Some parents have concern if their daughters were affected and they just haven't said anything. One mom says she's asked her [daughter] and her daughter said no." Another guest, clinical psychologist Michelle Golland, went much further: "My belief is that the coach . . . will probably be found out to . . . in some way be involved in something sexual with young boys." She continued: "We know what child sexual predators do, Drew. They watch it, they sell it, they use it, OK. And so I would not be at all surprised if at some point that this is going to be far bigger." The story was apparently so compelling to Pinsky that he stayed with it and was not able to cover other planned incidents "about a Michigan teen who had had his mouth stapled shut at a party and [a] Texas girl who was severely spanked at a school."

One might expect such stories to be covered on tabloid-style shows such as *Dr. Drew,* but this was by no means the rule; several stories caught the attention of nearly all the broadcast networks, but this was less true of the *New York Times.* In Tacoma, Washington, teacher Joe Rosi was reported to have orchestrated a bullying incident that was termed "of epic proportion" by attorney Joan Mell (CNN's *Issues with Jane Velez-Mitchell,* September 4, 2012). Several students caught the fifteen-minute incident on their cell phones; it shows Rosi allowing or encouraging other students to write on the victim's feet, pile chairs on him, stuff socks in his mouth, and cover his face with a pillow. (Rosi at least limited the humiliation by instructing the students to "leave [the victim's] pants on.") In response to the resulting uproar, Rosi wrote a letter in which he said: "I can honestly say that at the time I did not believe that any of the children were at risk of harm during their interactions, nor did I view the incident as anything more than harmless childhood horseplay." The story was reported on other CNN programs (e.g., *Saturday Morning News,* September 1, 2012), and by ABC's *Good Morning America* (August 31, 2012) and NBC's *Today* (September 1, 2012). A teacher in Brooklyn was accused of more direct and serious assaultive behavior against a student that was caught in an "outrageous video you have to see to believe" (CNN's *Issues with Jane Velez-Mitchell,* July 2, 2012). The video allegedly showed a student "brutally beat up by a teacher nearly twice his size" (the student was reported to weigh 110 or 112 pounds). The student was "thrown against a table" and thrown "to the ground a couple of times like a rag doll." Apparently, the difference in size between the teacher and the student was highlighted because the school had "tried to blame [the student] for the attack."

The widespread coverage of the two incidents just described may have been fueled partly by the existence of a video record, but the media also reported on nonvideoed incidents that were also less "vicious" (the word several journalists used to describe the content of the two videos just discussed). One such widely reported story involved a kindergarten teacher from San Antonio, Texas, who allegedly tried to teach her students that "bullying was bad" by ordering them "to beat up a so-called bully"; she told students to "take turns hitting him" and even to "hit him harder" (CNN's *Sunday Morning News,* June 17, 2012). Other CNN shows reported the story (e.g., *Starting Point with Soledad O'Brien,* June 18, 2012), as did ABC's *Good Morning America* (June 18, 2012) and NBC's *Today* (June 19, 2012). The boy's mother said that her child was a kindergartner, not a bully, and added that the school had never reported any behavior problems to her. A different story involved an elementary school teacher in Delco, Idaho, who instructed students who had succeeded at their writing goals to "scribble" with paint on the faces of students who had failed to meet those goals (e.g., CNN's *Saturday Morning News,* November 17, 2012).

The media sometimes pointed out that these types of incidents were extremely rare. Jane Velez-Mitchell said to Lorraine Connor, described as a teacher and anti-bullying coach: "We usually think of the victims of bullying as children and the perpetrators as other children. How common is this for a teacher to be an alleged perpetrator of bullying?" Connor responded: "It's not common, Jane. It really is not common, I promise you." However, Connor cited the statistic of 160,000 kids staying home from school every day because of child-on-child bullying and added that "the last thing they need to deal with is this kind of . . . behavior led by the adult in the room who's supposed to be the parent—in place of the parent during the school day" (CNN, September 4, 2012). Thus, the risk of teacher-on-student bullying was downplayed and then linked to concerns about student-on-student bullying.

While Lorraine Connor claimed that bullying by teachers is "not common," the available empirical evidence, while limited, suggests otherwise. One study of 116 teachers in seven schools reported that most (70.4 percent) of the teachers thought that they and other teachers bullied students "in isolated cases," while nearly one in five (17.6 percent) reported that such bullying happened "frequently" (Twemlow et al., 2006). (Thus, Connor's claim provides a rare case where an expert may have underplayed a bullying problem.) Another study, using a convenience sample, found that bullying of students by teachers (measured by teachers' self-reported behaviors and assessment of other teachers' behaviors) was positively related to the number of suspensions in the school (Twemlow and Fonagy, 2005). The authors of the study claim that this raises important questions about the role of teachers in fostering antisocial behaviors among students. As we discuss in Chapter 8, a more nuanced understanding of school bullying, grounded in a social-ecological approach, would require a more critical examination of how bullying by teachers works to support the use of bullying as a mechanism of social control among students.

Teacher wrongdoing was compounded in several cases by the institutional failure frame—claims that administrators did not respond appropriately or quickly enough, or even tried to cover up the behavior. Regarding the previously mentioned bullying incident involving teacher Joe Rosi, many parents and other commentators thought it outrageous that Rosi had not been immediately fired after the cell phone video recordings came to light. Lorraine Connor said: "I am absolutely shocked that this teacher still has a job" (CNN's *Issues with Jane Velez-Mitchell,* September 4, 2012). Regarding the previously mentioned Brooklyn incident, the student's mother claimed that she didn't learn of the alleged assault by the teacher "until the 'Daily News' knocked on her door, and she viewed the tape" (CNN's *Issues with Jane Velez-Mitchell,* July 2, 2012). An attorney guest, Alison Triessl, said on the same program that the school "can't claim [the teacher] as a rogue employee [because] there are many employees standing around. . . . So we know that there's a cover-up."

Importantly, all of these incidents were reported within a context of other, unrelated fears about schools. An episode of ABC's *Nightline* (January 30, 2013) illustrates how the news media agglomerates risks. The news show opened with a report about Charles Poland, who had shot a school bus driver and grabbed a child, taking him to an underground bunker. Coanchor Terry Moran said the incident is "raising some chilling questions about how safe children really are on the school bus." Reporter Jim Avila picked up the story by announcing: "School buses all too often are not the sanctuary they are supposed to be." As he continued, he strung together several unrelated incidents: the bullying of bus monitor Karen Klein; a father boarding a bus and threatening students whom he thought had bullied his daughter; and a bus driver in Almond, New York "who was so intoxicated the children asked her to stop the bus." He then added to the mix the results of an investigation by an ABC affiliate in Baltimore that caught on tape "hundreds of speeding buses, others running red lights." Avila said another affiliate in Cincinnati had conducted a similar study, and played a tape from an unidentified reporter there who said: "It scares me for the sake of our children." Avila responded: "Scary for good reason. Kids aren't required to wear seat belts in most school buses. This Ohio bus with an interior camera captured what can happen in an accident." A few months later, several news media broadcast a "disturbing video" that showed a school bus monitor "repeatedly bullying a 5-year-old boy with disabilities"

(CNN's *Starting Point with Soledad O'Brien,* April 1, 2013; see also ABC's *Good Morning America,* March 30, 2013; CNN's *Early Show,* April 1, 2013). Thus, the institutional failure frame was extended well beyond peer-on-peer bullying, with students also facing potential assault from teachers and risking a multitude of dangers while traveling to and from school. When this frame was combined with the discourse of indifference, school personnel were simultaneously constructed as not bothering to monitor students' behavior and over-monitoring through the application of their own bullying as a form of social control.

Parental and community fears related to the failure of schools to protect their children from the scourge of bullying served as an impetus for calls to remedy the situation. But the media, in their appeals for a remedy, paid relatively little attention to the broader aspects of school culture that might breed violence. Instead, they focused on four, sometimes interrelated influences: violence (which includes meanness and hyper-competitiveness and their portrayal in popular media), social media technologies, gender normativity, and homophobia. We address the first two here in Chapter 4, before turning to gender normativity in Chapter 5 and homophobia in Chapter 6.

The Discourse of Sociocultural Failure

Violence, Popular Media, and Bullying

As we have indicated, most news media poorly reconciled the ways that individual students, parents, school staff, and educational institutions contribute to the bullying problem. The addition of a sociocultural discourse provided further complexities that were also frequently unresolved. The expansion of explanatory frames to include social and cultural contexts worked to implicate the entire United States in the "still growing" problem of bullying in schools. Jane Velez-Mitchell asked on her CNN show: "Shouldn't we as a society look at the ugly truth that, we as a culture, you and me and everybody else, we're raising a generation of children who are addicted to violence?" (February 1, 2011). Los Angeles mayor Antonio Villaraigosa, responding to the Sandy Hook Elementary School shootings in Connecticut in December 2012, also referred to a "culture of violence" and considered bullying to be one aspect of it (CNN's *Newsroom,* January 14, 2013). Others implicated specific aspects of US culture, such as hyper-competitiveness. Rosalind Wiseman, as quoted in the *New York Times* (December 18, 2003), drew connections between a competitive culture and bullying, noting that "there's a tremendous competition for tying material goods to social status" and that "the competition is ruthless." Also in the *New York Times,* Natalie Angier enlarged the focus to include the international stage, suggesting that "it's perhaps a bit of delicious paradox" that while the "nation is seized with concern over school bullying . . . to the rest of the world, it seems, America is the biggest bully of them all" (May 20, 2001). Other claimsmakers focused in on popular culture specifically. Psychologist and "conflict expert" Susan Lipkins described what she called a "vulture culture" (NBC's *Today,* March 30, 2010). She went on to suggest that "we see [this] in the reality shows and a lot of television and media" and that we are "actually showing them [children] how to be demeaning and how to be degrading and how to bully."

However, even these broader sociocultural explanations were eventually brought back down to the institutional level. Even as explanations for school bullying expanded to include sociocultural contexts, responsibility for the creation of such contexts remained focused on families and schools. In the same *New York Times* article just quoted, Rosalind Wiseman went on to suggest that parents in the "New York–New Jersey metropolitan area" are much to blame for the ruthless competition we see among children, because "there is the tendency to see your kids as living, walking resumes" (December 18, 2003). Speaking on CNN's *Larry King Live,* Dr. Laura Schlessinger noted: "What you hear on radio . . . on television, in music and on the Internet is all mean. We have raised our children to believe mean is the norm. We really shouldn't be surprised. But we have to stop it" (April 8, 2010). Psychologist Michael Oberschneider also linked broader sociocultural trends to changes in parenting: "As a society, not to sound like a philosopher, but as a society, we're moving faster and faster. Parents don't have the time . . . to teach the values and morals that matter" (ABC's *Good Morning America,* November 6, 2010).

These types of claims were not new. Links between bullying and popular media were made after the Columbine school shootings and other mass violence in the 1990s. Phenomena such as heavy metal music and violent video games were blamed—or scapegoated (see Springhall, 2008)—for causing these events. However, the difference in some of the more recent discourse is an implication of a much broader range of popular media—for example, network television programs—rather than media consumed mostly by teenage boys. Thus, those who produce and consume much mass media—which is most of us—are implicated as contributing to various forms of cultural violence, including school bullying. Just as is the case with harsh and violent parents, children do as they see. And similar to the conflicting messages regarding parental and institutional failure, competing narratives sometimes emerged concerning popular cultural representations of bullying. For instance, one *New York Times* article identified the film *Mean Girls* as one of a number of "bully-centric teenage kiddie flicks" that contributes to the "media message that being mean is cool" (January 28, 2007). However, across the news media landscape, the film was also considered to have shined light on a long-hidden problem among school-aged girls. The film was based on Rosalind Wiseman's book *Queen Bees and Wannabes,* and Wiseman was consistently lauded for her contribution to the fight against bullying.

As we can see, in the turn toward sociocultural explanations, individual bullies, parents, families, and schools were not completely let off the hook even as their culpability was being partially mitigated by the consideration of these larger forces. As news media and other claims-makers advanced their explanatory frames to the sociocultural level, the kinds of responses they articulated often remained at the micro level. Sociocultural-level responses were rarely explored. Rather, the problem was framed as parents versus culture. This was true whether the claims-maker was a content producer or a parent. As to the first case, Randi Kaye interviewed Jo Overline, creator of a smart phone app called Ugly Meter Pro that "uses facial recognition technology to actually scan your face . . . to give you a beauty rating" (CNN's *Saturday Morning News,* May 5, 2012). In response to Kaye's question, Overline confirmed that "there's real science behind this." Kaye cited an example of a 14-year-old girl whose "friends" distorted a picture of the girl that "made her look fat" and then "wrote horrible things about her on [a] fake Facebook page." While this incident did not involve Overline's app, Kaye questioned whether it could become a bullying tool. Overline deflected the question in three ways. He first said that "bullies will be bullies" and that if they don't use the Ugly Meter, they'll just use something else. Later he said: "I think parents need to take responsibility for their own kids. . . . I don't need to . . . put the blame on apps or violence in movies or video games. I need to be a parent. And the other parents out there should do that too." When pressed further, Overline said: "Bullying is a hot topic. They like to find the next thing that they can try to blame bullying on. But it's completely fabricated by the press. There's never been any uses of Ugly Meter [in] bullying."

From the parental side, it seemed like an impossible task to battle against popular media, both because of its ubiquity and because of many parents' disconnection with it. Psychologist Wendy Walsh told CNN anchor Don Lemon a personal story during an interview (*Newsroom*, April 13, 2013). Walsh said that she had borrowed her daughter's iPod and gone for a run. Pressing the "25 most played song list," she encountered mostly lyrics with sexual messages, with "not one lyric about love, romance." She suggested that "every parent out there do [this] . . . to see what your voice is up against." Walsh was on the show to discuss a couple of recent cases of students sharing photos of girls being sexually assaulted. Lemon said the stories were "becoming more and more familiar" and asked Walsh: "What is going on here?" Walsh answered: "It's a kitchen sink of influences," including "male bravado," a decline of religion and moral teaching, and a lack of training in relationship, compassion, and emotional skills. She concluded: "Add that to the Internet, you got a big problem." Thus, the emergence of the cyberbullying frame brought forth a different kind of sociocultural failure focused on technological advances and the inability of adults to fully grasp or control youth behavior online.

Bullying Goes Viral

As a new form of bullying, cyberbullying reframed the discourse of an ever-growing and ever-worsening epidemic. Cyberbullying expanded traditional bullying's reach by spreading beyond the spatial and temporal boundaries of the school—defining bullying out. All of this was propped up by an increase in anxiety on the part of adults, who sometimes openly expressed their fear and lack of understanding of the technologies involved. In our analysis, cyberbullying emerged as a focus of news media attention in 2003 and rapidly took on a particularly prominent role in the construction of school bullying as a social problem. Part of this construction was the notion that cyberbullying represented a new, more dangerous form of bullying. Rosalind Wiseman, whose prominence as a bullying expert extended into the discourse on cyberbullying, seemed flummoxed when asked about bullying in "packs": "Oh, my gosh, absolutely. And the Internet makes it absolutely—I can't tell you. I can't tell you. . . . I mean, it's just—yes. Absolutely. The answer to your question is yes. In packs. With the Internet, it actually just—it swirls it to a frenzy" (NPR's *Talk of the Nation*, April 9, 2008). These kinds of claims regarding how much worse cyberbullying is compared to traditional school bullying were infrequently challenged even though research was both scant and methodologically problematic (see Thomas, Connor, and Scott, 2014). Recent, although limited, research that asks students to rate the seriousness of bullying behaviors suggests that the nature of the bullying (e.g., its public versus private nature) may be more important than its form (Bauman and Newman, 2013; Chen, Cheng, and Ho, 2013; Sticca and Perren, 2013). Other research that has measured students' actual experiences has sometimes found more negative mental health effects from cyberbullying than from other forms of bullying (e.g., Campbell et al., 2012).

As a sociocultural explanation, the elevated danger of cyberbullying was often attributed to the nature of the technologies involved. It wasn't so much that kids were changing, it was that the world around them was changing in ways that amplified their innate tendencies: "Kids have always had this tendency, this bullying sort of thing. The Internet just kind of distills it down, makes it bigger, faster, stronger, where kids have this instant response to these bullying tendencies they've always had" (Dr. Michael Bradley, speaking on ABC's *Good Morning America*, April 12, 2008). However, others likened it to a kind of transformation of children due to the technologies: "Kids without the Internet are catty. With social networking, they become monsters" (*NYT*, December 10, 2012). Similarly, a guest on Drew Pinsky's CNN show claimed: "Kids have a thing I call muscles, cyberbullying muscles, like beer muscles" (April 21, 2011).

What is cyberbullying? Definitions of cyberbullying were somewhat vague. For instance, the *New York Times* variously defined cyberbullying as "kids saying nasty stuff about other kids" (January 30, 2005), something that "invokes rumor and insults via the popular social-networking sites Facebook and MySpace" (January 28, 2007), and "an imprecise label for online activities ranging from barrages of teasing texts to sexually harassing group sites" (June 28, 2010). The lack of a clear and consistent definition of what constitutes cyberbullying contributed to bullying being defined up *and* down. In other words, behaviors that would otherwise be characterized differently began to be subsumed under the rubric of cyberbullying. The discourse on cyberbullying acted as a vacuum, sucking up a wide range of online behaviors deemed dangerous. This expansion extended to include the creation of fake websites or Facebook pages, classmates' posting of lists of girls that described them as "sluts," the reposting of a video of a young boy singing a song to a girl he liked, online and texted threats, and "sexting" (children sending nude or seminude photos of themselves to friends or current and former sexual partners). In some instances, claimsmakers struggled with how to categorize such behavior. An exchange between several claimsmakers on *The Bryant Park Project* morning radio newsmagazine (NPR, June 4, 2008) in response to an investigation of nude photo sharing at a school illustrates this point. Anchor Mike Pesca asked if the behavior could be likened to "bullying through nudity," suggesting that "it's a bullying package." Anchor Michel Martin replied: "Sounds like harassment . . . is maybe a better word . . . than bullying." Pesca and guest Laura Silver seemed to agree, with Silver summing up the negotiated definition by describing it as "a new form . . . cyber-cellular bullying." As reporting on sexting gained momentum, claimsmakers began to liken it to child pornography and prosecutors began to file charges in some instances, a somewhat troubling form of defining bullying up.

Similarly, cyberbullying was defined up to include other existing forms of serious online danger. For instance, Jane Velez-Mitchell said: "There's an epidemic of kids falling prey to *violent sex offenders* and young people resorting to unimaginable violence. . . . Teen girls *beating each other up* after accusations of trash talking. A feud that started on MySpace and ended up [in] *fisticuffs*" (CNN, February 9, 2010). Buzzwords such as "stranger danger," and fears related to kidnapping, abuse, and homicide, were used in conjunction with the cyberbullying frame in ways that heightened fear and evoked long-held emotional reactions associated with the vulnerability of youth. ABC's *Nightline* claimed that "there's a darker side to Facebook" and that "there's an increasing number of serious criminals online, looking for vulnerable individuals, particularly children. And the evidence of their activities, well, it's beginning to mount. From bullying to sexual assaults, even murder" (April 20, 2010). Another way in which cyberbullying worked to define bullying up that garnered a great deal of coverage in the news media was the video-recording and posting of physical fights on the Internet. The discourse framed this as cyberbullying by focusing on the posting of video on YouTube. Cyberbullying also served as a context in which previously held notions about the safety and sanctity of the home broke down, adding to the rising fear among (suburban) parents.

No safe harbor. In line with the construction of school bullying as a rapidly spreading epidemic, cyberbullying expanded the temporality and locus of traditional school bullying in ways that evoked greater fear among adults. Cyberbullying was consistently contrasted with school bullying or face-to-face bullying in ways that heightened its reach, in terms of both time and space. As discussed in Chapter 3, claimsmakers had been lamenting the growing threat of school bullying and its encroachment on nonschool spaces. With the emergence of cyberbully-ing, traditional bullying was reframed as primarily a school-based prob-lem. The juxtaposition of traditional school bullying and cyberbullying relied on two dominant narratives. First, cyberbullying was consistently positioned as being more vicious due to the ability of cyberbullies to escape detection. As CBS's *Early Show* host Jeff Glore pointed out: "Okay so we can be anonymous on the internet [*sic*] and kids can, too, which has increased vastly the amount of bullying or cyber bullying" (March 29, 2010). This anonymity was implicated in the increased viciousness associated with cyberbullying, compared to traditional school bullying. Second, there is the perceived inability of victims to escape their tormenters. Speaking on *NBC Nightly News* (April 3, 2010), author and frequent claimsmaker Barbara Coloroso stated: "There's no safe harbor. It used to be that we could go home if we were targeted, close our doors or even go out in our neighborhood and play and be free from the tormenting." So dominant was this frame that Anderson Cooper dedicated an entire week of coverage to it and said he had a good reason for calling the programming *Bullying: No Escape* (e.g., CNN's *Anderson Cooper 360,* October 4, 2010).

In terms of both place and time, then, cyberbullying was positioned as significantly more dangerous than traditional school bullying. Not only was there no escape, but the consequences of cyberbullying were longer-lasting. One mother of a cyberbullying victim suggested that a comment on the playground could be forgotten two weeks later but "kids save their I.M.'s [instant messages]. They not only save them, they cut and paste them and print them. It stays forever. If you say something mean, you can't take it back" (*NYT,* May 25, 2003). Others pointed to the disturbing trend of cyberbullies continuing to target chil-dren even after suicide to further emphasize the lasting effects of this new, more dangerous form of bullying: "And they're being bullied in death. I mean, they're being derogated in death. They're being defamed in death. I mean, it's not enough that their family has this pain visited on them, but think about these—these young men and women have taken their own lives, and still it doesn't stop. Still, they're being put down and derogated even in death, and that is absurd" ("Dr. Phil" McGraw, speaking on CNN's *Anderson Cooper 360,* October 29, 2010).

Even as cyberbullying was being constructed as more dangerous and wider reaching than traditional school bullying, the two were also linked together in ways that challenged the dominant cyberbullying dis-course and reinforced the epidemic frame. For example, on *CBS Evening News,* Beaux Wellborn of the Bully Suicide Project noted:

"Today, a kid will wake up and will have anonymous texts. They'll go to school and get bullied. They'll come home and they'll have messages on Facebook" (April 1, 2010). Like the other sociocultural explanations described in this chapter, with the emergence of the cyberbullying frame, blame for the bullying epidemic was no longer laid at the feet of parents and schools alone. Adults must worry about the encroachment of bullying into "every digital corner of a modern child's life" (*NYT,* August 19, 2010). The media's construction of cyberbullying interacted with existing fears associated with the danger and vulnerability of youth as well as the danger of new, unfamiliar technologies in ways that amplified adults' fears and generated a new sociocultural explanation.

The Wild, Wild Web. A general lack of understanding of the Internet, social networking, and new technologies among adults permeated the cyberbullying discourse. Claimsmakers and news media personalities seemed to struggle with wrapping their heads around what seemed like alien technologies poised to take over kids' lives in unprecedented ways. Speaking on his own Fox show, Bill O'Reilly stated: "This bullying is— it's 10 times worse than it was when I [was] a kid, 20 times than when you were a kid, because of the machines. You can do it on the machines now" (May 18, 2010). Similarly, on CNN's *Newsroom* (July 9, 2009), one host suggested that bullying had become much different than "when we were in school" because "now we got the Internet, the Twitters, the Facebooks, all of that." The media depicted parents as equally clueless. Writing about an online message board, a *New York Times* reporter noted that the father of a cyberbullying victim was aghast, since "like most other parents interviewed" he "had never heard of Formspring [a website allowing anonymous postings] until a reporter's call" (May 6, 2010). The father is quoted as saying: "It's just shocking that kids have access to all these things on the Internet and we don't even know about it." This lack of understanding and unfamiliarity led some to describe the Internet as a free-for-all in which there is no control over what children are exposed to or engage in. The *New York Times* (January 22, 2008) described children's online space as "a virtual Wild West, though conducted through cell phones, MySpace and Facebook." A few years later, Phil McGraw made the same point on CBS's *Early Show,* calling the cyberbullying environment "the Wild, Wild Web" (July 1, 2010).

This lack of understanding and the resultant inability to control children's behavior on the Internet worked to construct a vision of a new, unfamiliar society in which adults are ill-equipped to handle youth behavior. And, as with other sociocultural explanations, parents were not completely off the hook. As author Ryan Van Cleave pointed out on CNN's *Issues with Jane Velez-Mitchell:* "It's parents who allow their kid unsupervised access to social networking, Internet, video games. They are essentially buying bullets for a gun they didn't even know that their kids had" (March 29, 2011). Evoking strong emotional language associated with serious violence, the news media framed children's unfettered access to new technologies as part of parental irresponsibility and linked this frame to existing fears. In the context of cyberbullying, youth are constructed as being both out of control and vulnerable, in need of social control in an environment where adults are seemingly incapable of providing it. As one reporter on CNN's *American Morning* (April 8, 2010) pointed out, "We have a 21st century problem that's being dealt with [through] a 19th century mindset."

Counterclaims regarding parental fear of new technologies also emerged in the news media. In 2011, a *New York Times* article called into question the extent to which cyberbullying represented a real and lasting threat to children (June 26, 2011). In so doing, the newspaper related the seeming hysteria over cyberbullying to previous waves of adult fears. It referenced a variety of adult fears of media that went back generations. Like prior panics over comic books, the *New York Times* said that "the sky seems to be falling again," this time over digital threats. And yet, the newspaper reported, overall rates of juvenile crime, teen sex, and school violence have been declining since the 1990s. The article noted that David Finkelhor, director of the Crimes Against Children Research Center at the University of New Hampshire, "calls this distance between anxiety and reality 'juvenoia' and chalks it up to an 'exaggerated fear about the influence of social change on children.'" The article continued: "Parents and lawmakers are, in short, so worried about protecting our children that they can fail to distinguish between real threats and phantom ones." This dynamic is also similar to Woolgar's (2002) notion of *cyberbole,* a dialectic of hype after the introduction of a new high-tech product or service followed by counter-hype that there's really nothing all that new about it. In this sense, old problems related to traditional school bullying were redefined through the cyberbullying frame. Specifically, cyberbullying became a sociocultural discourse within which claimsmakers could bring forward concerns regarding time bombs and bullycides in ways that made them seem new, different, and increasingly common.

Sitting on some powder kegs. On CBS's *48 Hours* (September 16, 2011), cyberbullying was presented as a possible impetus for violent retaliation, such as in the case of time bombs (those who could erupt in mass violence). Journalist Tracy Smith said that "cyberbullying has turned up the heat on peer-to-peer abuse [and] we haven't seen the worst of it." Guest Kevin Epling responded: "Kids are just getting bombarded 24/7. I've talked with law enforcement in certain cities [and] we're probably sitting on some powder kegs. Something's going to happen. We need to [defuse] a lot of the tense situations in our schools, and we have to do it today." It is also possible that Epling's claim was made in regard to the link between cyberbullying and suicide. At other points in the show, the mother of a teen who died by suicide in response to persistent bullying online claimed that her daughter "was cyberbullied to death."

Other highly publicized instances of teen suicide were also linked to cyberbullying. For instance, 14-year-old Jamey Rodemeyer was claimed to have died by suicide "after online bullying and slurs against his sexuality" (CNN's *Anderson Cooper 360,* September 22, 2011). Phoebe Prince's suicide was at least partly attributed to online bullying, as was Tyler Clementi's suicide (although in the latter case the media were not consistent in describing exactly what had occurred online). Megan Meier's suicide and the subsequent prosecution of Lori Drew (the mother of another girl at Megan's school who was accused of bullying Megan via MySpace) were widely covered in the news media, which claimed that the filing of charges against Drew was the first prosecution of cyberbullying as a crime in the United States. On NPR's *Tell Me More* (July 8, 2008) it was claimed that there had been "a number of stories" of cyberbullying resulting in teens committing suicide. The presence of such stories implied a widespread problem, but evidence of an actual increase in bullying-related suicides other than reference to "a number of stories" was rarely, if ever, provided. Like the discourses of familial and institutional failure, the widely varied discourse of cyberbullying introduced additional conflicting narratives. Social media and other technologies were simultaneously positioned as dangerous tools employed by unmonitored and anonymous bullies and as malignant devices acting upon youth in ways that were beyond their control.

* * *

The combined result of all these conflicting messages has been a confused and somewhat contradictory set of policies, programs, and practices aimed at curbing the epidemic of school bullying at the familial, institutional, and sociocultural levels, a topic we take up in more detail in Chapter 8. But first we turn to two additional sociocultural explanations that we think are more appropriate frames for understanding school bullying, even though they were not often explicitly identified in the news media discourse during our study period. In Chapter 5 we explore the relationship between bullying and the enforcement of gender norms, using the case of Phoebe Prince as a springboard, and in Chapter 6 we turn to the relationship between bullying and heteromasculine norms, using the case of Tyler Clementi as a template. The bullying-related suicides of Phoebe Prince and Tyler Clementi served as watershed events that brought waves of media attention to bullying and highlighted the complex interactions among bullying, social control, gender, and sexuality.

Notes

1. Michael Greene was one of several educators and social service professionals whose letters the *New York Times* regularly published. He was identified as the director of the Center for the Prevention of Violence, a subdivision of the Youth Consultation Service in New Jersey.

2. Like other bullying statistics cited in Chapter 3, the source of the 85 percent statistic was never provided, and we also witnessed a migration in the application of this statistic. Kerry Kennedy said that in 85 percent of bullying incidents "there's no intervention or effort made by a *teacher* or *administration*" (NPR's *Tell Me More*, January 16, 2012). Psychologist Brenda Wade claimed more generally that 85 percent of "bullying incidents have no intervention. Nobody tries to stop it" (CNN's *Issues with Jane Velez-Mitchell*, March 28, 2011). However, there were several further permutations. Some stories stated that bystanders—those who are neither bullies nor victims—make up 85 percent of the student body (NBC's *Dateline*, September 13, 2010; CBS's *This Morning*, April 26, 1999; *NYT*, April 3, 1996) (the CBS story added that bystanders were "the silent majority," and the *New York Times* story added that bystanders "typically ignore" the bullying). If 85 percent of the student body were bystanders, this would mean that the remaining 15 percent of the school body constitutes either victims or bullies, but this would be quite inconsistent with media reports that 20 percent of children, at the very least, are victimized (and that some additional percentage bully). The statistic took on another meaning that seems more credible. NBC's *Today* reported that in 85 percent of bullying incidents, bystanders are *present* (June 6, 2007). CNN also made this claim, and added that "bystanders intervene in only 10 percent of bullying incidents" (*Anderson Cooper 360*, February 28, 2013) (strictly speaking, what CNN should have said was that bystanders intervene in 10 percent of the cases *that they witness*, meaning 8.5 percent of all cases).

5

Gender and Social Control

Popular girls, too, have to be socially confident and smart (but not too smart); they have to come from the right neighborhood, have the right style and, more important, the right hair. They cannot be poor, fat, masculine, prudish or promiscuous; they cannot be a teacher's pet or too opinionated, and they cannot have bad skin or try too hard at anything, especially at being "in."
—Fran Schumer (*New York Times,* December 28, 2003)

In Chapter 1 we described how the suicide of 15-year-old Phoebe Prince emerged as a watershed event in the ongoing construction of school bullying as a serious social problem. As we pointed out, part of what situated this story as a signal crime was the ability of news media and other claimsmakers to construct Prince as an ideal victim, worthy of a heightened sense of sympathy, and her alleged bullies as evil, unremorseful predators. In this chapter we put forth the argument that one reason for the greater attention paid to Phoebe Prince relates to gender ideologies regarding the relative vulnerability of girls compared to boys. The focus on Prince's physical appearance and vulnerability certainly comports with the broader discourse on the importance of beauty in regard to norms of femininity. It also taps into existing narratives regarding the need to protect young, pretty, vulnerable girls. The victimization of boys is acceptable (to a degree) as a rite of passage, while the victimization of girls is seen as more problematic. Moreover, there is at least some expectation that boys are better prepared to take care of and defend themselves compared to girls. Of course, these assumptions are the result of social constructions of gender rather than inherent differences between males and females with regard to resiliency.

Similar dynamics were at play in the construction of Prince's alleged bullies. Although two male students were charged in the case, the dominant construction of those who bullied Prince was that of a group of out-of-control girls. The students were frequently referred to as a "gang of girls" and "mean girls." In addition, the bullying that Prince endured was primarily described as resulting from relationships she engaged in with the two boys charged in the case. Prince, her alleged bullies, and their bullying behavior were all framed within the context of existing gender ideologies. From this vantage point, we are better able to understand one of the reasons this particular bullying-related suicide was constructed as a signal crime, resulted in the filing of criminal charges, and sparked a national news media frenzy.

The filing of criminal charges against Prince's alleged bullies was presented as a new development in the fight against bullying. A *New York Times* feature noted that "legal experts said they were not aware of other cases in which students faced serious criminal charges for harassing a fellow student, but added that the circumstances in this case appeared to be extreme and that juvenile charges were usually kept private" (March 30, 2010). The application of criminal justice sanctions in response to bullying is a vivid example of formal, legal social control of youth behavior. Moreover, the very nature of and purported impetus for Prince's bullying victimization suggests another layer of social control at work. Specifically, Prince was bullied for having violated the norms of appropriate sexual and relational behavior within her school. In other words, the bullying that Prince suffered illustrates the use of bullying as a mechanism for informal social control and the reinforcement of gender norms regarding proper behavior for young women. Similarly, the fact that Prince's primary bullies were also girls can be seen as an additional factor in the move toward filing criminal charges, illustrating how formal responses to bullying also serve as mechanisms for the social control of gender normativity more generally. In this case, we can see the convergence of three mechanisms of social control in relation to bullying. First, the discourse on bullying articulated in news media provides a mechanism through which essentialist notions of gender are reinforced. Second, the criminalization of bullying serves as a formal mechanism of legal social control through which violations of bullying-related gender norms are sanctioned. Finally, school bullying itself represents a mechanism of informal social control through which youth work to "police" one another's violations of gender norms.

Bullying and the Social Construction of Gender

Those who bullied Prince were cast as mean girls seeking revenge in the context of teenage relationship drama. The physical aspects of their bullying worked to both challenge the established frame of girls' bullying as primarily relational and tap into the more recent construction of the epidemic of girls' violence. The mean girls construction did not arise solely out of the coverage of Prince's suicide and the subsequent criminal investigation. By the time this case entered the news media landscape, the mean girls frame and purported epidemic of girls' violence had become entrenched narratives. The discourse of gendered bullying began with an early focus on comparisons between girls' and boys' bullying, which gave way to a "boys' crisis" narrative. This was followed by the emergence of a mean girls frame and its concomitant focus on relational aggression. Out of the mean girls frame, a focus on the growing problem of girls' physical violence emerged. It should be noted that these frames did not emerge as discrete, linear constructions. As the focus shifted, prior constructions remained part of the overall discourse on bullying. At each of these points, essentialist notions of gender were constructed and maintained. In other words, bullying serves as one mechanism through which gender normativity is constructed.

External events seemed to help shift the focus of news media and expert claimsmakers. The shift toward the boys' crisis emerged in conjunction with the purported rash of school shootings in the 1990s, nearly all by boys and young men. The mean girls frame, at least as covered in news media, emerged in conjunction with the publication of two widely read books about girls' relational aggression. The news media's focus on the supposed epidemic of girls' violence was driven by the shock associated with several viral videos of "gangs of girls" brutally beating other girls. Finally, as evidence in support of the epidemic of girls' violence failed to materialize (similar to the lack of evidence that school shootings had reached epidemic proportions), a return to relational aggression took place, this time with a focus on how much worse it was than physical aggression.

Establishing Sex Differences

In the early and middle 1990s, news media primarily relied on expert claimsmakers who articulated sex-based differences in bullying. As quoted in the *New York Times* (October 28, 1993), professor of educational psychology Jan N. Hughes noted: "Aggression in boys is different from aggression in girls. . . . Girls are aggressive by excluding others and saying mean things. Boys are aggressive by hitting and getting into fights." Similar claims were made by psychologists acting as claims-makers in the broadcast media. Boys were implicated in physical (and verbal) aggression, while girls were implicated in relational (and indirect) aggression. Even as claimsmakers challenged the notion that bullying among girls was worse than among boys, the establishment of clear sex differences in bullying styles was maintained. The following exchange between CNN host Bobbie Battista and school psychologist Penny Peterson illustrates this point (*Sunday Morning News,* December 6, 1997). Battista asked: "Some would say that girls are even worse than boys because I think they tend to victimize a little bit more through mind games or emotional games [whereas] boys tend to be more physical. Do you think that's true?" Peterson replied: "Actually research indicates that there are more boys that bully than girls, but there are definitely a lot of girl bullies and [teasers] and . . . it may take different forms."

The establishment of these sex differences in bullying, which were at least partially grounded in the existing academic literature, worked to construct particular expectations about the behavior of boys and girls. Violation of these expectations were sometimes constructed as particularly troubling, as illustrated by assistant professor of psychiatry Eugene V. Beresin: "I'm more concerned about grade-school girls than boys who fight with peers. . . . If I see a 10-year-old girl who's getting into fights, I start thinking about underlying biological problems. Adding to those problems might include attention-deficit hyperactivity disorder or depression" (quoted in *NYT,* March 24, 1994). As this excerpt suggests, physical aggression on the part of boys is not only expected, but also seen as normative. Among girls, however, physical aggression is viewed as a symptom of biological or psychological abnormalities in need of medical social control. This kind of essentialism played a significant role in the framing of the epidemic of girls' violence. However, before the focus on girls' violence emerged, the purported epidemic of school shootings perpetrated by boys was linked to bullying and tied into a boys' crisis.

The Boys' Crisis

Driven by several high-profile school shootings, including the 1999 shooting at Columbine High School, bullying was further implicated in the perpetration of serious violence among boys. These extreme forms of violence, purportedly in response to bullying victimization, became additional evidence of a growing boys' crisis. Speaking on CNN's *Larry King Live,* clinical psychologist and author William Pollack claimed that "there is a real national crisis of boyhood in America" (May 6, 1999). He would repeat this claim on several broadcast media shows. Beginning in 1998, but picking up momentum after the Columbine shooting, several experts began articulating the need to explore the inner lives of boys in relation to bullying and other forms of aggression.

Author Michael Thompson made similar claims. Both he and Pollack drew attention to aspects of gender socialization that put boys at risk for increased physical aggression. In particular, Thompson noted that challenges to boys' sexuality and masculinity could be linked to physical aggression and bullying. A failure to focus on the interior lives of boys was implicated as part of the problem. Direct links between gender socialization among boys and bullying were offered in the news media, and boys were framed as potential time bombs: "We don't allow our boys to shed tears. And some boys who can't cry, cry bullets" (William Pollack, quoted on ABC's *World News Tonight,* January 15, 1999).

As the fervor over the school shootings began to dissipate (at least temporarily), the boys' crisis lost newsworthiness and was soon supplanted by the mean girls phenomenon. In a gendered analysis that was not uncommon at the time, while boys' aggression was linked to cultural constraints on their ability to express their emotions (i.e., boys don't feel enough), girls' aggression was linked to their inability to control their emotions (i.e., girls feel too much). This contrast certainly fit within broader cultural notions regarding gendered emotionality. It also served to position girls who bullied as being particularly catty, manipulative, mean, and ultimately dangerous and in need of more formal, legal mechanisms of social control.

Mean Girls

The 2002 publication and subsequent coverage of two widely read books—Rosalind Wiseman's *Queen Bees and Wannabes* and Rachel Simmons's *Odd Girl Out*—helped to shift the focus of news media from boys' bullying to girls'.[1] Both of these books were the focus of a 2002 *New York Times* feature (February 24) that emphasized the notion that girls' bullying primarily involved relational aggression and was, in this sense, different from boys' bullying. The feature quoted from Simmons's book: "Unlike boys, who tend to bully acquaintances or strangers, girls frequently attack within tightly knit friendship networks, making aggression harder to identify and intensifying the damage to the victims." And: "Within the hidden culture of aggression, girls fight with body language and relationships instead of fists and knives." The suggestion here is that girls' aggression and bullying are less apparent yet more harmful than boys'. These kinds of constructions are not too dissimilar from early theories of female criminality. For instance, in the 1950s and 1960s, Otto Pollack put forth the theoretical argument that criminality among women could be explained by their greater ability to hide their crimes through the use of deceit (see Belknap, 2007).

Some news media claimsmakers recognized the potential danger of the mean girls construction. In the same *New York Times* article just quoted, a counterclaim was offered:

> On the one hand, it is kind of satisfying to think that girls might be, after their own fashion, as aggressive as boys. It's an idea that offers some relief from the specter of the meek and mopey, "silenced" and self-loathing girl the popular psychology of girlhood has given us in recent years. But it is also true that the new attention to girls as relational aggressors may well take us into a different intellectual cul-de-sac, where it becomes too easy to assume that girls do not use their fists (some do), that all girls are covert in their cruelties, that all girls care deeply about the ways of the clique—and that what they do in their "relational" lives takes precedence over all other aspects of their emerging selves.

The mean girls construction could be seen as a mechanism through which girls were liberated from constraining notions of timidity. It could also work to support existing gender essentialism by filtering all girls' bullying behavior through the lens of relationships and friendship networks. It appears from our analysis that the latter of these two possibilities materialized in news media discourse. Stories regarding girls' bullying were overwhelmingly presented through the mean girls construction. Moreover, the news media continually described girls involved in bullying as catty, nasty, and manipulative members of cliques, supporting the framing of girls' bullying within existing essentialist notions of gender.

As time progressed, the mean girls construction became an accepted reality. The focus on mean girls and girls' bullying in general has remained the dominant gendered lens through which bullying has been viewed in the news media. Those who bullied Phoebe Prince were similarly situated. Jane Velez-Mitchell asked bullying expert and regular claimsmaker Barbara Coloroso, who also happened to conduct anti-bullying training at the very school Prince attended: "Is this group of middle class teenagers a gang? You know, gangs aren't just in the inner city. If it quacks like a gang, is it a gang?" To which Coloroso replied: "It's criminal bullying is what it is" (CNN, March 30, 2010).

The juxtaposition of the mean girls and boys' crisis constructions resulted in a continuation of established gender essentialism, suggesting inherent differences between girls' and boys' performances of bullying. While some claimsmakers recognized the cultural and social roots of this essentialism, many simply accepted it as fact. Even in the academic literature, these essentialized notions of bullying were often left unexplained, as pointed out by Carrera, DePalma, and Lameiras (2011). Once established, those who violated the gender norms of bullying were cast as even more sinister than those who bullied from within its confines.

To return to our case study, as Prince's suicide took hold as a signal crime, news media and other claimsmakers could reach into the readily available reservoir of the mean girls discourse in order to assist in the construction of her alleged bullies as evil predators. But her alleged bullies also violated the basic mean girls construction by engaging in what had been previously established as boys' domain—physical and direct verbal bullying. The result: an increased sense of outrage within the community and troubling expressions of vigilantism.

At least one parent of one of Prince's alleged bullies reportedly removed her daughter from school following the filing of charges, fearing for the safety of her child. The girl's defense attorney, Colin Keefe, appeared on ABC's *Good Morning America* (April 6, 2010) days after the district attorney's press conference, describing the response his client received from the public and her fear of reprisal: "She has been receiving significant harassment over the Internet and in other ways. My client and her family are very concerned for their overall well-being." Later interviews with this alleged bully, 16-year-old Sharon Velasquez, corroborated such stories of harassment. On NBC's *Dateline* (April 1, 2012), Ann Curry asked Velasquez about an alleged incident involving a rock being thrown through the window of Velasquez's home, which Velasquez confirmed: "Yeah, it was smashed. And there was a bullet through it so I—we found the bullet shell so we didn't know if they shot first and then threw a rock or, we didn't know."

We suggest that the vitriolic community response aimed at the girls accused of bullying Prince was partially fueled by their violation of gender normativity in relation to bullying. In this sense, the bullying discourse served as a mechanism of informal social control through which gender normativity was reinforced, bolstered by the imposition of formal, legal social control in the form of criminal charges. What was perhaps lost on those who responded with such vitriol was the possibility that they too were sending a message to the youth in their community and nationwide—that those who are implicated in bullying deserve to be treated the same way they treat others. The news media and other claimsmakers, in their own attempt to reinforce the seriousness of bullying as a social problem, also reinforced the very problem that formed the basis of their anger. Vicarious victimization grounded in a collective sense of grief ultimately led to a situation in which bullying *among* youth was met with the bullying *of* youth.

Girls Get Violent

Girls who engage in violence are constructed as a particular kind of mean girl. This was especially the case as videos of girls engaging in relatively serious forms of violence went viral. These videos received particularly wide coverage in the broadcast media, perhaps fueled by the ability to replay the videos, adding to the newsworthiness of such events. Girl fights, as they were often called, were initially presented as rare occurrences that deviated from the much more common relational bullying associated with girls. As Nancy Grace noted in response to one such viral video: "And it's very rare that you see girls with a pack mentality actually physically attacking someone" (CNN, April 15, 2008). Two weeks later, Grace would connect the same video to the established mean girls frame: "Tonight: Real, live 'mean girls' takes on a whole new meaning after a brutal all-girl gang attack on a teenage honor student cheerleader all caught on video" (CNN, April 29, 2008).

The framing of these videos as part of the mean girls phenomenon and the growing epidemic of girls' violence led news media and other claimsmakers to search for explanations. Among them was the notion that girls were somehow becoming masculinized, as psychologist Jennifer Hartstein suggested: "They're really following the boy—boys always fought physically. Girls fought with social aggression, and slander, and making rumors and all that kind of stuff. And now it's just going this further step. But they fight mean and they fight dirty and it's hard to watch" (CBS's *Early Show,* February 2, 2010). This led host Maggie Rodriguez to ask, "Why are they becoming more like boys?"

A month later it was noted that girls were not only becoming more like boys, they were "doing boy" better. Speaking with author and bullying expert Rachel Simmons, NBC's Natalie Morales noted: "What's interesting is you say that girls actually are more physically aggressive than boys. Is that true? I mean, why do you think that is?" To which Simmons replied: "It's true. Recently we saw some research that now about 25 percent of girls have been involved in a violent altercation. And I think it's a combination of things. I think they're consuming a lot of media that shows violence as a form of power" (*Today,* March 23, 2010).

In addition to suggesting a masculinization of girls, some claims-makers harkened back to now-defunct theories suggesting that the purported escalation of girls' (and women's) violence was rooted in their growing equality with boys. Speaking on NPR's *Day to Day* (January 15, 2008), Dr. Louis Kraus of the Rush University Medical Center in Chicago noted: "We see more girls interacting in competitive sports. We've seen girls get into more fights. We've seen the leveling off of male gang behavior, but an increase in female gang behavior." This was then linked to rates of fighting among high school girls: "And in the 2007 federal report on school crime and safety, 28 percent of high school girls said they've been in a fight. It's not clear why this is happening. But these 13-year-olds see it as a sign of their growing equality with boys."

We can, of course, make a strong argument as to why getting into a fight does not qualify as bullying per se. As discussed in Chapter 1, definitions of bullying in the research literature are quite specific in terms of the repetitive nature of bullying and the requirement of a power imbalance between the bully and the victim. This did not, however, prevent news media and other claimsmakers from conflating girl fights with bullying. In some instances, like the following excerpt from CNN's *Nancy Grace* (April 6, 2011), news media claimsmakers actively negotiated the link between violent physical attacks and bullying: "Bombshell tonight, live, Pennsylvania. Real, live mean girls, a brutal all-girl gang attack on another teen caught on video. We have the video." As this show continued, local news reporter Joe Gomez stated: "Nancy, this shocking video, you know, it all began with, apparently, some boy gossip that turned bad. Right now, a couple of mean girls apparently chased another group of girls that they felt were—" Grace interrupted her guest mid-sentence: "Wait! Wait! Wait! Gomez, you may call them mean girls. I call them felons. This is an aggravated assault in any law book. Go ahead." To which Gomez conceded: "That's right, Nancy. Well, I mean, this group of bully teenage girls." Grace herself had begun the broadcast by referring to the attackers as "mean girls," as she had in previous broadcasts, but then challenged this very construction by positioning the attackers as "felons." Her guest, Gomez, then responded to this challenge by referring to the attackers as "bully" girls. A similar exchange happened later in the same show, with Grace once again challenging the construction of these girls as "mean girls" and elevating their status to that of a "gang." In response, Gomez again reestablished their construction as "bullies." Grace later asked: "Are these so-called mean girls actually junior felons?"

This exchange is a microcosm of the overall construction of girls' violence and its relationship to the mean girls narrative. Girls' bullying is first constructed in ways that emphasize their inherent differences from boys in their tendency to engage in relational aggression. Girls who violate these established norms by engaging in physical aggression are both incorporated into the mean girls frame and positioned as something different and worse. In so doing, claimsmakers are able to both reinforce the gender norms associated with the mean girls frame as well as contribute to the construction of a "growing epidemic" of girls' violence.

Prince's case fit this particular narrative. Her bullying took place in the context of so-called relationship drama. Prince was bullied, the dominant narrative suggests, because she dated two popular boys in school. The boys' girlfriends were not pleased and retaliated through bullying. Their actions, however, were described as "beyond the pale." The final day of Prince's life received significant attention in part due to the nature of the bullying that occurred, which included a soft drink can being thrown at her from a moving car. The criminalization of bullying in the Prince case, we suggest, was partly informed by the combination of the mean girls frame and the purported escalation in the epidemic of girls' violence.

At the press conference where the charges against Prince's alleged bullies were presented to news media, the district attorney, Elizabeth Scheibel, described their behavior in ways that intensified the discourse. Scheibel's description of the bullying Prince endured was referenced in several broadcast shows and *New York Times* articles. For example: "The events of January 14th were not isolated. Rather they were the culmination of a nearly three-month campaign of verbally abusive and assaultive behavior and threats of physical harm towards Phoebe on school grounds by several South Hadley High School students" (CNN's *Campbell Brown,* March 30, 2010). And: "The prosecutor brought charges Monday against nine teenagers, saying their taunting and physical threats were beyond the pale and led the freshman, Phoebe Prince, to hang herself from a stairwell in January" (*NYT,* March 30, 2010).

As mentioned in Chapter 1, news media and other claimsmakers, drawing on the initial description provided by Scheibel, honed in on the seriousness of the bullying as well as its prolonged nature, consistently referring to the bullying as consisting of "physical threats," "verbal abuse," "harassment," and even "torture," and employing terms such as "relentless." Darby O'Brien, spokesperson for the Prince family, amplified the bullying discourse even further: "The word bullying is probably not even accurate. I mean, really, when you look at what happened with her, it's persecution. I mean, this thing was a hate crime" (CNN's *Rick's List,* March 31, 2010). Speaking on *Anderson Cooper 360,* CNN legal analyst Lisa Bloom also illustrated this elevation of bullying to more serious forms of criminal and violent behavior: "For all of these kids who have been abusing this girl—and I don't like the word bullying, I think it underplays what's going on. It's child abuse. It's harassment. It's stalking. It's threatening behavior" (April 1, 2010). This escalation in the language conformed to existing narratives related to the so-called wave of girls' violence and meanness. It also corresponds to our suggestion that violations of gender norms related to bullying (i.e., girls engaging in physical as opposed to relational bullying) result in the imposition of more formal, legal mechanisms of social control.

The Mythical Wave of Girls' Meanness

Similar to the purported epidemic of school shootings in the 1990s, the so-called epidemic of girls' violence does not seem to hold up to critical inspection, as pointed out by some counterclaimants in the news media. In a 2010 *New York Times* opinion piece titled "The Myth of Mean Girls" (April 2, 2010), researchers Mike Males and Meda Chesney-Lind present significant counterclaims to the alleged increase in girls' violence after first referencing the reaction to Phoebe Prince's suicide and resulting criminal charges. They suggested: "This mythical wave of girls' violence and meanness is, in the end, contradicted by reams of evidence from almost every available and reliable source." They went on to note that "news media and myriad experts, seemingly eager to sensationalize every 'crisis' among young people, have aroused unwarranted worry in the public and policy arenas." In the end, they ask: "Why, in an era when slandering a group of people based on the misdeeds of a few has rightly become taboo, does it remain acceptable to use isolated incidents to berate modern teenagers, particularly girls, as 'mean' and 'violent' and 'bullies'? That is, why are we bullying girls?"

Those who study crime trends and the relationship between gender and crime should not be surprised by these counterclaims. Feminist criminologists and others have long been pointing to the myth of an epidemic of girls' violence. Early notions that women's liberation would lead to some sort of masculinization of women and girls and an increase in their commission of "men's crimes" simply did not pan out. Yet, as Males and Chesney-Lind point out, popular and news media discourse continues to emphasize this phantom epidemic. These counterclaims did not derail the construction of the mean girls frame nor the associated construction of an increase in girls' violence. And, in line with Males and Chesney-Lind's opinion piece in the *New York Times,* Prince's bullying-related suicide was followed by a more punitive response.

Applying a gendered lens to the analysis of bullying in news media discourse suggests that constructions of and responses to bullying serve to create and reinforce norms of gender. The ways that some news media and expert claimsmakers have articulated the relationship between gender and bullying corresponds to broader essentialist notions of gender in the lives of youth. Physical bullying and violence are constructed as strictly male behaviors, while relational and psychological bullying are constructed as strictly female behaviors. More important, those who violate these norms are exposed to vitriolic responses and calls for more severe sanctions.

As suggested earlier, this leads us to the conclusion that constructions of bullying articulated in the news media serve as a mechanism for the informal social control of gender normativity, leading to increased calls for the imposition of formal mechanisms of control (e.g., school and legislative policy, criminal charges) in order to reestablish the status quo. If this is the message sent by those in positions of authority (e.g., news media, bullying experts, and justice administrators), then is it any surprise that boys and girls also recognize the need to establish and police the boundaries of gender normativity? And if young people witness the ways these same adults treat one another, is it any surprise that they turn to bullying as one mechanism through which they are able to police those boundaries?

Bullying and the Social Control of Gender

In addition to serving as a context within which gender is constructed, bullying is also employed as a mechanism of informal social control through which established gender norms are policed. Youth who violate these gender norms are seen as ripe for bullying victimization. In our study period, even when such victimization did not actually occur, parents were challenged around their willingness to expose their children to potential victimization when allowing or encouraging them to explicitly violate established gender norms. Dr. Drew Pinsky went as far as accusing parents who were raising their child in a gender-neutral fashion as "experimenting on a child" (CNN, May 24, 2011).

CNN's Joy Behar (November 16, 2010) made similar kinds of assertions when she asked a young boy who competes in beauty pageants: "What do your friends say at school about you being in the pageant, Zander?" After the young boy denied any problems with his peers, Behar asked the boy's mother: "Do the children bully your son at all or tease him about it?" The boy's mother also denied any problems from peers, even noting: "All I've heard is, wow. That's cool. Girls chasing him on the playground, all positive right now." Behar seemed to begrudgingly accept these responses, stating: "OK. That's fine." She then made a claim that directly contradicted the experiences of her guests: "The thing about it is, unfortunately there is a stigma attached to boys when they do traditionally girlie things. When they play with dolls or they put on tiaras or dress like girls or whatever. They have a little bit of trouble with their peers." She then again asked the boy's mother: "Are you—are you concerned about that at all?"

Even when faced with evidence to the contrary, the assumption of potential bullying victimization remains. Behar's interview was not the only instance in which news media claimsmakers challenged parents who supported their children in explicitly violating established gender norms. Parent and author Cheryl Kilodavis, whose son inspired her book *My Princess Boy,* was confronted with these kinds of challenges in two television interviews (NBC's *Today,* January 3, 2011; CNN's *The Joy Behar Show,* January 7, 2011). In both instances, hosts questioned Kilodavis regarding the potential for bullying. As we will see in Chapter 6, this assumption is not wholly unfounded. Boys who are perceived to violate hetero-normativity are certainly bullied. The point here, however, is that news media and other claimsmakers seemed to carry this forward by lamenting the possibility of bullying, even in the face of direct evidence to the contrary.

Girls were also seen as potential victims for bullies when they violated gender norms. During an interview with one mother who was writing a book about bullying, NPR's Michel Martin described how the woman's daughter was "teased for carrying a Star Wars water bottle to school by kids who told her that Star Wars was only for boys" (*Tell Me*

More, January 24, 2012). More common, however, was coverage of the bullying of girls who challenged established gender norms regarding appearance and sexuality. As discussed previously, the bullying of Prince seemed to fit within this framework. As author and expert claimsmaker Rachel Simmons pointed out regarding Prince: "She rocked the boat. And that's actually really what went down here. Upper classmen girls went after her because she threatened the social order" (CNN's *The Joy Behar Show,* April 6, 2010). Simmons went on to connect this to broader gender norms: "And part of the story here is that girls grow up in a culture where on reality television shows women are competing over men and basically treating each other like second-class citizens," and also to Prince's suicide: "That's what you saw play out where the senior girls felt like they had the right to dehumanize Phoebe because she dared to date an older boy." Sadly, this is not all too uncommon. Bullying, in this sense, operates as a mechanism through which youth enforce gender norms related to physical appearance and promiscuity among girls.

Bullying and the Female Body

While some may consider the use of plastic surgery on young boys and girls in response to bullying a bit extreme, others find it to be an important factor in their ability to heal and minimize future bullying. The very notion that children and their parents are willing to go to such drastic measures illustrates one of our major findings—that bullying is employed as a mechanism of informal social control through which youth police gender norms related to physical appearance. This seems to be especially the case for girls and young women. Perhaps we should not be too surprised to find that youth judge girls and young women by their looks, considering the continued objectification of women's bodies in US culture.

In fact, when confronted with young women who report bullying, news media and other claimsmakers sometimes reinforce the expectation that only those who don't conform to gender norms of appearance would be subject to bullying. In our study period, this was the case even when attempts were made to challenge such constraints. Kathy Lee Gifford, during her interview with founder of Girl Talk and author Haley Kilpatrick, began: "It's hard to look at you and think that you were once a victim in middle school of this sort of bullying from mean girls." Gifford went on to lament the difficulty young women have in living up to the standards of beauty set by Hollywood. Others, however, recognized that both those who underconform and those who overconform to these norms are potential targets for informal social control in the form of bullying. For instance, speaking on NPR's *Tell Me More* (April 5, 2010), Nicholas Carlisle, executive director of the organization No Bully, noted: "So the kids who are less attractive, the kids who are more attractive, they both seem to get targeted by bullies." While this might initially seem contradictory, we can understand why both more and less attractive kids are exposed to informal social control in the form of bullying when the phenomenon is placed in the context of the sociological study of deviance. According to Heckert and Heckert (2002), rate-busters are seen as deviant due to their overconforming to social norms (in this case being "too pretty"), while negative deviants are those who underconform to social norms (in this case being "not pretty enough"). This also fits with more recent research, discussed in Chapter 2, in which bullying is understood as a form of social jockeying, with those in the middle of the social hierarchy bullying both those below and above them in order to achieve status among peers.

Given the power of these kinds of messages coming from news media and other claimsmakers, as well as the cultural pressures placed on youth, especially young girls, to live up to normative standards of beauty, the use of bullying as a mechanism for the informal social control of gender norms related to appearance becomes less surprising. The power of these messages and the harm associated with bullying are perhaps most clearly illustrated by those who turn to suicide in response. In discussing a suicide pact among two 14-year-old girls, Drew Pinsky noted: "The teens' families say they were both the victims of merciless bullying from classmates. They were targeted for weight, hair color, and their friendship" (CNN, April 22, 2011).

When the threat of serious self-harm as a result of bullying is added to the mix, it may be even less surprising that youth and their parents are willing to go to seemingly extreme measures to protect themselves. In 2012, ABC's *Good Morning America* ran a story titled "Teen Bullied into Plastic Surgery" (August 9; also covered on ABC's *Nightline,* August 14, and CBS's *This Morning,* December 4). In his lead-in to the story, George Stephanopoulos stated: "You know, we've got a very different kind of story now about teens and plastic surgery. You know, usually it's not the kind of thing we encourage. But for one young woman in Georgia, it seemed like the only way to end years of bullying." This was followed by an interview with the young woman, who spoke about being teased and bullied because of her ears and said that she had even contemplated suicide. When asked if there were concerns that this would send "a message to other bullied children that they, too, need to have plastic surgery to overcome the bullies," the young girl's mother claimed, "It's no different than somebody having teeth that . . . require braces."

This young woman and her mother were not unique in their response to either real or potential bullying around physical appearance. Stories of young people having plastic surgery or losing significant amounts of weight in response to bullying were not at all uncommon beginning in 2010. On NBC's *Today* (March 30, 2010), Ann Curry interviewed several young people who had undergone plastic surgery in response to bullying. One young woman made the connection between her sense of self, her body image, and the bullying she endured: "Well, like all my life I knew that my nose was my negative aspect to my face. And all the bullying and the Facebook, like negative comments just made me like more insecure and self-conscious. So it came to the point where I had to get my surgery done, and I'm so much happier."

Stories like this were covered on other broadcast shows. ABC ran a story about a young woman who had undergone plastic surgery on her nose at the age of 15 (*Good Morning America,* January 12, 2011) and about another young girl who was considering plastic surgery on her ears because of the potential for bullying (*Good Morning America,* April 14, 2011). ABC also ran a story, titled "New Face, New Year; Back to School Surgery," in which reporter Bill Weir claimed: "Well, back to school means new classes and fresh notebooks and [for] an increasing number of American teens, a new face" (*Nightline,* August 14, 2012). NBC and CBS ran similar stories, including one about a young girl considering having her ears pinned back in response to being a target for bullying at school (NBC's *Today,* May 24, 2011) and another about a young girl who had actually done just this (CBS's *This Morning,* December 4, 2012). Some young women took other measures in response to bullying about their bodies. For example, as covered in an ABC feature story (*Good Morning America,* December 10, 2012), a fifth-grade girl talked about having lost sixty-six pounds partly in response to having become a "target for bullies." Perhaps rightly, this young girl and her parents were praised for their dedication to a healthy lifestyle change, as articulated by host George Stephanopoulos: "You look, you look so great right now, you look so healthy and happy."

Many of these stories were accompanied by testimonials from young people and their parents articulating the positive impact that body modification had on their ability to function at school, and on their self-image. Speaking on NBC's *Today* (March 30, 2010), one young woman responded to questions about whether her breast-reduction surgery had diminished the harassment she was experiencing: "Yeah, absolutely. And the physical handicap [that] having large . . . breasts places on . . . a young person who's athletic and I was a dancer and that kind of thing has definitely gone away. The harassment was mostly sexual for my problem." Another young woman, in response to questions about the impact of her nose surgery, explained: "I have more confidence. I can actually have my head high up and be pretty" (ABC's *Good Morning America,* January 12, 2011). She went on to state: "This was just something to make me feel better, to make me happy, to make me feel like a beautiful woman."

That a young girl's sense of self and happiness would be linked to her body image, though troubling, should not be too surprising. A wealth of research has shown that the cultural messages young girls (and boys) receive regarding their bodies place immense pressure on them to live up to gender norms of appearance and beauty. Some examples may serve to better illustrate how reinforcement of gender norms of appearance and beauty can lead to bullying as a mechanism for the informal social control of those norms among youth.

In Georgia, a 2012 advertising campaign targeting childhood obesity included images of obese children in tight clothing with captions such as "It's hard to be a little girl if you're not" (CNN's *Newsroom,* January 5, 2012). In response, branding and social media consultant Peter Shankman expressed concern that such an approach would in fact lead to increased bullying of kids who didn't conform to normative standards of appearance, suggesting: "I think there is a better way to do it that is just as effective and just as shocking but may not cause such problems with those children."

In a more recent story (NBC's *Today,* May 22, 2013), clothing retailer Abercrombie & Fitch and its chief executive officer, Mike Jeffries, experienced a public backlash when confronted over the company's practice of selling men's but not women's clothes in extra-large sizes. In this story, Jeffries was quoted from a 2006 interview as stating: "Candidly, we go after the cool kids. Are we exclusionary? Absolutely."

ABC's *Good Morning America* (May 23, 2013) ran a story about a young girl who was punished by her parents for bullying a classmate about her appearance. The parents forced her to wear "thrift store clothes" to school and endure teasing from peers for two days. Some challenged the parents' punishment approach, suggesting that instead of increasing this young girl's capacity for empathy, the punishment would in fact have a negative impact on her own self-esteem. Others, however, supported the parents' approach and lauded their willingness to take creative steps to teach their daughter a lesson. While none of the parenting experts or news media claimsmakers in this story questioned the broader message this punishment sent, one viewer did. As Josh Elliot (of *ABC News* and who was present on the *Good Morning America* set) said off-camera: "I had somebody tweet me, though, this morning saying they weren't sure about it because they thought it might equate wearing [second-hand] clothes . . . with being bad. That somehow that was a bad thing." The response to this viewer comment seemed to ignore its underlying premise. Instead of carefully considering the impact of situating those who wear second-hand clothes as somehow bad and worthy of contempt and bullying, the experts and news media claimsmakers discussed how they had grown up wearing second-hand clothes and that it wasn't that big of a deal. In fact, they used this as justification for why the punishment was laudable, as Karyn Gordon, a relationship and parenting expert pointed out: "Right. You know what I find interesting, . . . I grew up wearing second-hand clothes. . . . How is it so bad? I mean, you know, it'd be different if . . . the mother is making her daughter wear clown costumes. She's simply getting her to wear second-hand clothes." The problem with this punishment and the way it was framed within this story is not the actions of the parents per se, but the manner in which news media and expert claimsmakers ignore larger cultural contexts. Not only does this type of punishment reinforce the contradictory notion that bullying a bully is an effective strategy to reduce bullying, but it also reinforces the notion that those who dress in second-hand clothes (or who do not live up to gender norms of appearance) should expect some level of ridicule and bullying from peers.

In another example, both CNN (*Newsroom,* February 28, 2013) and CBS (*This Morning,* March 2, 2013) ran stories about a "controversial tactic in trying to bring childhood obesity under control." Schools in several states were sending students home with letters documenting their body mass index (BMI). The idea behind this policy was to alert parents if their child's BMI was considered too high or too low. We can see how such a policy could work to reinforce the notion that only bodies of a certain type are acceptable. Combined with the existing evidence that youth who violate gender norms of appearance are at risk for bullying, this kind of practice could serve to further reinforce the use of bullying as a mechanism of informal social control.

Having considered the relationship between bullying, gender norms, and body image as articulated in news media discourse during our study period, it is clear to us that youth do in fact use bullying as a mechanism for the informal social control of gender norms. This, in itself, is of course troubling. However, the dominant responses presented in the news media that we analyzed suggest additional troubling dynamics. By focusing attention on the behavior of individual youth as bullies and on the reactions to that bullying on the part of individual youth, news media and other claimsmakers wittingly or unwittingly ignore the larger social and cultural influences that give rise to bullying as a mechanism of social control among youth as a whole. Those who engage in bullying in response to violations of gender norms of appearance are framed as somehow deviant and in need of correction. Equally problematic, those who are bullied because of their violation of those norms are also seen as deviant and in need of correction. As Tammie Jackson, the mother of a young girl who was being bullied because of her breasts, describes, a school official reinforced this kind of message in response to her requests that something be done: "[The official told me] that I could transfer my daughter to different schools but since her boobs are so large that she's going to always get teased. And then, she told me the only suggestion that she could make is for my 13-year-old daughter to get a breast reduction. It makes me feel like now you're telling me it's my fault or it's God's fault the way that he made my daughter?" (CNN's *Dr. Drew,* January 23, 2013).

By focusing on those youth who employ surgery and other forms of body modification in response to bullying, gender norms of appearance are implicitly reinforced. In no way are we suggesting that those who undergo plastic surgery in response to bullying are wrong or blameworthy; however, by highlighting these kinds of stories, news media and other claimsmakers are able to sidestep the more difficult task of confronting the broader social and cultural sources of bullying related to gender norms of appearance. Instead of asking what it is we need to change about a young woman who is bullied to the point of considering plastic surgery or even suicide, we should be asking what it is we all do to create and support a culture in which school bullying emerges as a mechanism of social control aimed at reinforcing established gender norms. We may ask the same kind of question when bullying is employed as a mechanism for the social control of young women who violate sexual norms.

Viral Victim Blaming

In addition to controlling the appearance of girls' bodies, bullying may also be seen as a mechanism to control their use of their bodies. This seems to be particularly true when looking at the phenomenon of "slut shaming." Speaking on *All Things Considered,* Melissa Block described slut shaming in the following manner: "We're going to explore now the social media equivalent of a scarlet letter. These days, it's called 'slut shaming,' and it involves harassing and humiliating girls by posting explicit photos or videos of them online" (NPR, January 7, 2013). When combined with the threat of bullycide, the nexus of bullying and social media technologies marks a new turn in the discourse surrounding the control of female sexual behavior. As discussed earlier, Phoebe Prince's suicide is one example of how young women who are perceived to have violated sexual and relationship norms are met with bullying. More recent suicides illustrate the phenomenon of slut shaming as well.

On September 12, 2012, 15-year-old Audrie Pott died by suicide after enduring humiliation related to photos of her sexual assault being distributed to peers via e-mail. Similar to coverage of Phoebe Prince's suicide, news media attention did not focus on Pott's suicide until after criminal charges were filed, in April 2013, against three boys accused of sexually assaulting her. Just a few days prior to coverage of the charges filed in the Pott case, the suicide death of 17-year-old Rehtaeh Parsons in Canada also sparked news media coverage in the United States.

At age 15, Parsons was allegedly gang raped by four boys at a party. The boys distributed photos of the assault, and Parsons was subsequently subjected to prolonged bullying on social media sites. Describing the bullying that Parsons endured, her mother, Leah Parsons, noted: "One girl that was her friend put on her status, 'Sluts need to leave this school anyway'" (CNN's *Around the World,* April 10, 2013). Even after leaving the school, however, Parsons was unable to escape the constant bullying, as host Suzanne Malveaux discussed: "I understand, too, that she had moved away from her school . . . because of social media, because of those visuals and those messages that she was still traumatized by all of that. She could not get away from it." Similar to the criminalization of bullying and passage of legislation in response to Phoebe Prince's bullying-related suicide, Canada passed cyberbullying legislation at least in partial response to Rehtaeh Parsons's suicide. Thus, once again in the cases of Pott and Parsons, young women who violated gender norms were met with bullying as a mechanism of informal social control, which in turn triggered legal mechanisms of social control to deal with those who initiated the bullying.

For Pott and Parsons, as well as others, the trauma associated with the alleged sexual assault and rape they suffered was compounded by the distribution of photographic evidence via the Internet. This viral victim-blaming through cyberbullying became an important focus of the news media discourse surrounding these two tragic suicides. As Kyra Phillips, anchor of CNN's *Raising America,* said: "And if these girls, if this happens to these girls that they are raped and these pictures go on the internet [*sic*] then that's hard enough as a female, as a young girl to see that, right? . . . But when these boys and these girls start calling her a slut and sluts aren't welcome here and you know, this is all your fault, imagine what it's like for a teenager to have to listen to and have to deal with [that]" (quoted on CNN's *Newsroom,* April 13, 2013).

From this vantage point, bullying emerges as another mechanism through which victims of rape and other forms of sexual violence are constructed as blameworthy. As Dunn points out, victims of sexual assault are sometimes constructed as "the agents of their own downfall" (2010, p. 55). The post-victimization bullying reflected in the slut-shaming phenomenon certainly fits this model. Moreover, the construction of victims of sexual violence as blameworthy has been linked to high rates of underreporting. For instance, in *Transforming a Rape Culture,* Buchwald, Fletcher, and Roth note several reasons why women do not report sexual assaults, including "keeping the assault as a personal matter, fear of reprisal, and protecting the offender" (2005, p. 7). What is perhaps most troubling about the phenomenon of slut shaming and the use of social media to spread digital evidence of sexual assaults and promiscuity is the additional lack of control over reporting. While we are certainly concerned over the degree to which many sexual crimes go unreported, this at least provides some level of protection for women and girls who do not want to be re-victimized by the stigma of blameworthiness. Through the process of slut shaming, however, even this little bit of power that women and girls are able to employ to protect themselves from reprisals is removed.

The slut-shaming phenomenon may serve as additional evidence for the existence of a rape culture as articulated by Buchwald and her colleagues. In our study period, those who did attempt to address this broader cultural context within which slut shaming occurs focused on various explanations. For instance, in response to a viral video of a 14-year-old girl in Baltimore performing oral sex, defense attorney B. J. Bernstein noted: "My first concern is how the judgment around this act focused on the girl, not the boy in the sexual act and not the boys who did the videotaping. And so I think it's very much about this what is called Lolita Effect, that we hypersexualize our very young girls and then we turn around and call them whores" (speaking on NPR's *Tell*

Me More, October 31, 2011). Others, such as CNN's designated "human behavior expert," Wendy Walsh, pointed to multiple explanations simultaneously:

> You know, it's a kitchen sink full of influences here. We are talking about young teenage boys, who tend to not be showing a lot of compassion anymore. We have taken prayer out of the schools but we haven't replaced it [with] any other kind of moral teaching. Then you talk about the gender question. Research shows that young men and boys and teenagers believe that women have a greater comfort level with sexual activity than women report they do. So the guys are thinking it's fun. Maybe they're posting these pictures because of male bravado, not necessarily to shame them, but to brag about their conquests. . . . Anyway, again, the Internet and people not understanding the emotional consequences of digital typing, and then you just add the whole culture that we are in. It's so sexual with TV and film, and songs. (CNN's *Newsroom,* April 13, 2013)

Walsh was perhaps getting at something when noting that slut shaming works to both stigmatize young women and bolster the reputation of young men. On NPR's *All Things Considered* (January 7, 2013), one young man, when asked about his own involvement in slut shaming, noted: "Yeah. After it happened, there was a lot of, like, yeah, man, that was awesome." When confronted regarding his seeming lack of remorse, he continued: "I regret doing it to her. But still, I didn't have to go to jail. Porn websites do it every day, so. Even the girls gave me props, but there was about, like, 1 percent of them that, you know, that thought I did the wrong thing."

This young man's experience suggests that the issue of slut shaming cannot solely be explained as a problem of socializing young boys to exert control over girls and ultimately women in the form of sexual violence and exploitation. His gain in status among both male and female peers indicates that both boys and girls support the employment of bullying as a mechanism for the informal social control of women's sexuality. Further evidence of this is that being labeled a "slut" doesn't always result in shaming. In fact, in some instances the label confers status. The coverage of a "slut list" posted on the Internet by female students at a "top-ranked New Jersey high school" illustrates this point: "While any form of bullying or hazing is bad, experts, school officials and most parents agree, the added element of not just sexuality but promiscuity has many of them particularly concerned" (*NYT,* September 27, 2009). What seemed to shock parents and news media claimsmakers even more was that "the whiff of sexual prowess actually raises the status of girls on the forbidden list among their high school peers. It's a celebration of machismo, but for girls only." A recent graduate of this New Jersey high school reinforced this idea: "Being on the list means you are rich, you wear expensive clothing, and probably fall under the general umbrella of attractiveness. Essentially, the slut list is the Goldman Sachs daughters list, a distorted assertion of wealth and power within a highly pressured upper middle class environment." Perhaps parents, school administrators, and experts should not have been so shocked. Paraphrasing Terry O'Neill, president of the National Organization for Women, the author of this same article suggested, "The language of the slut list borrows from the objectifying way men have often talked to other men about women. It not only makes it O.K. now for boys to continue to do this, she said, but it confuses girls."

Gender, Bullying, and Social Control

As suggested at the beginning of this chapter, women are caught in a double bind in which their sexual lives are judged against a limited range of acceptable behaviors. Girls who don't live up to these sexual norms risk corrective action, through informal social control, in the form of slut shaming (for those who are deemed too promiscuous) or relational and emotional bullying (for those who are deemed not promiscuous enough).

The relationship between bullying and gender is complex and dynamic. In one sense, our analysis suggests that the discourse of bullying serves as a context for the construction of gender normativity. Over time, academic and news media constructions of bullying have led to essentialist notions of gender. Boys are understood as participating primarily in physical forms of bullying, while girls are understood as participating primarily in relational and emotional bullying. From a constructionist framework, we would suggest that the articulation of this distinction indeed reflects some aspects of reality. In other words, there is research to support the existence of general differences in patterns of bullying behavior among boys and girls.

However, we would also suggest that the articulation of this distinction within news media and popular discourse also helps to create this reality, because as this distinction becomes further entrenched within the collective psyche, people begin to seek out evidence in support of such claims. But what of evidence that contradicts these claims? Our analysis suggests two possible outcomes. First, such contradictory evidence may be ignored or de-emphasized. Second, such evidence may serve as a trigger point for mechanisms of formal and informal social control. As we have seen in this chapter, girls who violate essentialist notions of gendered bullying, by engaging in violence or physical bullying, are viewed as more dangerous and in need of formal social control (e.g., criminal charges).

In addition to serving as an arena for the continued construction of gender, bullying also serves as a mechanism for the informal social control of gender normativity. In particular, bullying is in part a mechanism for the control of girls' bodies. Similar to those who violate gender norms associated with bullying behavior, those who violate gender norms of appearance and sexuality are viewed as being in need of correction. It is not unreasonable to assume that the broader discourse among adults regarding what is or is not proper behavior for boys and girls finds its way into the day-to-day lives of young people. Bullying, as a predominant form of informal social control among adolescents, serves as one mechanism through which gender normativity is reinforced. Parents and youth are then warned that any deviation from the established norms will result in increased exposure to bullying. A self-fulfilling prophecy emerges in which kids are forced into, blamed for, and victimized by the reinforcement of gender normativity through bullying.

Complicating the problem, attempts to challenge the use of bullying as a mechanism for the informal social control of gender normativity triggers the discourse of existing culture wars. For instance, correspondent Claudia Cowen noted: "As part of a program said to combat bullying, Redwood Heights Elementary brought in Gender Spectrum, an activist group whose mission is to create more gender sensitive environments for kids. . . . Critics say these lessons amount to indoctrination by activist groups" (*Fox News,* May 27, 2011). In response to this elementary school program, Brad Dacus of the Pacific Justice Institute stated: "Public schools are here to serve children and educate children on behalf of the parents, not to cross the line and violate the rights of parents and families. . . . This school is taking an extreme position in inculcating these children at a very young age with gender confusion as opposed to gender identity." Cowen concluded by stating: "The school maintains [that] most parents, teachers, and students had no problem with what was taught. But critics say there are not multiple genders, just boys and girls." Even as local communities support programs and policies aimed at minimizing or eliminating the use of bullying as a mechanism for the informal social control of gender normativity, the broader news media discourse sometimes problematizes these efforts and, in effect, reinforces existing essentialist notions of gender. As we will see in the next chapter, these same kinds of constructions take place in relation to both perceived and real challenges to hetero-normativity among boys.

Note

1. The full title of Wiseman's book is *Queen Bees and Wannabes: Helping Your Daughter Survive Cliques, Gossip, Boyfriends, and Other Realities of Adolescence* (New York: Crown, 2003); and the full title of Simmons's book is *Odd Girl Out: The Hidden Culture of Aggression in Girls* (New York: Harcourt, 2002). Following the publication of these two books, both Wiseman and Simmons emerged as regular expert claimsmakers, in both the print and broadcast media, with regard to girls' bullying. Wiseman's book was also the impetus for the 2004 feature film *Mean Girls*.

6

Constructing
the Gay Victim

It may sound extreme . . . but Tyler Clementi is someone who died
in a battle that many clergy and religious people are fighting. For
inclusion. For our understanding of what God wants the world to
be.

—Reverend Audrey M. Connor
(*New York Times,* October 9, 2010)

We don't support . . . special rights for people based upon their sexual
behavior.

—Tony Perkins of Focus on the Family
(CNN's *Newsroom,* February 19, 2012)

As discussed in Chapter 5, the suicide of Phoebe Prince in January
2010 resulted in extensive media coverage and a "national discussion" about school bullying. That discussion encompassed a wide variety of issues, but anti-gay bullying[1] was not front and center. The suicide of 18-year-old Tyler Clementi on September 22, 2010, very quickly shifted the media focus onto the bullying experiences of LGBT youth generally, and LGBT bullycides more specifically. (This was the case even though the question of whether Clementi had actually been bullied was a matter of some media debate.) As pointed out in Chapter 1, our media samples are replete with illustrations of the profound impact of Clementi's death. It "sparked a chain reaction generating a media and cultural firestorm" (ABC's *20/20,* March 23, 2012) and led to the creation of the "It Gets Better" project. Media attention remained focused on Clementi's death for an extended period due to criminal charges being filed against parties whose

actions were said to have led to the suicide, following the same pattern we saw in the case of Phoebe Prince. In addition, the media linked together other suicides related to anti-gay bullying that occurred both before and after Clementi's death into an "epidemic" of LGBT bullycides. Through this shift of focus, the media constructed anti-gay bullying as a largely separate social problem with its own set of claims and counterclaims.

Our exploration here of how this "problem within a problem" was framed will lead to an exploration of the reverberations of Clementi's death among the news media, which constructed a picture of LGBT youth that was based mostly in a discourse of suffering and suicide. This construction of gay youths (and their putative problems) did not represent a "discovery" by the media and experts. Rather, the media defined the category of gay youth into being—they were "making up people" through a process referred to as "dynamic nominalism" (Hacking, 2004, p. 106). Part of making up people is the notion that there are interactions with the classification and its subjects, thus creating a mutually reinforcing "looping" process. It is also important to recognize that the power to define suggests the ability to control. Therefore we conclude the chapter with a discussion about hetero-normativity and how anti-gay bullying became caught up in culture wars as a forum through which LGBT activists and sympathizers would situate larger concerns about LGBT rights while anti-gay commentators would warn of the "Trojan horse" of forcing acceptance of a "deviant lifestyle" onto unsuspecting and innocent schoolchildren through legislation and policy.

This discourse frequently pitted teaching tolerance on the one hand versus a putative respect for parents' rights on the other. The tolerance message was: "It's OK to be different." However, this framing of the issue as involving tolerance only did not address either the question of "different from *what*" or why the "what" was still situated as the norm from which LGBT people differed. Thus there was almost no media attention focused on the *purposes* that anti-gay bullying serves. As discussed in Chapter 1, anti-gay bullying taps into a powerful discourse whereby students police each other's performances of masculinity and ridicule (and worse) any violations of hetero-masculine norms. Thus, the media mostly assumed that the victims of anti-gay bullying were gay (with some notable exceptions). In this way, the media missed an opportunity to examine how the policing of hetero-masculine norms is a central part of boys' social lives.

The Problem Within a Problem

As mentioned, the death of Tyler Clementi caused a quite rapid shift in focus from the problem of bullying in general to the related but distinct problem of anti-gay bullying. Most obvious was the emergence of a new group of LGBT bullycide victims and the backgrounding of non-LGBT victims. However, there were many other differences. New claimsmakers emerged, including a host of celebrities both gay and straight (but mostly the former), while some prior claimsmakers (such as LGBT activists and groups opposing gay rights) were awarded additional airspace and column inches. In explaining the roots of anti-gay bullying, the media tended to favor a societal level of focus (cultural homophobia and discrimination) that was more "macro" than that found in most prior bullying discussions. Thus the media also typically situated the prevention of anti-gay bullying within remediation of anti-LGBT discrimination. This is not to say that competing constructions of causes and solutions were not considered. We explore clashes around macro causes in our discussion of culture wars at the end of the chapter.

Considering anti-gay bullying as a separate problem had both risks and rewards. For example, LBGT activists' linking of bullying to discrimination and homophobia offered a way to combat the larger cultural and social problem and one of its putative manifestations at the same time. However, making anti-gay bullying just a "gay issue" risked overreaching and marginalizing the cause, and drawing the wrath of groups opposing expansion of LGBT rights. As to the "gay issue" problem, research demonstrates that the media tend to carve out some news stories and assign them to particular demographic categories. For example, Entman (1994) showed how the media treat certain issues as "black news," and "ghettoize" African American news commentators as mostly black news experts. During our study period we saw efforts by both LGBT activists and the news media to emphasize the special plight of LGBT youth while also trying to bridge the divide between LGBT concerns and more universal ones, a tactic that can be attributed to this risk of marginalization. This tactic reflects how LGBT activists' strategies in general have shifted from an "us versus them" to an "us and them" approach as we have entered the supposedly "post-gay" era (see Ghaziani, 2011). We also found evidence that groups who opposed LGBT rights sought to discount the "specialness" of LGBT bullying as well as to marginalize LGBT concerns as being out of touch with mainstream values.

Our media sample provides many examples of the (sometimes awkward) efforts to universalize the experiences of LGBT people while at the same time emphasizing their unique suffering. The screenwriter of *Milk,* Dustin Lance Black, demonstrated this balancing in an interview on CNN's *Issues with Jane Velez-Mitchell* (December 6, 2011). Black was asked about his reaction to an "It Gets Better" video recorded by a 13-year-old boy, Jonah Mowry, who considered suicide after repeatedly being bullied for being gay. The video at that time had been viewed nearly 6 million times on YouTube. Black first universalized his reaction: "Oh, boy, I was so inspired by this. I was weeping. I think probably a lot of people were; not just gay and lesbian people. I don't think anyone out there . . . really felt completely comfortable in high school, and we all had that moment where we felt really different, right?" However, he immediately turned to the uniqueness of the LGBT experience: "But for gay and lesbian kids, there's this isolation thing . . . where we do feel so incredibly different. We don't have parents who are gay and lesbian most of the time. We are hearing these messages from the church and government that aren't exactly supportive and bullies are listening to that."

A similar sort of back-and-forth occurred among two *Today* hosts and their guest Andy Cohen from the Bravo network (NBC, October 4, 2010). Cohen was discussing the "It Gets Better" project and said that "this is a project that I took part of and a lot of gay celebrities . . . and . . . just gay people everywhere are posting videos on YouTube, talking about their experiences growing up gay." He added that the singer Jewel had recorded a video. Kathy Lee Gifford responded: "Well, she's not gay, so it's open to everybody," and Cohen agreed, saying that "everybody can do it." But he immediately returned to the LGBT focus, adding: "But 9 out of 10 gay kids report getting bullied in school." Another such "bridging" moment occurred on CNN during a discussion about Ricky Martin's "coming out" (*Showbiz Tonight,* November 10, 2010). The host lauded Martin's interview with talk show host Ellen DeGeneres, saying that the "fact that Ricky is talking about [anti-gay bullying] can only help people . . . on both sides, whether they're straight or gay." While seemingly striving for inclusion, these kinds of responses also work to support essentialist and dichotomous constructions of sexuality, as discussed in Chapter 1.

We also sometimes witnessed attempts to both particularize and universalize the Tyler Clementi case. Some commentators suggested that if Clementi had been heterosexual and had engaged in sexual behavior with a woman, the webcam incident would not have occurred, because his roommate would likely not have taken such an interest in Clementi's request to be alone. And as noted earlier, the media repeatedly linked Clementi's suicide to the bullycides of other LGBT youth. On a deeper and more subtle level, the intense focus on how Clementi's sexuality had been exposed surreptitiously likely tapped into hetero-normative assumptions that gay sex is inherently and particularly shameful. It seems that video of a heterosexual college student "making out" with a woman had been streamed online in the same surreptitious way, the media would have had a harder time understanding suicide as a response. Thus, the news media often depicted Clementi's sexual orientation as a central feature. However, at other times, commentators appeared to attempt to minimize its salience. On an episode of ABC's *20/20,* Chris Cuomo first described Clementi as a shy violinist and then added: "Tyler also *happened to be* gay" (March 23, 2012). This seemingly offhand but actually strained reference belies the fact that Clementi's sexuality was always at the center of discussions about the case. Cuomo's reference is akin to whites' reluctance to identify African Americans based on their race, which turns out to be a counterproductive strategy (see Norton et al., 2006).

Nevertheless, the media mostly treated Clementi as an ideal victim (perhaps because he was a white college student), and thus found ways to universalize his ordeal. For example, Nancy Grace said on her CNN show, referring to Clementi: "I don't care who the victim is. I don't care if he is Caucasian, African-American, I don't care if he's gay, I don't care if he's straight. I don't care if he's green from Mars. What he endured and the humiliation was uncalled for. It was wrong" (May 21, 2012). Claimsmakers and the media thus sought to connect with the public by universalizing anti-gay bullying; however, they were simultaneously constructing it as being much worse than other forms of bullying.

The Special Dangers of Anti-Gay Bullying

One way that anti-gay bullying was constructed as a parallel but separate social problem was through claims that it was much more widespread and harmful compared to other types of bullying. Such claims were presented in both qualitative and quantitative terms. In the former category, anti-gay bullying was described as being a "special problem" (CNN's *Starting Point with Soledad O'Brien,* April 16, 2012) that can have "especially tragic circumstances" (ABC's *World News,* April 17, 2009). Some stories were more specific as to extent or harm. The *New York Times* (September 27, 2009) reported (without explanation) that an

academic study conducted at an all-male school found anti-gay bullying
to be "the most psychologically harmful type." Similarly, Thomas
Krever, director of an LGBT youth services agency, said that "we still
live in a society where the most base derogatory taunt that a young person perhaps 11 or 12 years of age can come up with is calling another
young person gay" (CNN's *Anderson Cooper 360,* April 14, 2009).
Only occasionally was a specific explanation offered as to why anti-gay
bullying was qualitatively worse—usually because such bullying was
especially isolating due to lack of support from families or schools.
Gary Takesian, director of the documentary *Teach Your Children Well,*
about anti-gay bullying, said that this type of bullying is "the worst of
its kind" because

> if a young person is bullied because of a racial issue or because of an
> ethnic issue, they can go home to their family and they can talk about
> it and they will get support. But if you're gay, and your family hap-
> pens to be homophobic, then you run into a situation where you don't
> have anywhere to turn. You have no support. And these are the situa-
> tions where we see so often where when the person has nowhere to
> turn, they become very lonely, and these are when suicides happen.
> (CNN's *Saturday Morning News,* May 19, 2012)

Dustin Lance Black offered a similar alienation thesis, as discussed previously. (Note that Black's analysis—like that of most commentators—
assumed that the only targets of anti-gay bullying are gay). Anderson
Cooper pointed to schools' complicity with bullying (also a kind of isolating or marginalizing factor) when he said that a school would immediately discipline a child for a racial slur but that the "F word" is "still
kind of accepted" (CNN, May 13, 2010).

Many stories also quantified the prevalence of anti-gay bullying.
Sometimes this was done imprecisely, whether in absolute terms (e.g.,
"significant majority" or "common") or as compared to the rate for all
students ("higher rate" or "top three groups"). Many stories were more
specific; the most common statistic cited was that "9 in 10" LGBT (or
gay/lesbian) students experienced bullying (or "harassment," in some
stories). Only a few stories that used the "9 in 10" figure cited the
source, which appears to be the National School Climate Survey
(NSCS), commissioned by the Gay, Lesbian, and Straight Education
Network (GLSEN). Both the 2007 NSCS (Kosciw, Diaz, and Greytak,
2008) and the 2009 NSCS (Kosciw et al., 2010) reported the same
approximate "9 in 10" figure. This figure had significant staying power,
with citations continuing into 2013. It stands as a dramatic reminder

that LGBT youth face outsized discrimination risk; however, the figure without context is difficult to generalize from. It does not indicate how frequently incidents occur (the figure reflects any experience, even a single incident, in the previous year), and the seriousness of the incidents is broken down into only three categories: verbal, physical harassment, and physical assault. Some reports did not separate the risks even in this limited way; for example, the *New York Times* (October 4, 2010) reported that "9 in 10 [LGBT] students suffered physical or verbal harassment in 2009, ranging from taunts to outright beatings."

None of the stories we located explained how GLSEN obtained the data supporting this figure. According to GLSEN's 2007 report, the survey was not randomized; rather, paper surveys were sent to LGBT community groups, and youths were sought through advertisements on MySpace (Kosciw, Diaz, and Greytak, 2008, p. 7). While such methods are not uncommon in reaching "hidden populations" (see Muhib et al., 2001) such as LGBT youth, they raise validity and reliability issues that none of the news media sources we found explored, much less mentioned. There were other methodological concerns. The NSCS theoretically includes students in the "9 in 10" figure who were "harassed" only once in the year prior to the survey, thus not meeting the repetition element of most definitions of bullying. Also, the NSCS findings do not match up well to the limited population-based data available regarding LGBT youth. For example, in a 2005 national population survey discussed in GLSEN's 2007 report, 22 percent of LGBT students reported feeling unsafe at school (versus 7 percent of non-LGBT students), while the figure for LGBT students in the 2007 NSCS was over 60 percent (Kosciw, Diaz, and Greytak, 2008, p. 37). Also, in the 2005 national study, 90 percent of LGBT students reported that they had been victimized, but fully 62 percent of non-LGBT students reported that they too had been bullied (pp. 37–38). Clearly, anti-gay bullying is both widespread and particularly harmful; in a review of the literature, Mishna writes: "There is strong evidence that homophobic bullying is pervasive, insidious, and starts early" (2012, p. 48). At the same time, an uncritical and cursory reading of the results of GLSEN's research might suggest that LGBT students face a dire situation in which the vast majority are constantly besieged and in fear for their safety.[2] This is exactly the narrative that the media tended to construct during our study period.

In addition, the focus on bullying behaviors per se ignored the many "microaggressions" that LGBT people, including schoolchildren, are regularly subjected to. "Microaggression" is a term coined to describe the "brief and commonplace daily verbal, behavioral, or environmental indignities (whether intentional or unintentional) that communicate hostile, derogatory, or negative racial slights and insults" (Nadal and Griffin, 2011, p. 4). The term is often used in reference to any oppressed group who suffer the effects of this subtle form of discrimination. In the case of LGBT persons, the unfortunate proliferation of the expression "that's so gay" is one example of a microaggression (see Woodford et al., 2013; Woodford et al., 2012). Researchers have found a correlation between experience of microaggression and negative outcomes in LGBT persons, including negative health outcomes (Woodford et al., 2012). Importantly, microaggressions often go unnoticed by those who aren't their indirect target. For example, one study documented that only 16 percent of a national sample of school psychologists reported that they observed or heard anti-gay bias at least once a month, but that fully 43 percent of the same sample reported hearing "that's so gay" and similar phrases in the same period (McCabe, Dragowski, and Rubinson, 2013). Thus, even many school professionals who ought to be attuned to derogatory comments and a hostile environment seem to perceive homophobic statements as normative background noise.

This connects back to our earlier point about the lack of attention to the motivations of anti-gay bullying. As discussed, during our study period the news media presented such bullying as being particularly widespread and harmful. A common explanation for the particularity of this harm was that bullying of LGBT students resulted in isolation of those students, because they had nowhere to turn for safety. However, this analysis—while it may have some validity—is highly victim-centric and thus does not address such questions as why LGBT and gender-nonconforming students are targeted to begin with, and why anti-gay bullying is so prevalent. Anderson Cooper was likely correct in pointing out that students' use of the word "fag" is still condoned in many schools, even by administrators and teachers, but again, the question is: Why is this so? As discussed in Chapter 1, anti-gay bullying—particularly that directed at boys—exists and has been accepted because it reinforces larger cultural expectations around boys' (and men's) performances of masculinity (see Renold, 2002). Here, gender and sexuality are conflated, and boys who violate gender norms—whether they identify as gay or not—are labeled as gay. This conflation assumes that "feminine" boys must also be gay (and vice versa). The narrative equates femininity with weakness; the marking of a child as a bullying victim further entrenches this weak and feminized construction (Payne and Smith, 2013, p. 8). These are likely important components of the news media's construction of a suicide narrative that depicted gay youth as universally fragile and vulnerable.

Creating an LGBT Suicide Narrative

As mentioned at the outset of this chapter, the media linked Tyler Clementi's suicide with those of several other LGBT youth, creating a new "epidemic" narrative. It is an indication of the overwhelming amount of coverage of Clementi's death that the news media could not agree in retrospect as to whether that coverage marked the *culmination* of concern about LGBT youth suicide or its *genesis*. On the one hand, Chris Cuomo reported on ABC's *20/20* that Clementi's death "coincided perfectly with a cresting wave of public outrage against bullying of gay teens and a series of headline grabbing suicides" (March 23, 2012). On the other hand, Jeff Rossen reported on NBC's *Today* that Clementi's death "seemed like a horrible but isolated case" but since then "a rash of new cases" had occurred, including the suicide of Corey Jackson, a 19-year-old student at Oakland University (October 23, 2010). On CNN's *Newsroom*, Aaron Hicklin made a similar observation: "In the days *after* Tyler Clementi's suicide, there were many other suicides actually that came into the media spotlight" (May 21, 2012). Cuomo's "culmination" assessment probably appeared to him sensible in hindsight, because before Clementi's death there had been *some* media coverage of anti-gay bullying as well as of some individual bullycides.[3] However, our research supports the "genesis" thesis. After Clementi's death, print and broadcast news media linked together suicides, some of which had occurred weeks, months, and in a few cases years before Clementi's, as part of a "string," "rash," or "disturbing wave," or, most alarmingly, as part of an "epidemic." Successive suicides continued to be added to the pattern. Anderson Cooper's statement was typical of much reporting at the time when he pointed to these deaths as evidence of "cruelty that has spiraled out of control not only just in our schools, but also beyond" (CNN, October 4, 2010).

The media also almost always found the anti-gay bullying to be the direct and sole cause of the suicide, similar to what we reported in Chapter 3 about the link between other kinds of bullying and suicide.[4] The *New York Times* reported that "bullying related to sexual orientation or perceived sexual orientation [was] *the* cause of some of the recent suicides" (May 29, 2011). CNN reported on youth "who were gay, or thought to be gay . . . harassed, tormented and bullied to the breaking point" (*Newsroom,* October 15, 2012). Similarly, NPR reported on "a spate of recent suicides of gay students pushed to the edge by bullying" (*Tell Me More,* October 12, 2010). Reporting was the same for individual cases. Carl Walker-Hoover Jr., whom fellow students apparently considered effeminate, was said to be "bullied at school . . . until he couldn't take it anymore" (CNN's *Newsroom,* April 15, 2009), and it was the online streaming of Tyler Clementi's "intimate moments" that "[drove] Tyler to suicide" (NBC's *Today,* October 23, 2010).

Reporting of the actual number of LGBT bullycides that constituted the putative "string" varied. Many stories did not specify a number, using terms such as "several" or the even more vague term "shocking number" (CNN's *Newsroom,* October 1, 2010). *ABC Nightly News* (September 30, 2010) reported that there had been three such cases in the weeks before Clementi's suicide, while *CBS Evening News* (October 1, 2011) reported that the number was five. NBC first reported that there had been three cases, (*Today,* October 1, 2010) but then reported the number as five the following day (*Nightly News,* October 2, 2010). The *New York Times* (October 1, 2010) first discussed two other suicides along with Clementi's: that of Seth Walsh, who was bullied for being gay and took his life in September 2010, and that of Jessica Logan, whose suicide occurred in 2008 after her ex-boyfriend circulated nude photos that she had "sexted" him. A few days later, the *New York Times* (October 4 and 9, 2010) turned its focus solely to suicides by "young gay teenagers," mentioning three victims (including Walsh) in addition to Clementi. The newspaper continued to refer to this "rash of suicides" involving anti-gay bullying well into 2011 (e.g., July 15, 2011). Most of the news media outlets eventually settled on five as the number of suicides in 2010 related to anti-gay bullying, and all the victims were boys: Ty Smalley (May 13), Justin Aaberg (June 9), Billy Lucas (September 9), Seth Walsh (September 19), and Asher Brown (September 20).

However, adding to the uncertainty of this number was the fact that some news media considered only LGBT bullycides as part of this "string," while others linked together suicides of all LGBT youth (in high school, college, and sometimes beyond). For instance, *CBS Evening News* (October 16, 2010) reported on "suicides by gay high school and college students" being "an all-too-familiar tragedy," with "at least a dozen such deaths nationwide since the beginning of September." ABC's *Good Morning America* (October 3, 2010), reporting on the death of Raymond Chase, a 19-year-old college student in Rhode

Island, said: "And while his brother tells [us] *the suicide wasn't brought on by bullying,* he is one of at least five gay teens to kill themselves across the country in the last three weeks alone from Texas to Indiana to California." Similarly, the *New York Times* (November 6, 2010) reported on the suicide of Joseph Jefferson, a gay 26-year-old. The article opened with the observation that "in the lives of gay people" the link between bullying and suicide "has never been stronger than of late." However the newspaper did not find Jefferson to have been bullied, and reported that the death of his mother and other "setbacks," coupled with his depression and a prior suicide attempt, were likely contributors to his completed suicide.

The news media thus constructed LGBT bullycides as the new epidemic. At the outset, there were some comparisons made to the Phoebe Prince case; for example the *New York Times* (October 1, 2010) noted that Clementi's death, like Prince's, has "stirred passionate anger," together with calls for serious criminal charges. However, the two cases were rarely discussed together after this in the *New York Times* or elsewhere; Prince's death was rarely mentioned alongside the suicides of Ty Smalley, Justin Aaberg, Billy Lucas, Seth Walsh, and Asher Brown. This emphasis fed into preexisting cultural ideas about the "tragedy" of gay life and may have reinforced a "suffering suicidal script" (see Savin-Williams, 2001) that ignores the possibility of resilience in LGBT youth. The fact that the news media pulled in examples of LGBT persons who were not even bullying victims suggests that an overarching narrative was at work.

Bullying and the Social Construction of Sexualities

The news media were of two minds about the lives of LGBT youth, presenting a confusing story of youth bullied to the point of suicide, against a backdrop of progress in gay rights. Juju Chang was one of many journalists to contrast "the public strides made by gays and lesbians in recent years" with the "climate of hate and fear" that was said to exist in many schools (ABC's *Good Morning America,* October 7, 2010). Tyler Clementi's death brought increased news media attention but was hardly the start of this conversation. Michel Martin interviewed writer Benoit Denizet-Lewis a year before Clementi's suicide about the writer's article in the *New York Times Magazine* titled "Coming Out in Middle School." Martin asked whether the "glass was half-full or half-empty," continuing:

On the one hand, you report some kids—and you did a lot of reporting in the Bible Belt, it has to be said—that even when some kids came out at ages that a lot of people would consider very young, they were stronger, more resilient, comfortable in their own skin, did not feel that they were necessarily set up to be victims or outcasts or anything of that sort.

On the other hand, you point out that there have been a number of horrific incidents of kids even being killed by other kids and that there are still kids who report in surveys being essentially terrorized at school, that it's just something to be endured. (NPR's *Tell Me More,* September 29, 2009)

After Clementi's death, the resilience narrative became much harder to find, and the news media increasingly constructed LGBT youth as universally fragile, vulnerable, and besieged.

The Construction of "Gay" as "Suffering and Suicidal"

Both the *New York Times* and the broadcast news media repeatedly made sweeping claims about the lives of LGBT youth, frequently presenting their experiences as unvaryingly bleak. One *New York Times* editorial (February 24, 2007) claimed that LGBT youth are "some of the nation's most vulnerable young people" and another (March 26, 2008) claimed that LGBT youth suffer "abuse at school, abuse on the playground and then disgrace at home." CNN reported that bullying and humiliation were "a way of life for" LGBT students (*Newsroom,* October 2, 2010) and that they "are terribly alone" and "feel so isolated" (*Anderson Cooper 360,* May 13, 2010). Adding to the plight of these students was an additional "hidden bias when judged by school and legal authorities," who, it was claimed, tended to punish them rather than their bullies (*New York Times,* December 7, 2010).

When diversity of the LGBT youth experience was in fact recognized, it sometimes led to an even more dire pronouncement, as when the *New York Times* reported that "experts say the stress can be even worse in rural places, where a lack of gay support services—or even openly gay people—can cause a sense of isolation to become unbearable" (October 4, 2010). Other reports noted how much worse it is for LGBT youth who have nonaccepting families. The suffering narrative may have reached its peak when the *New York Times* (October 9, 2010) reported about a minister, Audrey M. Connor, speaking about Tyler Clementi "in the Christian context of martyrdom." As quoted at the beginning of this chapter, Connor said: "It may sound extreme . . . but

Tyler Clementi is someone who died in a battle that many clergy and religious people are fighting. For inclusion. For our understanding of what God wants the world to be." This is one of the clearest examples of constructing the ideal victim that we found. However, such extreme and deterministic constructions of LGBT youth have the effect of denying their agency (the ability to act on their own behalf); they were doomed to a fate over which they had no control, passive and helpless "martyrs" in a battle not of their choosing.

The construction of LGBT persons as fragile and vulnerable (and thus, prone to suicide) stems from a combination of social and cultural factors. Waidzunas (2012, p. 210) identified several contributing factors, including the (self) construction of LGBT persons as socially oppressed, and the pathologizing of homosexuality both as a psychiatric disorder until 1973 and then again starting in the 1980s by way of association with HIV/AIDS, as discussed in Chapter 1. The myth of the "innately self-destructive homosexual" found in popular culture is an additional factor; it too has been revived by linking the myth to HIV/AIDS (e.g., Magnusson, 1990). Another important and more specific contribution is Gibson's seminal report about suicides by gay and lesbian youth; emblematic of the report is Gibson's claim that "lesbian and gay youth are the most invisible and outcast group of young people with whom you will come into contact" (1989, p. 117).

As noted earlier, we found no shortage of claims similar to this one in our news media sample, twenty years after Gibson's report. Gibson also claimed that gay and lesbian youth were "two to three times" more likely than heterosexual youth to attempt suicide and that 30 percent of the youth in his sample had attempted suicide; these risk figures have come to be cited as scientific fact although their methodological basis is problematic, something Gibson (1989) himself acknowledged. For example, Gibson used a clinical rather than a random sample; one would expect to find more suicidal ideation and behavior in a clinical sample. Waidzunas (in citing Latour, 1987) described how Gibson's figure became "black-boxed," a term that captures "how facts become constructed, moving from qualified to unqualified claims," to end up being stated conclusively and without citation (2012, p. 208). Continual unquestioning citation of Gibson's figures has had social effects that have served to reinforce the statistics in a process referred to as "co-production" (Jasanoff, 2004). Co-production suggests that scientific knowledge and social life are intertwined. Thus, Gibson's statistics were employed in supporting new and more methodologically sound research and in reforming state policies to include anti-discrimination provisions.

Also, Gibson's numbers have morphed in curious ways; for instance, his finding that 30 percent of his sample had attempted suicide may be the source for widely cited claims that 30 percent of all youth suicides are by LGBT youth. Best (2012) effectively shows why that estimate is probably grossly exaggerated.

We found some references to Gibson's risk estimate of "two to three times," but were more likely to find a significantly higher ratio in discussions of either attempted or completed suicides. As to attempts, the news media reported the risk of suicide for LGBT youth as being variously at least two times, two to three times, two to four times, up to four times, four times, and as much as seven times the suicide risk for non-LGBT youth. Likelihood of a completed suicide among LGBT youth was reported to be "significantly higher," "far higher," 30 percent higher, and also variously three times, four times, seven times, and, in the case of a nonaccepting family, nine times higher than the suicide risk for non-LGBT youth. Aaron Hicklin, editor-in-chief of *Out* magazine, said that "the majority of suicides in high schools and universities" are by LGBT youth (CNN's *Newsroom,* May 21, 2012). This exceeds even Gibson's likely inflated 30 percent figure. We located only one story that challenged the idea that LGBT youth have a heightened suicide risk (discussed later when we turn to the "resilience" narrative).

The media's discussion of suicide risk poses interesting questions as to how statistics come to be presented as decontextualized facts and also how such statistics can vary so wildly, even within the same media source. Some of this confusion is understandable. A recent in-depth review of the literature concerning the risk of suicide-related outcomes (SROs) in the LGB[5] population discussed many factors that make any broad conclusions problematic (Haas et al., 2011). (SROs include suicide attempts, suicidal thoughts, plans for suicide, and the lethality of prior attempts.) As to completed suicides, the relative risk is simply unknown, because death records do not routinely include the deceased person's sexual orientation. In fact Haas and colleagues state that among the "most pressing" knowledge gaps is "whether LGBT people are overrepresented among suicide deaths, and if so, why" (2011, p. 28). As to suicide *attempts,* many nationally representative studies show elevated risk among LGB persons compared to the non-LGB population. However, some find the risk to be adolescent-limited, others lifelong, and yet others timed to the age at which gay men and lesbians "come out." For example, King and colleagues (2008) examined twenty-five studies and found a lifetime elevated risk that varied substantially among the studies; Haas and colleagues (2011) also found significant variation among the studies as to the magnitude of the increased risk for LGB persons (two to seven times compared to the non-LGB population) as well as differences in risk between gay men, lesbians, and bisexuals within and across studies. As to suicidal ideation, Haas and colleagues cite one study that found a relationship between suicidal ideation and suicide attempts in lesbians but not in gay men (2011, pp. 18–19).

Importantly, King and colleagues point out that the studies they examined "were limited by small samples or selection bias" and that "all of the studies failed to meet several of our quality indicators" (2008, n.p.). Another methodological issue is the meaning of "sexual orientation"—that is, whether it is measured by same-sex attraction, sexual behavior, or self-identification (a phenomenon we alluded to in Chapter 1). These are important distinctions, because suicide risk varies depending on which measure is being used. Stone and colleagues pooled five surveys of urban youth and found that "the prevalence of SROs varied significantly on the basis of sexual identity and sex of sexual contacts among both males and females" (2014, p. 2). Little can be said about suicidal risk among transgender persons or the effects of race and ethnicity due to small sample sizes or use of nonrandom samples. It is also important to note that in many studies a high percentage of respondents do not answer questions about sexual orientation or suicide. Stone and colleagues (2014) reported that, across the five surveys they pooled, about 2 percent of males identified as gay, 1.4 percent of females identified as lesbian, and 2.2 percent of males and 5.7 percent of femalies identified as bisexual. However, about 6 percent of respondents in each survey did not answer the question about sexual orientation, and a significant percentage did not answer the questions about SROs (ranging from 1.1 percent to 19.7 percent across the five surveys).

Adding to the difficulty in assessing risk is that suicide is a complex phenomenon involving both protective factors and risk factors. Mental disorders and substance abuse are among the most significant risk factors, and LGB persons have been found to have an increased risk of depression, anxiety disorders, and substance abuse compared to the non-LGB population (King et al., 2008). However, mental disorders and substance abuse are themselves correlated with social factors. For instance, discrimination against LGB persons at the individual, institutional, and societal levels has been shown to be correlated with mental health problems and SROs among this population (see Haas et al., 2011, which collects the findings of studies on this topic). For example, LGB persons living in one of the nineteen states that lacked legal anti-discrimination protections during the time of the study by Haas and colleagues "were almost five times more likely than those in other states to have two or more mental disorders" (2011, p. 24). As well, the institutional environment can be either a risk factor or a protective factor regarding suicide. Hatzenbuehler (2011) found that schools lacking supportive LGBT policies, such as policies prohibiting anti-gay bullying, had a rate of LGBT suicide that was 20 percent higher than that found in more supportive schools. At the family level, nonrandom studies have found an elevated risk of suicide attempts by gay and lesbian youth if they have rejecting families (Haas et al., 2011, p. 22). Cover (2012a) also notes the contribution of social factors, but takes a very different approach, framing his argument within queer theory. He acknowledges that youth suicide among the queer population can be explained in part as a response to an oppressive hetero-normativity. However, Cover also claims that such suicides can represent a response to the social pressures of being required to choose *any* sexual identity as well as result from an inability to conform to expectations from the mainstreamed gay community. Thus, LGBT youth may feel constrained and pressured by both hetero-normativity *and* homo-normativity.

We discuss the LGB and LGBT suicide research in some detail here because it is important to try to view suicide as the complex phenomenon that it is. We also do so to echo Waidzunas (2012), who points out that even well-meaning but perhaps methodologically careless uses of Gibson's (1989) statistics (and the statistics of others) have led to unintended consequences. First, "they have led to the homogenization of the identity category 'gay youth' as universally denoting people at risk for suicide" (Waidzunas, 2012, p. 203). Second, wide use of suicide statistics can act as a self-fulfilling prophecy whereby gay youth "augment their reported level of suicidality, enacting . . . a 'suffering suicidal script' as a rite of passage" or conversely react by developing "'resilience' narratives" (p. 204). Waidzunas reports that one researcher (Savin-Williams, 2001) found that LGBT youth exaggerated their suicidality due to societal expectations. Finally, Waidzunas warns of "the potential for the redeployment of decontextualized numbers in ways that can possibly repathologize homosexuality" (2012, p. 204). We would add another twist to the use of these statistics in the media reports we reviewed. While elevated suicide risk theoretically should apply only to youth who are *actually* LGBT, the media cited the statistics unproblematically when explaining suicides of youth who were bullied over *perceptions* that they were gay. This conflation with the substance and the target of the bullying is left unexplained. It may actually be that anti-gay bullying, even when directed at youth who are not self-identified as LGBT, increases the risk for suicide as compared to other forms of bullying. This is consistent with limited studies that suggest that anti-gay bullying directed at boys causes more harm than other types of bullying (e.g., Swearer, Turner, and Givens, 2008). However, the subject/object conflation went unexplored in media reports that purported to report suicide risk for LGBT youth rather than for youth subject to anti-gay bullying. Sanjay Gupta of CNN raised but did not resolve this distinction when he reported that parents of two children who had died by suicide "say their teenagers were bullied over their *perceived* sexuality. And that's not uncommon among teen suicides nationwide" (*Anderson Cooper 360*, July 20, 2011).

Waidzunas's second point about youth acting out a suffering suicidal script is outside our research, but we did find evidence of his first and third points. As to the first, the news media almost always implied that all LGBT youth faced similar experiences and dealt with those experiences in similar ways. Thus the news media presented the link between LGBT youth status and suicidality as direct, unproblematic, and monolithic. The *New York Times* reported that "it should come as no surprise" that LGBT youth had higher suicide rates (September 22, 2011) and that "an awareness of how closely [bullying and suicide] can be linked in the lives of gay people has never been stronger than of late" (November 6, 2010). It is worth noting that in our sample, the *New York Times* had reported on a total of four LGBT bullycides in the several months prior to its 2010 article. It went on in the same article to report the non-bullying-related suicide of Joseph Jefferson, discussed earlier, whose suicide seemed puzzling to the article's author because Jefferson's "life fit no clean narrative of fragile disempowerment."

The broadcast news media were no different, whether reporting general risk of suicide or individual cases. On her CNN show, Jane Velez-Mitchell (September 30, 2010) said that being a teenager is "difficult enough. Add that to being gay and the odds can be sometimes stacked against you." Clinical psychologist William Pollack asserted that "gay white males are the most likely people to kill themselves across America," without a further discussion of risk factors (ABC's *Good Morning America*, October 7, 2010). ABC reported that another Rutgers student had died by suicide within a year before Clementi did, and according to Rutgers professor Rob O'Brien "that suicide also centered around sexual orientation" (*Good Morning America*, October 2, 2010). O'Brien's comment suggests a direct link between orientation and suicide in each case; thus, Clementi's suicide "centered around" his sexual orientation rather than the invasion of his privacy, his own risk profile, or other factors. These stories strongly imply two things: that risk is uniform among all LGBT youth, and that LGBT orientation alone somehow precipitates suicide. This news media narrative is consistent with Cover's finding that stories in the Australian news media about LGBT youth suicides sometimes implied that "nonnormative sexuality was *in itself* causal of suicide risk" (2012b, p. 1176, emphasis in original).

This homogenization of risk and assumption of a direct link between sexual orientation and suicide likely occurred without any conscious homophobic intent; in fact, this conflation was frequently made by LGBT advocates. However, the connection between homosexuality and suicide was occasionally used in the manner predicted by Waidzunas's (2012) third unintended consequence—as an attempt to repathologize homosexuality. One example comes from Anderson Cooper's interview of Tom Prichard, president of the Minnesota Family Council, concerning Prichard's purported statements about the suicide of a gay student (CNN, October 5, 2010). Cooper said: "You say the bullying had nothing to do with it and that he and other gay teens who kill themselves die because they have adopted, in your words, 'an unhealthy lifestyle.'" On a different program, Tony Perkins, president of the Family Research Council, claimed: "There's no correlation between in-acceptance of homosexuality and depression and suicide." (Presumably, by "in-acceptance" Perkins meant general social intolerance or family rejection.) But for "these young people who do identify as gay or lesbian," he continued, "we know from the social science that they do have a higher rate of depression and a propensity to suicide *because of that internal conflict*" (NPR's *All Things Considered,* October 26, 2010).

Perkins's reference to internal conflict is obviously incomplete, because it does not address the source of that conflict (if it exists at all). Identity conflicts occur because of a disjuncture between internal states and external demands (e.g., the "in-acceptance" of LGBT people). As we demonstrated earlier, familial and institutional rejection and oppression may be factors fueling mental health problems and, possibly, suicide. These relationships are quite complex, but in our study period the news media tended to focus on LGBT suicides in deterministic, cause-and-effect terms that tied anti-gay bullying to an individualized response of suicide. Only occasionally was the idea presented that LGBT youth had access to protective factors that could buoy their resilience; sometimes this came from unlikely sources.

The Resilience Narrative

Dharun Ravi, Tyler Clementi's dorm mate, provided an interesting rejection of the fragility narrative in his interview on ABC's *20/20* (March 23, 2012) that occurred after the jury returned a verdict but before his sentencing. At one point the interviewer, Chris Cuomo, asked Ravi whether he had "misunderstood how fragile [Clementi] was." Ravi responded: "I really don't think he was very fragile. I think he just didn't like talking to people. . . . Just because he's gay doesn't mean he's automatically fragile and can't deal with anything." While this statement can easily be interpreted as merely self-serving, it nevertheless stands as a rare counterpoint to the news media constructions of Clementi and other LGBT youth discussed previously. While uncommon, this "resilience" construction was not entirely missing from our sample. We did find some examples where LGBT youth were constructed as resilient or even thriving, and on a few occasions we found the uniformly "fragile and suffering" construction of LGBT youth directly challenged.

Perhaps the strongest telling of the resilience narrative came in two feature articles in the *New York Times* (August 27, 2009, January 4, 2011). The first was a lengthy piece (more than 6,500 words) by Benoit Denizet-Lewis, whose NPR interview was quoted from earlier. This article was based upon a rare source for the *New York Times* and most other news media: interviews with a number of LGBT youth and their parents who reported on their actual lived experiences. The result was a "complicated" picture of LGBT middle school children. The article cited oft-used statistics on rates of bullying and suicide among this population and noted: "For many gay youth, middle school is more survival than learning." It also depicted children who had been rejected by their families. However, the article included interviews of many middle school students who were "out" at home and at school, and who were grappling openly with finding gay friends and romantic partners. The article said that "young people with same-sex attractions are increasingly coming out and living lives that would be 'nearly incomprehensible to earlier generations of gay youth'" and that "being young and gay is no longer an automatic prescription for a traumatic childhood."[6] The article was rare in its normalization of sexual attraction among LGBT youth. It ended with the story of "Austin," a student in Michigan whose father agreed to take him to a gay pride parade in Chicago. Austin's mother said: "Austin warned his dad, 'You can't get mad at me when I scream at cute guys in Speedos!' And boy, did Austin scream. He was in gay teenage heaven.'"

The later article (January 4, 2011) focused on what academic research suggests about the resiliency of LGBT youth and included interviews with two researchers: Dr. Ritch Savin-Williams, a professor of developmental psychology at Cornell University, and Lisa Diamond, a psychology and gender studies professor at the University of Utah. This article directly challenged the strength of the evidence that LGBT youth are more prone to suicide and mental health problems. It noted that a problem with the suicide statistics commonly cited is that the research they were taken from "focused on clinical populations—people who sought help because they were troubled, had attempted suicide or professed suicidal tendencies." This skews the results and makes the actual risk "hard to measure." (We made this point earlier with respect to the Gibson statistics.) Savin-Williams said: "We don't hear about normal gay teens. It's hard to get studies published when researchers don't find differences." In fact, says Diamond, research shows "more similarities than differences among gay and straight adolescents." For example, she said that studies showed that gay youth "had as many friends and were just as popular and socially connected as other teenagers," and that the risk factors for suicide—including mental illness, family dysfunction, and access to means of attempting suicide were also the same among both gay and straight youth. While studies do show that gay teenagers are somewhat more likely to suffer severe emotional distress compared to straight teenagers, Savin-Williams claimed that "the effects of bullying and discrimination are often overplayed in the news media." He said that "a direct link between bullying and suicide among gay teens has not been shown," and also strongly cautioned against claiming such links: "I'm concerned about the message being given to gay youth by adults who say they are destined to be depressed, abuse drugs or perhaps commit suicide. . . . I believe the message may create more suicides, more depression and more substance abuse. I worry about suicide contagion. About 10 to 15 percent are fragile gay kids, and they're susceptible to messages of gay-youth suicide." Savin-Williams took direct issue with the "It Gets Better" project, saying that the message of just surviving adolescence "is a disservice" and that "the message should be that your life can be good right now." He said many gay teens live happy, healthy, and productive lives, and that many can name positive attributes that have accrued to them because of their sexual orientation.

This resilience narrative was fairly difficult to find in other articles in the *New York Times* and in broadcast stories. While news media featured some "success" stories about LGBT youth, the "fragile and suffering" construction dominated, so that if a bullycide wasn't being reported, then a near-bullycide was. News media ran many survivor stories about teens who were coping after having attempted suicide or seriously thought about it. One gay student was said to be doing well after he got help from the Trevor Project after contemplating suicide (*NBC Nightly News,* October 2, 2010). A transgender youth said that he too had considered suicide (*CBS Evening News,* October 1, 2010). These stories were not limited just to the weeks or months after Tyler Clementi's death. One gay teen's story was featured on *CBS Evening News* in 2000 (October 19); he had been bullied and become "depressed and confused" and "swallowed a whole bottle of pills" in an attempted suicide.

Particularly resonant were the stories that showed LGBT youth apparently getting along in their lives, but only to have tragedy strike. Several stories about LGBT bullycides depicted parents who said that they had accepted their children's sexual orientation and had complained to the school system about bullying. Asher Brown's father said that he was accepting when his son came out to him, and that his son seemed relieved and returned to school with a better attitude, only to commit suicide shortly thereafter. A similar story, and the one that received the most news media exposure, was the suicide of Jamey Rodemeyer. Rodemeyer made a video for the "It Gets Better" project in which he claimed he had been bullied for years. In it he said: "I promise you it will get better. I have so much support from people I don't even know online. I know that sounds creepy. But they're so nice and caring [and] they don't ever want me to die" (CNN's *Anderson Cooper 360,* September 20, 2011). Despite this support, Rodemeyer killed himself after the video was posted, resulting in a large number of media stories that aired portions of the video in reporting his death. This story and others like it reinforced the construction of LGBT youth as fragile; even with the support of family and the public, these children could still be bullied into suicide.

Fragility's Unintended Consequences

Fragility claims were perhaps the ones most calculated to elicit empathy (and thus action, including policy change); however, as we have noted, there can be unintended consequences of such a construction, three of which we touched on earlier. First, LGBT youth come to be seen as a homogeneous category of individuals who all have the same elevated suicide risk compared to heterosexual youth. This could overly alarm all parents of LGBT youth as well as obscure a more appropriate focus on the 10 to 15 percent of LGBT kids who are actually fragile, if Savin-Williams is correct. Second, there is a danger of creating a "suffering suicidal script" that normalizes suicide as a response to bullying. Thus, LGBT youth can come to perform the script and feel suicidal over their suffering, but this increases their risk, as Savin-Williams (2001) demonstrated, of actually attempting and even completing suicide. Third, there is the danger of the misuse of fragility claims by finding pathology in homosexuality itself rather than in societal reactions to it. We present examples of this when we venture into culture wars at the end of the chapter.

There could be other unintended consequences, some related to these three. Constructing all LGBT youth as universally besieged fails to take into account the wide diversity of experience of these youth in terms of both individual and structural factors. Individually, LGBT youth may be very resilient, may have supportive families, and may be leading fulfilling lives, as the research discussed previously demonstrates. On the structural level, presenting school environments as highly, and equally, dangerous to all LGBT youth is both inaccurate and harmful. First, it overlooks initiatives that schools have taken to improve their climate, such as staff training and the creation of gay-straight alliances and LGBT-inclusive curricula. In fact, the most recent research—from the 2011 NSCS—shows some overall improvement in school climate in this regard (Kosciw et al., 2012). A second and related point is that constructing school environments as uniformly LGBT-hostile may suggest the notion that anti-gay bullying is so ingrained as to be impervious to change and thus may give license to anti-gay bullies who may equate "widespread and normative" with "accepted and condoned." This would encourage the continued peer policing of heteronormativity and would also complicate one successful strategy for changing youth behavior—the social norms approach. Studies have shown that changing students' perceptions of social norms (for instance, publicizing accurate but poorly understood norms such as "most students on this campus don't binge drink") is an effective method of changing their behavior (see DeJong et al., 2006).

Another effect of constructing LGBT youth as fragile is reinforcement of cultural notions of homosexuals as being weak and self-destructive; such notions suggest that bullying victims are completely helpless and must endure their victimhood. School responses such as the creation of "safe spaces" and "gay days" may be important, but may also reinforce the notion that LGTB kids are marginalized persons (Payne and Smith, 2013, p. 16). A cursory look at the "It Gets Better" project may fuel these ideas and thus also give license to children who may receive the unintended message that anti-gay bullying is normative: "It only 'gets better' for my LGBT classmates later; I'm expected to bully them now." In addition, and importantly, conflating the subject and the object of anti-gay bullying ignores the fact that such bullying is directed at both LGBT youth and young people who do not conform to gender norms. While GLSEN's National School Climate Surveys have reported on anti-gay bullying as well as bullying regarding nonconformity to gender norms, the news media in our study period focused almost exclusively on findings about the former.

All of this is consistent with the news media's pattern of ignoring the peer-policing functions of anti-gay bullying. The focus on victims' reactions to bullying, on promises that things will eventually change, and on victims' general vulnerability serves to distract from a more important focus: the problematizing of anti-gay discourse. The avoidance of why anti-gay bullying is so prevalent, and the social purposes it serves, is likely due to a number of factors related to social discomfort with seeing children as sexual beings and also related to the powerful force of hetero-normativity in conflating LGBT persons with their (shameful) sexual identities.

Squeamishness, Reductionism, and Hetero-Normativity

News media reporting on the bullying of youth who are LGBT or who are perceived to be LGBT occurs at the intersection of several cultural attitudes about sex and sexuality. First, it comes up against the reluctance in the United States and some other Western cultures to address children's sexuality at all, due to assumptions about their presumed innocence (see Reynolds, 2005; Schalet, 2006). Second, cultural norms of hetero-normativity and homophobia result in a strong resistance to accept the chance that children are nonheterosexual unless they have expressly claimed otherwise. Finally, there is a tendency toward reductionism of sexual identity, in several ways. In our study period, LGBT youth typically were constructed as either homosexual or heterosexual. If homosexual, their sexual orientation became the only salient characteristic in defining them (see Epting, Raskin, and Burke, 1994), and then their sexual orientation was reduced merely to sexual behavior.

One example involved the case of 11-year-old Carl Walker-Hoover Jr., whom fellow students considered feminine and as a result had been subjected to "gay slurs." He died by suicide by hanging himself in early 2009. His mother, Sirdeaner Walker, when interviewed on CNN, said that she did not ask her son if he was gay, but offered: "Some people may say he was flamboyant. He was very dramatic" (*Newsroom*, April 15, 2009). Two days later, Walker appeared on *Anderson Cooper 360* along with Mel White, founder of Soulforce Inc. (CNN, April 17, 2009). When White asked Cooper what he thought of Walker-Hoover's suicide, Cooper responded that it made him "sick" because "we've buried so many young gay guys." Ms. Walker immediately corrected Cooper:

> WALKER: First of all, you know, with all due respect, Carl was not gay. He didn't have any quote, unquote, "gay tendencies." He was just a young 11-year-old boy.
> COOPER: Sure.
> WALKER: Who was full of life, who loved life, who was the type of kid that would give his teacher a hug, you know, upon seeing her, greeting her in the morning. So people—other children took that as . . . he wasn't tough. But, you know, he was never, you know, he never expressed any kind of tendencies towards being gay towards me.
> COOPER: And I mean, he was 11 years old.
> WALKER: He was 11 years old.
> COOPER: Right.
> WALKER: He was just in the beginning of his life.

Similarly, Kyra Phillips said on CNN that "Carl was just 11 years old, not really old enough to know or care about his sexual orientation" (*Newsroom*, May 14, 2010). It is thus interesting that in the *same newscast*, Randi Kaye reported that Larry King, a gender-nonconforming boy who was murdered by another student, had "come out at age ten." A similar denial was heard in the case of bullycide victim Samantha Johnson. Her mother described her as a "tomboy" and "perceived as gay" (CNN's *Newsroom*, July 21, 2011). When the interviewer asked if Samantha *was* gay, her mother responded: "No. We don't think she was gay. She was 13."

Another example is that of Paige Moravetz and Haylee Fentress, two 14-year-old eighth-graders in Minnesota who killed themselves in an apparent suicide pact. The girls were described in many news media stories as being exceptionally close friends. A cousin of Fentress, Patrick Martin, appeared on *Today* (NBC, April 21, 2011) and was asked "if the girls felt more strongly about themselves, more than just a friendship, and they were confused by those feelings and maybe felt a little ostracized." Martin replied: "I don't want to say that we have anything that, you know, tells us that that's definitely the case. But, you know, there are things that suggest that." This was a rare acknowledgment of even a potential LGBT identity, but the next day, on *Dr. Drew* (CNN, April 22, 2011), Fentress's aunt, Robin Settle, denied anything more than a friendship, adding: "It has been turned into the question of homosexuality or a deeper relationship, and I really just don't believe that that's the case." Pinsky responded: "And I want to say, Robin, that *you don't need to bring that element in* to just say that this was a dependent relationship where they found, as you said, a mirror in one another and they could find refuge against this bullying."

By discussing these cases, we are not claiming that any of these children were nonheterosexual; rather, we are pointing out the reluctance to consider this possibility through use of the pretext of age in the first two cases (in the last case, there was a suggestion of shamefulness or squeamishness as well—there is no "need to bring that element in"). Because there were other stories in the broadcast news media and in the *New York Times* discussing youth who had come out between the ages of 10 and 13—in fact there were stories that specifically focused on children coming out at earlier ages than in the past—it seems fair to conclude that the focus on the age of Walker-Hoover and Johnson as precluding gay or lesbian sexual orientation appeared to be rooted in hetero-normativity. We applaud the news media for sometimes recognizing that anti-gay bullying can be directed at any child who violates gender norms, but it is equally important to recognize that pre-teens may be developing an LGBT identity, and that this identity is not a badge of shame. Otherwise, news commentators are tapping into and reinforcing the homophobic attitudes they claim to find repugnant.

While the news media tended toward hetero-normativity as the default, if a child had "come out" they tended to completely reverse course and engage in essentialism (see Fuss, 1989) by emphasizing sexual orientation over all of that child's other characteristics. Non-normative sexuality was thus constructed as a sort of "master status" (Becker, 1963) in that other aspects of the youth, including other reasons for their bullying victimization, were overlooked. There were some exceptions, though. For example, there were several stories about how bullycide victim Asher Brown was bullied for multiple reasons. His father said that his son was gay and then added: "He was also a Buddhist. He was also a child with a disability" (CNN's *Issues with Jane Velez-Mitchell*, September 29, 2010). Jeff Rossen reported on *Today* (NBC, October 1,

2010) that "bullies picked on [Brown] for everything: because he was short, because he had a lisp, because he liked to read," and Brown's father said that the bullies "made fun of his size, him being small. They made fun of his ears. They made fun of his religion when they found out he was Buddhist." The *New York Times* also reported that Brown endured "years of harassment for his small size, religion and perceived sexuality." However, the great majority of stories simply added Brown to the "string" of suicides of gay youth, elevating one status as his sole status.

Essentialism arose in broader contexts such as policy discussions. There, anti-gay rights advocates regularly reduced sexual orientation to only "sexual behavior." This process illustrates how identity politics, which groups enter in order to claim rights, can also be used against those groups as a form of social control. Social control over the lives of gays and lesbians has a long history and has been enforced through a societywide confluence of the mass media, scientific-medical and moral-religious discourses, and the criminal justice system (see Wittman, 1970). Homosexuality has been normalized to an extent in the United States as public opinion has shifted and as formal social control mechanisms have been relaxed or reversed. However, as Seidman (2005) points out, cultural messages still retain a distinction between the "polluted homosexual" and the "normal gay"; the latter individual conforms to generalized heterosexual sexual norms. The American Psychiatric Association removed homosexuality from its list of mental disorders in 1973, the Supreme Court found laws against same-sex sexual behavior unconstitutional in 2003, same-sex marriage was first made legal in Massachusetts in 2004, the armed services began accepting openly gay members in 2011, and the Supreme Court found the federal Defense of Marriage Act unconstitutional in 2013. However, the ghosts of formal social control still haunt the culture; for example, it is common to still hear claims opposing homosexuality that are rooted in psychological or biological pathology. In fact, as LGBT rights continue to advance, they are sometimes met with great resistance and backlash.

One of the most contested spaces over the past generation has been the schools, where proponents of "teaching tolerance" have come up against those advocating "parental rights." Such conflict has arisen over a number of issues; we witnessed it occurring in the context of anti-gay bullying legislation and policies. Anti-gay claimsmakers paradoxically framed LGBT persons as inherently defective and self-destructive, while also claiming that these persons were not in need of "special protections." Attempts were made to pathologize homosexuality and to conflate sexual behavior with sexual identity, thus framing the issue as one of "sex education," an aspect of the curriculum over which parents have perhaps the most control. LGBT claimsmakers constructed anti-gay bullying as particularly widespread and harmful, and also emphasized that anti-gay bullying is directed at any child who is perceived to be gay. Bullying was thus pulled into the battlefield of culture wars, where claims and counterclaims flew like bullets.

Culture Wars and the Social Construction of Sexuality

The bulk of objections to anti-bullying policies occurred in the context of larger issues involving LGBT people, issues that are often part of culture wars. It was in this context that we witnessed pitched battles as anti-gay activists and legislators proposed or enacted policies that would increase formal social control over how homosexuality is discussed in the schools. Some proposals went much further, illustrating the extremes of anti-gay activists' social control agenda. For instance, a bill proposed by a Tennessee legislator would have required schools to "inform parents if their students engage in homosexual activity" (Fox's *The O'Reilly Factor,* January 31, 2013).

In these debates we witnessed the clearest examples of contested claimsmaking about anti-bullying policies, and we thus frame our discussion here in the constructionist language of social problems. One point of contention was a basic one—whether anti-bullying policies should include specific attention to sexual orientation/identity. Arguments for inclusion were based on many of the assertions discussed in this chapter, including the assertion that anti-gay bullying is worse than other forms of bullying; bullycide horror stories were also invoked to buttress these arguments. Counterclaimants mainly argued against "special rights" and suggested that generally worded policies would protect all students. Jonathan Saenz, director of legislative affairs at the Liberty Institute, ostensibly appealed to fairness when he said a proposed bill was "'not about bullying' but about creating 'new classes of people and giving special protections to some categories and not others'" (*NYT,* March 4, 2011). This argument is a type of tactical criticism (Ibarra and Kitsuse, 1993)—it agrees that there is a problem (here, bullying) but disagrees on the proper means of redress (here, "special protections"). Counterclaimants also employed moral arguments drawing on the rhetoric of rectitude (see Best, 1987). Tony Perkins of Focus on the Family said his organization is opposed to laws that "normalize" homosexual behavior and added that it is also opposed to normalizing promiscuity and adultery (CNN's *Newsroom,* February 19, 2012). Perkins's argument appears to be that LGBT-inclusive anti-bullying policies would protect same-sex *behavior* rather than prohibit anti-gay *bullying*. Perkins reinforced this interpretation when he said "we don't support . . . special rights for people based upon their sexual *behavior*." Perkins's focus on same-sex sexual behavior rather than status or identity is a common rhetorical technique of groups opposed to LGBT rights.

Proponents for inclusion had two responses to these counterclaims. The first is that anti-gay bullying is not prevented by enacting general anti-bullying prohibitions. Eliza Byard, executive director of GLSEN, claimed that her organization's research demonstrates that only LGBT-inclusive anti-bullying statutes reduce anti-gay bullying (CNN's *Anderson Cooper 360,* September 1, 2010). The second response involved the observation that children are bullied based on perceived, not actual, LGBT status, and that such bullying is particularly harmful. Dr. Warren Throckmorton, associate professor of psychology at Grove City College, noted that most children who commit suicide after anti-gay bullying are not gay, saying: "The common element is anti-gay harassment" not gay identity (NPR's *All Things Considered,* October 26, 2010). Psychologist Susan Swearer emphasized the special harm of this type of bullying when she claimed that research showed "the kids who were bullied because other kids called them gay had higher levels of anxiety and depression and a more negative view towards school and really felt ostracized" (CBS's *Sunday Morning News,* January 9, 2011). Thus, the argument goes, an inclusive statute would protect many heterosexual children who are perceived as LGBT. This counterclaim, if accepted, at least partly neutralizes the assertion that "special protection" is being sought only for LGBT students. However, it may not assuage those who claim that the "homosexual agenda" would still be advanced by such statutes, which was an argument that we also found prevalent.

A debate on Fox's *Hannity & Colmes* (July 19, 2000) represents another illustration of these types of claims and counterclaims. The show was introduced as a discussion about whether GLSEN's initiative to "combat what it sees as anti-gay bias in Southern schools" was actually a "real agenda . . . to normalize homosexuality in the minds of children." The guests on the program were Wayne Besen of the Human Rights Campaign and Christine O'Donnell of the Savior's Alliance for Lifting the Truth. The hosts were Pat Halpin (sitting in for Alan Colmes) and Sean Hannity. The program began with a discussion about safe-sex education, but Halpin turned the conversation to bullying of LGBT youth when he asked Besen how serious a problem it was and Besen replied that it was "incredibly serious." O'Donnell immediately de-privileged LGBT bullying by responding: "Dorks and freaks get teased, and nerds." After some cross-talk, Besen again universalized his claim by pointing out that "a lot of people who are getting harassed for this reason are accused of being gay." (Besen likely inadvertently used the term "accused," which stigmatizes non-normative sexuality.) O'Donnell responded: "It's kids being kids, that's it." Similarly, Robert Newman of the California Christian Coalition said of bullying: "It's part of growing up. It's a part of maturing" (CNN's *Anderson Cooper 360,* September 20, 2011). He added: "I hardly think bullying is a real issue in schools." O'Donnell's and Newman's claims are naturalizing strategies that suggest the condition is normal or inevitable rather than a problem (see Ibarra and Kitsuse, 1993). Such claims also contradict forty years of bullying research; ironically, however—and as already discussed—these claims inadvertently have some truth to them; namely, that some kinds of bullying, including anti-gay bullying, appear to be a normative component of children's lives. Though as we also hopefully make clear, normative should not mean acceptable.

News media also reported a number of other conflicts involving initiatives in different states. Two of these appeared to be the most frequently discussed: the "neutrality policy" of Minnesota's Anoka-Hennepin School District, and a proposed Tennessee statute that would have protected religious expression from claims of bullying. The neutrality policy represents an attempt at social control over teachers' discourse around homosexuality; the second was presented as a matter of religious freedom but was seen by LGBT claimsmakers as opening the door for informal social control of LGBT youth through bullying framed in religious discourse. In news media coverage of the debates over each of these policies, a number of claims and counterclaims arose that are representative of those raised in other cultural conflicts.

Anoka-Hennepin School District's Neutrality Policy

The Anoka-Hennepin School District encompasses the city of Minneapolis and is the largest district in Minnesota. According to the *New York Times,* the district expanded its anti-bullying policy by adding gay and lesbian students to the other target groups already named, acting in the wake of "at least two suicides by gay students" in a year (November 7, 2010). The two suicides were among seven that were eventually reported to have occurred over a two-year period (*CNN Presents,* October 9, 2011). However, to "placate religious conservatives," the school district also required that "teachers must be absolutely neutral on questions of sexual orientation and refrain from endorsing gay parenting." Rights groups and several students sued the district, and the US Justice Department opened an investigation (*CNN Presents,* October 9, 2011). The *New York Times* ran several stories about the neutrality policy, and while CNN was the only broadcast network to report on it, the coverage was extensive. The intent and effect of the policy were debated at some length on several CNN programs, providing insight into the claims and counterclaims frequently employed around policies prohibiting anti-gay bullying.

Those in support of the neutrality policy argued that it was fair because it did not allow faculty and staff to either condemn or support homosexuality. The superintendent of the school district was paraphrased as claiming that "the neutrality policy is a reasonable response to a divided community" (CNN's *Anderson Cooper 360,* July 20, 2011). Such a claim invokes the rhetoric of entitlement because of the appeal to fairness (Ibarra and Kitsuse, 1993). However, opponents reframed the putative "neutrality" policy as biased, unfair, oppressive, and dangerous. This claim relies on the perversity thesis (Hirschman, 1991), which posits that an intended solution to a problem has actually made it worse. For example, one teacher called it a "censorship policy" that was "contributing to a hostile, toxic environment" (*CNN Presents,* July 24, 2011). Thus children were vulnerable to bullying and had nowhere to turn for help. Some were quite pointed about the effect of the policy. Ashleigh Banfield said on CNN's *Early Show* (March 6, 2012) that the school district "had this . . . neutrality policy . . . [and] all of a sudden there were all these bullying cases. People can call [them] gay or fagots [*sic*], and things [were] happening with these kids, kids committing suicide." Anderson Cooper also dramatically illustrated this alleged imbalance when he said that Kyle, a particular student he had interviewed, "was trying to survive in a climate where teachers could not even talk to Kyle in whispers about what bullies were shouting in his ears" (CNN, December 13, 2011).

In response, parents employed a rights discourse. Yvette Schue, a parent from the school district, said: "Parents have a right to raise their children the way they want to and the school district doesn't need to be sitting there telling kids your parents are wrong" (*CNN Presents,* July 24, 2011). Underlying this rights discourse were claims based on the rhetoric of endangerment (Ibarra and Kitsuse, 1993) that constructed

LGBT issues as "controversial" topics that also necessitate discussions about sex or are meant to "promote homosexuality," or both. Candi Cushman said that her organization, Focus on the Family, supported parents' rights to "determine and control when, how and if their children are exposed to controversial sexual topics like homosexuality, gay marriage" (CNN's *Anderson Cooper 360,* July 20, 2011). Calling something "controversial" is a kind of perspectivizing strategy that characterizes an opponent's claims as being mere opinions that need not be shared (Ibarra and Kitsuse, 1993). Some news media commentators appeared to recognize the politics involved in the labeling of LGBT issues as controversial. Anderson Cooper referred to the school district as considering "*what they're calling* a controversial topics curriculum policy" (CNN, December 13, 2011), and Dr. Drew Pinsky referred to a discussion "on what are *called* controversial topics like homosexuality" (CNN, December 14, 2011).

Reducing all LGBT-related issues to controversy over *sex* is a commonly employed counterstrategy, as noted earlier; it appears designed to raise concerns about protecting children from sensitive topics and also to discomfit some non-LGBT persons who are directed to thinking about sexual acts rather than sexual identity (or ascribed identity) and affection. This is sometimes accomplished in a general way by using the term "homosexual" rather than "gay or lesbian," such as when the term "homosexual agenda" is employed as shorthand for a host of evils. The term "sexual agenda" has even been employed (e.g., *NYT,* September 27, 2009, quoting Finn Laursen, executive director of the Christian Educators Association). One letter to the editor in a newspaper in the Anoka-Hennepin School District went much further, invoking the pathology discourse: "It is irresponsible for educators to promote the 'It's OK to be gay' message to students when homosexuality is such a high-risk behavior"[7] (reported on *CNN Presents,* July 24, 2011). However, most claimsmakers conflated sex and identity rather than warning of "high-risk behaviors." Along these lines, Tony Perkins of the Family Research Council said: "You should not be able to bully a student based upon . . . *what they do sexually*" (CNN's *Newsroom,* February 9, 2012). Candi Cushman, in discussing opposition to the neutrality policy, said "parents should have a choice when it . . . comes to sex education and sexuality topics in the classroom" (CNN's *Dr. Drew,* December 14, 2011). Thus it is interesting that Anderson Cooper on his show referred to conservative groups opposing "what they call a pro-gay agenda" (CNN, September 1, 2010). Here, Cooper uses the less-charged word in defining the opposition, a word that "they" would actually *not* use.

A similar rhetorical pattern emerged in discussions about other policies, in which familiar claims, counterclaims, and rhetorical strategies were asserted. There were conflicts involving policies designed to change the cultural or institutional climate around LGBT issues and thus to reduce anti-gay bullying in an indirect way. These included a law in California requiring the teaching of gay history (discussed on CNN's *American Morning,* July 6, 2011). More generally, there was discussion in news media about how progress in LGBT rights would "trickle down" and reduce students' anti-gay biases.

Tennessee Bill 370

The formal social control process took a decidedly different turn, with claimants reversing their rhetorical strategies, when lawmakers introduced Tennessee House Bill 370, which "would prohibit bullying because of a student's sexual orientation, race or religion" (CNN's *Anderson Cooper 360,* September 20, 2011). In advocating for the bill, claimsmakers used a rights-based discourse that expressed respect for students' religious beliefs and the First Amendment protections afforded to them. Republican representative Mike Harmon presented a hypothetical conversation wherein a student might say that "homosexuality is a sin" (CNN's *Anderson Cooper 360,* September 20, 2011). Harmon said that "we don't want that child to be labeled a bully just because they had that particular belief," but went further, turning the LGBT activists' argument on its head, when he added: "We don't want that child to be *bullied* because they have a certain moral or religious belief."

The bill's supporters used the counter-rhetoric of hysteria by suggesting that opponents had irrational concerns. David Fowler, president of the Family Action Council of Tennessee, said that the bill merely codifies "the First Amendment rights that students have according to our courts. . . . So I don't know why there's such a controversy that [this codification] is a license to bully." When another guest objected to his characterization, Fowler appeared to go out of his way to assuage opponents. He said that "words even cloaked in political or religious terminology certainly can constitute bullying" and that "if it needs to be clarified to make it so, then that's fine." But he concluded more defiantly: "And if there is a problem with the bill, then they have a problem with our courts and the First Amendment, not with me." Here Fowler is attempting to depersonalize the argument while simultaneously validating his claims by invoking a higher authority.

The bill drew opponents who claimed that the legislation was really a Trojan horse, meant to permit bullying of LGBT students under the guise of religious freedom. This counterclaim, based in the rhetoric of insincerity, is interesting because it mirrors the argument made by those who claimed that a "homosexual agenda" was being advanced in the guise of anti-bullying policies. Michelle Bliss, a board member of the Tennessee Equality Project, said: "Unfortunately, this bill provides a giant loophole . . . for a child to say anything to another child. We're not talking about civil discourse. We're talking about nasty, ugly language that apparently you can preface by saying, my politics or my philosophy or my religion says this. Therefore, I can say this to you" (CNN's *Newsroom,* January 6, 2012). Some journalists also questioned the bill's real intent; Randi Kaye had begun the just-referenced CNN story by asking: "Should there be a legal right to bully in school? Some state lawmakers in Tennessee seem to think so."

Kaye's commentary is indicative of her staunch opposition to bullying—in fact, Kaye had been airing a regular weekly feature about bullying for some time before this report. Other journalists expressed similar outrage toward the proposed bill. This indicates that the media had, following the Clementi case, come to recognize the most blatant forms of anti-LGBT policies even if they frequently ignored the many subtle ways that such bias exists elsewhere in the culture generally and in their coverage specifically. Kaye's commentary also illustrates that news media commentators can themselves become primary claimsmakers and have the power to frame issues and advance causes, and thus shape public opinion.

* * *

Most broadcast journalists expressed deep skepticism of, if not outright hostility toward, both the Anoka-Hennepin School District's neutrality policy and Tennessee Bill 370 (though there were many notable exceptions among the journalists at the Fox network). This is reflective of the changing landscape of news reporting. Journalists are increasingly involved not just as reporters but also as interpreters and opinion leaders; they even sometimes speak about issues from deeply personal perspectives. Thus it is not surprising that most journalists' attitudes are reflective of changing public attitudes about sexuality, and that they espouse positions favoring the protection of LGBT students and the reduction of homophobia generally, although, as we've discussed, their lack of attention to hetero-normativity and to the peer-policing functions of bullying is troubling. In the following chapter we turn to this changing role of broadcast journalists and other aspects of news production, focusing not only on the content of news stories but also on how and why journalists report them. Through the news production process itself, the media helped to propel bullying to prominence as a social problem worthy of national attention.

Notes

1. We use the term *anti-gay bullying* for the sake of efficiency. By use of this term, we mean to include bullying behaviors directed at both youth who are lesbian, gay, bisexual, or transgendered, and at youth who are perceived to be LGBT.

2. We found many examples of the use and misuse of other statistics. For instance, clinical psychologist William Pollack said that gay students are "taunted and teased" an average of twenty-six times per day (ABC's *Good Morning America,* October 7, 2010). This appears to be a misstatement of a 1998 finding that students heard anti-gay slurs twenty-six times a day, or about once every fourteen minutes during a six-hour school day (see Bart, 1998).

3. There were occasional stories before Clementi's death, particularly on CNN, that grouped together several bullycides. Some of this reporting followed in the wake of Phoebe Prince's suicide (e.g., CNN's *Newsroom,* May 14, 2010). Anderson Cooper mentioned the suicides of at least four youth (one of them, Ryan Harrigan, had died by suicide in 2003) on his program when discussing specific prohibitions against LGBT bullying (CNN, September 1, 2010). However, reports such as these were not particularly frequent, were not always about LGBT youth, and did not usually use the "epidemic" language that emerged after Clementi's death.

4. We also recognize that the media linked suicide and bullying in general, as documented in Chapter 3. The difference here is that the media seized on bullied LGBT youth as being particularly prone to suicide at least in part because there was a preexisting frame linking suicide and LGBT persons. No other bullied demographic group was singled out in this way.

5. We at times use the acronym *LGB* rather than *LGBT* in order to make clear that studies typically do not reach conclusions about transgender youth due to small sample sizes.

6. The interior quote in the sentence is from the book *The New Gay Teenager* (Cambridge, MA: Harvard University Press, 2006) by Ritch Savin-Williams, who was among those interviewed in the second *New York Times* article discussed here.

7. We find some fault with this argument. First, as discussed, sexuality (of every kind) involves at least three components: identity, desire, and behavior. Second, same-sex sexual behavior need not be high-risk, and schools can help to teach safer-sex practices. Third, normalization of homosexuality may actually reduce risky sexual behaviors; research shows that gay men who were exposed to anti-gay bias were more likely to suffer psychological stress that in turn led them to engage in more "difficult" sexual situations involving increased health risks (Díaz, Ayala, and Bein, 2004).

7

The Anti-Bullying Industry

I want to show you some really horrifying video.
—Joy Behar (CNN, February 1, 2011)

I never planned on being a celebrity. It's weird.
—Karen Klein, bullied bus monitor
(CNN's *Newsroom,* June 24, 2012)

U p to now we have mostly taken the approach that news media more or
less reflect social concerns. However, news media do more than simply reflect reality. In this chapter we take up the ways that the news production process has independent effects on what events are covered and
how they are covered. We also discuss how coverage begets more coverage through positive feedback loops, and how coverage and events are
interdependently linked through the process of interactive momentum. We
then examine how particular news values influence how stories are
selected and how they are told. Finally, we detail how the news media
were involved in the rise of the anti-bullying industry, and how they act as
an instrument of informal social control. The news media provided a moral
frame for the bullying problem through which particular people and events
were selected as subjects of "moral outrage" and "gonzo justice." We first
turn to a discussion of the process by which events set off coverage.

Trigger Events and Media Waves

In describing the pattern of news media attention to bullying, we intentionally avoid the terms "moral panic" and "media panic" because of

155

their theoretical and methodological weaknesses (see, respectively, Jewkes, 2011; and Buckingham and Jensen, 2012). Rather, we employ and expand upon concepts put forth by European academics in describing the media's sudden and intense attention to a particular issue. This pattern has been variously termed a "media hype" (Wien and Elmelund-Præstekær, 2009), "media cascade" (Walgrave and Vliegenthart, n.d.), "media storm" (Walgrave, Boydstun, and Hardy, 2011), and "media wave" (Paimre and Harro-Loit, 2011). These formulations have somewhat different emphases but share a conceptual core. We employ the term "media wave" for reasons that will become clear, but we also cite research that uses other terms. The start of a media wave involves a trigger event that generates strong emotions and is capable of making a complex problem understandable, such as by drawing upon preexisting and well-known cultural frames. The trigger event is also one that is able to be covered from multiple angles and is suitable for public debate.

In the case of school bullying, we must necessarily expand the notion of a media wave, because we are chronicling a span of multiple years of coverage rather than a response to a single event. At the beginning of the twenty-first century, there was a relatively low tide in this wave of news media coverage of school bullying. Beginning in 2008, the tide rose modestly. Then in 2010 and continuing into 2013, an irregular rhythm of news waves emerged, the cumulative effect of which raised the tide of between-wave coverage, creating a new equilibrium. The beginnings of these waves were marked by some very dramatic trigger events, including but not limited to bullycides. Such events were covered by multiple news media outlets that very quickly produced both follow-up stories involving coverage of similar events and ancillary stories such as editorials and features. Sometimes a media wave dissipated and reformed later, such as when criminal charges in some of the bullycide cases were filed or resolved. Thus the entire span of coverage itself resembles a giant swell within which individual waves rise and fall. As of this writing, this high tide of coverage has lowered but not yet dissipated.

We saw many trigger events over the course of our research period. As detailed in Chapter 3, during the time bomb era these consisted of mass school shootings that were linked to school bullying. However, these trigger events set off relatively small waves, at least as far as they concerned discussions of bullying specifically. Trigger events of the bullycide era set off much larger waves. The most significant trigger events, of course, were the deaths of Phoebe Prince and Tyler Clementi in 2010, as discussed in Chapter 1, and the subsequent coverage of the criminal trials involving their alleged bullies, as discussed in Chapters 5 and 6. The initial waves from their suicides lasted several weeks, with ripple effects lasting much longer. Bullycides fit the elements of trigger events in that they generated strong emotions and became a stark and simplified symbol of the harms of school bullying. Since both bullying and suicide are behaviors that are largely invisible to the general public, bullycides provided a dramatic trace of bullying, and the media in turn provided a dramatic trace of the bullycides. Clementi's death was particularly impactful, because it changed the substance of the conversation to anti-gay bullying. Bullycides clearly had media interest—they were dramatic and violent events befalling ideal victims. However, there were other aspects to bullying that lent themselves to coverage from a number of perspectives; some of these were "new" aspects (e.g., cyberbullying and mean girls) while others tapped into existing cultural frames (e.g., anti-gay bullying and culture wars).

Bullycides and school shootings were not the only trigger events. In the first half of 2012, by which time bullying frames had become well established, we saw four trigger events that together represented more than one-third of the overall stories for that period. The first was a throwback to the time bomb era and involved widespread but temporally brief coverage of a school shooting in Hadron, Ohio (e.g., ABC's *World News,* February 28; *CBS Evening News,* February 28). The second trigger event played out over a longer period and involved reporting about a controversy over the "R" rating of the documentary *Bully* assigned by the Motion Picture Association of America (MPAA). That event is discussed later in the chapter. The third trigger event caused a sudden but short-lived wave. It began with a *Boston Globe* story during the 2012 presidential campaign alleging that Mitt Romney had bullied a fellow student when the two were in boarding school. We found at least eighteen stories about the alleged incident that ran from May 10 to May 15, and three follow-up stories on *Fox News* toward the end of May. The fourth media wave was much larger and long-lasting; it was triggered by the bullying of school bus monitor Karen Klein. Video of the incident showed several middle school boys hurling invectives at Klein for more than ten minutes. A fund that was set up to send Klein on a vacation quickly reached more than $700,000 in donations, a fact that fueled further coverage. Klein then appeared on several television programs, resulting in more coverage and more donations. She was incredulous at all the attention and her celebrity status, as captured in the quotation at the beginning of this chapter.

The fact that the four trigger events of the first half of 2012 were not bullycides and were rather tangential to the typical focus on contemporary peer-on-peer school bullying (involving a candidate's distant past and a bus monitor victim) or very short-lived (as were the first two stories) demonstrates how the bullycide era had given way to a period of briefer and more fractured accounts. One additional focus was on human-interest stories. In one example, a news wave was started in late September 2012 when a high school student, Whitney Kropp, was voted homecoming queen by her classmates as a prank (NBC's *Today,* September 25). After the *Today* report, nearly every other broadcast network ran more than one story about Kropp (e.g., ABC's *Good Morning America,* September 30; Fox's *The Five,* October 1; CNN's *Early Start,* September 28). Another news wave that erupted at about the same time involved Jennifer Livingston, a news anchor in Lacrosse, Wisconsin, who read aloud a letter from a viewer who claimed she was "not a suitable example for this community's young people" because she was overweight. The first report in our sample to feature Livingston's interview was *NBC Nightly News* (October 2). Stories ran the following day on ABC, CBS, CNN, and Fox. Many commentators framed the discussion in terms of "bullying" (e.g., Elizabeth Vargas on ABC's *Good Morning America,* October 3), while others felt it was more a matter of rudeness; this difference of opinion only created more discussion of the case, focusing on as to whether "bullying" was the right term (e.g., CNN's *Showbiz Tonight,* October 3).

However, bullying also remained linked to serious incidents such as mass shootings (including at a movie theater in Aurora, Colorado, and at Sandy Hook Elementary School in Newtown, Connecticut). Nevertheless, there was no central focus to the coverage—the news threshold had been lowered to the point that a sense of proportionality was mostly lost. The news media ping-ponged from celebrity anti-bullying projects to "feel good" features to follow-up stories involving prior dramatic cases to one-off stories about particular bullying incidents (some of them quite minor). In fact, the breadth of bullying stories was so wide that it is difficult to capture here. Even much of the focused coverage in 2012 and 2013 can better be classified as "wavelets" rather than waves, and these had a variety of subjects (e.g., there were eleven stories about Whitney Kropp and twelve involving Jennifer Livingston). At the same time, though, dramatic incidents still received outsized attention, driven by news media appetite for particular stories that contained certain leading *news values.*

Bullying and News Values

A number of commentators have offered lists of various news values that they claim help determine the content and the style of reporting. McGregor (2002) offers just four that we agree are particularly salient in the media landscape of late modernity: celebrification of the journalist, emotion, "visualness," and conflict. McGregor writes that, of the first three, the "most dominant news value of our times is visualness." We address the first three news values in turn here, while giving attention to conflict throughout the discussion.

Celebrification of the Journalist

The idea of the journalist as an objective mediator "has been well punctured" (McGregor, 2002). This is particularly true of broadcast journalists. Studio anchors, hosts, and reporters in the field have become part of the news by offering analysis, personal commentary sometimes rooted in self-disclosure, and outright advocacy. We found many examples of journalists inserting themselves into bullying stories by sharing their own bullying history or stories about their own children. It was also common for journalists to offer their personal support for anti-bullying efforts and to openly express strong emotions in response to bullying stories.

An extreme type of advocacy journalism is when the reporter becomes the story. An example of this occurred when CNN anchor Carol Costello interviewed Bryan Fischer of the American Family Association about "Mix It Up at Lunch Day," an initiative launched by the Southern Poverty Law Center (SPLC) (CNN's *Newsroom*, October 16, 2012). According to the SPLC's website, the initiative's purpose is to have students "move out of their comfort zones" and make "interconnections across group lines." During the interview, Fischer claimed that the initiative is "a thinly veiled attempt to push the normalization of homosexual behavior in public schools" and to punish students who find homosexuality objectionable. Based on our reading of the transcript, Costello seemed to find Fischer's statement odd, noting: "There is absolutely no mention of homosexuality at all and this program has been going on for 11 years." Fischer later went on to discuss a book that claimed that Hitler recruited homosexuals to be his storm troopers. Then, when Fischer began to talk about the "health risks" of homosexuality, Costello cut him off, saying: "OK. That's just not true. I'm going to end this interview now, sir. I'm sorry because that's just not true. Mr.

Fischer thanks for sharing your views, I guess." Less than a week later, Costello followed up the story, announcing that after the program Fischer "came after me" (*Newsroom,* October 22, 2012). She played a video clip (of unannounced origin) wherein Fischer called homosexual behavior immoral, unnatural, and unhealthy, claiming this to be a "simple straightforward statement of fact," and added that Costello was part of the "gay Gestapo." Costello then said: "Well, Mr. Fischer if that's the definition of the gay Gestapo, then I'm a proud card carrying member."

This type of personal involvement—where the journalist becomes the story—was rare. More commonly, journalists offered their own experiences with bullying. CNN anchors, contributors, and reporters were most likely to do this; among those who claimed to have been bullied were Joy Behar, Brooke Baldwin, Larry King, Don Lemon, Kyra Phillips, Steve Perry, and Drew Pinsky. Some such disclosures were perfunctory. CNN anchor Brooke Baldwin told her viewers: "I want to let you in on a little something about me," and revealed that she had been bullied about her height and then said: "You couldn't pay me enough to go back to then" (*Newsroom,* August 9, 2011). Joy Behar reported several times on her show that she had been bullied in school (e.g., April 6, 2010, September 13, 2011). Behar conducted an interview of Marc Lamont Hill, a professor of anthropology at Columbia University, about the proper response to bullying (November 4, 2010). Behar said that when she was a kid, she once stood up to a bully: "I took her fingers, I bent them and made her fall to the ground. I enjoyed that so much." Hill responded: "I don't think that's in the handbook, Joy. I don't think that's in the psychological handbook. I agree with you though."

Such revelations were not limited to CNN. Michel Martin of NPR said that she was reluctant to reveal a personal story, but went on to say that when she was in school she had been "miserable at recess because there were just too many bullies, and that the bullies ruled the playground. . . . There was nothing fun about it" (*Talk of the Nation,* April 6, 2010). Bullying experiences were also shared several times by the hosts on Fox's *The Five.* Kimberly Guilfoyle said she had been bullied at school and added that it was also now happening to her son, who was in kindergarten and being picked on by older boys (April 6, 2012). Another host, Andrea Tantaros, gave a detailed account of a violent childhood fight between girls when she had defended a bullied friend (April 3, 2012).

Only a few journalists admitted to having bullied others as a child. CNN's Don Lemon said he had been a "smart aleck" and "got my shots in" (*Newsroom*, May 23, 2010). Fox's Greg Gutfeld said he had "defi-nitely" been a bully (*The Five*, June 4, 2012). But overall, broadcast journalists appeared to identify with the victim. The result was emotional resonance at the cost of objectivity. However, journalists' childhood recollections were shared from a significant temporal distance and thus were somewhat emotionally muted. Current stories offered a greater immediacy. While some reporting was dispassionate, journalists expressed increasingly stronger emotional reactions as the bullycide era progressed.

Emotion

Reporting on school bullying has a potential to be rather dull, as academic discussions of prevalence statistics and public policy are not inherently exciting. In addition, most instances of bullying take place outside of camera range, and school-age victims are generally not readily accessible. However, bullying involves conflict and violence and is thus ripe for exploitation, which was especially so in the bullycide era. Thus journalists used a number of practices to draw out the emotional content from the story. There was wide use of interviews of family members of bullycide victims and of experts who had particularly strong views and provided good sound bites. Journalists openly displayed emotion (shock, empathy, anger, and outrage) in response to the events they were covering.

Anderson Cooper was at the forefront of CNN's coverage, conducting many interviews of family members, bullying victims, and experts. He also was not hesitant about sharing his own experience and emotional reactions. In 2010 he opened his program with an interview of Tami Carmichael, mother of bullycide victim Jon, by saying: "I'm so sorry for your loss. I mean, I have lost a brother to suicide and I know it's . . . an inexplicable thing" (March 31, 2010). Cooper also publicly "came out" in 2012 in a letter posted on Andrew Sullivan's blog on the news site *The Daily Beast*, writing: "There continue to be far too many [incidents] of bullying of young people. And I believe there is value in making clear where I stand" (ABC's *Nightline*, July 2, 2012). Thus Cooper appeared to be personally motivated to respond both to anti-gay bullying and to bullycides generally. Nancy Grace of CNN also revealed a personal connection during a report on Tyler Clementi's death (May 21, 2012). She said she "understood as a crime victim of violent crime myself" what the Clementi family wanted. She also said that his death "really broke my heart," adding: "You know how I feel about John

David and Lucy, my twins. To think that you would send your son off to somewhere like Rutgers . . . thinking you're doing the best you can for him, and now this happened." Many other journalists also spoke from their position as parents. Sanjay Gupta of CNN opened a story about bullycides by saying: "More breaking news tonight on a subject that frankly terrifies me as a father" (*Anderson Cooper 360,* July 20, 2011). In another story on his own CNN show about sibling bullying, Gupta said: "I tell you, as a dad of three daughters, three young girls, this story really did strike a chord with me" (June 22, 2013). On another CNN show, Kelly Ripka, cohost of the syndicated program *Live with Kelly and Michael,* responded to several students after they told their bullying stories: "I have to tell you as a parent I'm sitting here and I'm stewing with rage. . . . I care about you. And I really feel touched for your experience. Really" (*CNN Presents,* October 9, 2011).

In many other cases the reaction was less personalized but nonetheless heartfelt. Josh Elliot reported on the suicide of Jamey Rodemeyer, saying that "the anguish of those parents is so heartbreaking," and Diane Sawyer replied: "Crushing, crushing what is happening to some of these teens" (ABC's *World News,* September 22, 2011). Ed Henry, CNN's senior White House correspondent, said that "it's heartbreaking when you hear all of these stories" (*Newsroom,* March 10, 2011). Soledad O'Brien of CNN reported on a boy who died after another student punched him: "My God, what a terrible, terrible story. . . . Just breaks my heart." (*Starting Point,* March 5, 2013). There was also widespread emotional reaction to the documentary *Bully.* Soledad O'Brien interviewed Lee Hirsch, the director of the documentary (*Starting Point,* April 6, 2012). She said about one segment of the film: "As a parent I tell you I was bawling watching this," adding that she had watched the film with her children: "It was really impactful for them. It made a big, big difference. You did a lot for my kids, you should know that." Film critic Grae Drake said: "Just the thought that this is actually happening is horrendous to me," adding that it "had me in tears over how brutal these kids' lives are" (CNN's *Newsroom,* April 7, 2012). Kimberly Guilfoyle said of the film: "It's so upsetting to me. It breaks my heart. I find it to be very depressing that this goes [on]" (Fox's *The Five,* April 6, 2012).

The depth of emotion in response to *Bully* is not surprising given the stories it tells and, perhaps most important, given the medium it tells them in. Visual media have the most potential to provoke an emotional response, and we saw news media running stories that had a visual record even when the events depicted were relatively common; capturing an event on video was much more likely to make an event a "story," allowing it to break through the news threshold and emerge into relevance just by the nature of its capture.

The Primacy of the Visual

In early 2013, two guests on CNN's *Dr. Drew* were discussing the practice of young people posting videos to YouTube showing incidents of bullying and fighting (January 14, 2013). Lisa Wexler said: "Why is it that this generation thinks that unless they videotape themselves doing something, it didn't really happen?" The other guest, Jillian Barberie Reynolds, responded: "Right. They're not alive if they haven't videotaped." On another CNN program, Don Lemon was discussing a mother in Belgium who had posted to Facebook a video that showed some girls bullying her daughter. Lemon introduced the segment by saying: "I want to show you something that just came in this week. . . . It's a bit hard to watch." He later asked his guest if it was a good idea "for the mom to post this" (*Newsroom,* June 30, 2012). These examples demonstrate how unaware those in the broadcast media are of their own fetish for the visual. Lemon was showing a video on a national news program even as he questioned whether the clip should have been posted on Facebook. Wexler and Reynolds were incredulous at teenagers' habit of posting incendiary or self-inculpating video; the irony is that the media sometimes played such videos for their viewers even while they questioned why the video was made, or was made available, and even as they pointed out that posting to YouTube and Facebook may serve to encourage similar incidents.

Video sometimes seemed to take on a life of its own. Margaret Hoover reported a story about the widely viewed video that was shot of a Rutgers basketball coach abusing his team members. Hoover said: "And I think the key here and the point is viral video; viral video is now holding Rutgers accountable" (*CNN Live Event/Special,* April 3, 2013). Indeed, the most dramatic images typically came from field sources rather than the networks. In some cases the video was captured by government surveillance, such as in the heavily reported story involving James Jones, the father who boarded his daughter's school bus and said: "I'm gonna [censored by network] you up. This is my daughter, and I will kill the [censored by network] who fought her" (ABC's *Good Morning America,* September 17, 2010). Videos also came from the perpetrators (sometimes, as discussed earlier, through the perplexing practice of posting their videos on YouTube or Facebook) or from bystanders. News media commentators narrated these videos with a sense of alarm and dire warnings to viewers: "We are gonna begin with some shocking video out of Washington state" (ABC's *Good Morning America,* August 31, 2012); "We'll show you the shocking video tonight" (CNN's *Issues with Jane Velez-Mitchell,* July 2, 2012); "We want to warn you, much of the video is disturbing" (CNN's *Newsroom,* March 14, 2013); "We have a disturbing story now out of Colorado and it may be tough to watch" (CNN's *Starting Point with Soledad O'Brien,* March 14, 2013).

Robin Roberts on ABC's *Good Morning America* (February 1, 2011) showed viewers "a disturbing case of bullying caught on tape" wherein 13-year-old Nadin Khoury was "dragged through the snow, tossed as you see there into a tree, left hanging by a group of seven teens." She added: "This is so disturbing to see continued stories like this." Many other news programs covered this incident; most of them used various forms of heightened language both in describing the incident generally (e.g., "I want to show you some really horrifying video" [CNN's *The Joy Behar Show,* February 1, 2011]), and in depicting the bullies (e.g., "a pack of teenage thugs" [CNN's *Issues with Jane Velez-Mitchell,* February 1, 2011]). A few days after the incident, Khoury also appeared on several television programs, including ABC's *The View,* where according to CNN (*Newsroom,* February 5, 2011) several Philadelphia Eagles players gave him an autographed jersey.

While the attack on Khoury did appear to be traumatizing, prolonged, and potentially dangerous, Khoury was not seriously physically injured according to CNN (*Newsroom,* February 4, 2011), and it appears unlikely that this incident would have been covered on national news programs in the absence of the existence of video documenting it. The same likely can be said of the video recordings of several "girl fights" (some of which we discussed in Chapter 5), which were also the subject of extensive television news reports in which news media used heightened language. The Karen Klein story, in addition to its clear demarcation of good and evil, also surely owed its primacy to the power of video. In another story, a reporter was interviewing a boy who said he had been bullied, and the bullies returned and assaulted him again during the interview, making for dramatic coverage that emphasized the audacity of bullies and a sense of how out-of-control bullying had become (CNN's *Starting Point with Soledad O'Brien,* October 9, 2012). Airing dramatic and violent videos helped to frame bullying as involving significant physical risks and requiring a strong and punitive response. This was the case even as the news media were reporting that bullying had taken on less physical forms such as cyberbullying and social exclusion.

Random violent events were not the only source for videos. Another significant source comprised the many video testimonials recorded as part of the "It Gets Better" project. One that became particularly poignant was made by Jamey Rodemeyer, a 14-year-old freshman at Williamsville North High School in Buffalo, New York, who had "come out" at school as bisexual (and whose suicide we discussed in Chapter 6). Many reports claimed that he had been bullied since the fifth grade (e.g., *CBS Evening News,* September 21, 2011). Rodemeyer blogged regularly about his troubles and made several videos. He appeared to be despondent and suicidal at times but seemed to rebound; he recorded a video that he ended by saying: "I promise you it will get better" (CNN's *Anderson Cooper 360,* September 20, 2011). Anderson Cooper recognized the significance of Rodemeyer's video record when he said on his show: "Now, often when kids die, there's no record of their pain. There's no record of what they have been through, of their suffering. But Jamey did leave us a message" (September 20, 2011). Parts of that "message" were played on Cooper's show as well as more than a dozen others in our sample, and the story was also covered internationally (e.g., *London Daily Mail,* September 21, 2010). His death was probably the most-covered single bullycide outside those of Phoebe Prince and Tyler Clementi, and was called "the most haunting in hindsight" of the "It Gets Better" videos (NBC's *Today,* September 27, 2011). Rodemeyer's death also had many ripple effects beyond the initial coverage, illustrating interactive momentum, a concept that we explore later in the chapter. While Rodemeyer's death provided a powerful call to action in many ways, the news media also presented it as a particularly painful version of the tragic, suicidal gay teen, as was discussed in Chapter 6: even with his family behind him and his message of "It Gets Better," Rodemeyer did not survive.

Although the news value of many of these stories was heightened by violence or the threat of violence, many stories were aired that were much less dramatic, such as the racial taunting of a boy with autism (CNN's *Newsroom,* February 16, 2012) and the mocking of a girl with cerebral palsy (CNN's *Dr. Drew,* October 18, 2012). This demonstrates that the news media had lowered their threshold for what was considered bullying "news."

News Themes and the Lowering of News Thresholds

In a media wave, once a theme is established, the news threshold is lowered and reporters set out to find similar cases to link to the trigger event (regardless of whether these cases occurred before or after the event) and even fit dissimilar cases into an expanded narrative. One outcome is that "the scope of the problem gets broader by the day" in a "spiral of social amplification" (Vasterman, 2005, pp. 517, 525). Sometimes an epidemic narrative emerges, in which later incidents can more readily become trigger events and create more news waves. We detailed in Chapter 6 how the news media, after the death of Tyler Clementi, first linked together bullycides of LGBT youth into an "epidemic" narrative and then brought in cases of suicides of LGBT persons who had not been bullied, thus expanding the frame to LGBT persons' suicides generally. In Chapter 8, we detail how the media defined bullying up to include single incidents of assaults and "consensual" fighting.

Thus we saw the media linking similar events but also broadening their coverage as they competed with each other to cover these events and also to develop features that showed an exclusive and unique angle. As competition increased, the news threshold was lowered even further as the media began to cover much less serious incidents. The media also created feature stories that were sometimes only minimally linked to the original event. For instance, CNN featured a story of a male student who was bullied over his cheerleading (*Newsroom,* September 24, 2010) and a story of a junior high school girl who "was bullied so much her mother had her switch schools" (*Saturday Morning News,* December 1, 2012). Each of these stories was deemed worthy of a national news feature. This magnification of issues was governed by two important processes: positive feedback loops and interactive momentum.

Positive Feedback Loops

The trigger event initially leads to intense coverage, which then spurs further coverage as the story self-replicates in a cascading fashion in the form of positive feedback loops, sometimes referred to as "inter-media agenda setting" or more colloquially as "pack journalism" (see Boydstun, Hardy, and Walgrave, n.d.). However, the term "loop" doesn't quite capture the potential dynamics. In addition to looping, coverage can also emanate outward in a cascading, increasingly multipronged way, as aspects of stories provide fodder for further stories. These further stories can then create loops of their own.

Positive feedback loops can occur either within or between media outlets. As an example of the first type of positive feedback loop, suppose that CNN's *Newsroom* program initially reports on an event. That reporting may then generate regular updates on the same program throughout the day and on succeeding days. *Newsroom*'s attention to the event at some point may inspire Anderson Cooper or Drew Pinsky to do a longer feature piece on some aspect of the event. These features are then promoted on *Newsroom* and are linked to stories involving new events; they also are later re-aired using the same cross-promotion feedback loop. CNN.com also gets linked into this process at various stages, through either its own content or CNN journalists' on-air promotions, such as when they direct viewers to the website to take a viewer poll. In the second type of positive feedback loop, coverage is propagated between media outlets, in various ways. In the most basic case, outlets first "pile on" reporting of the trigger event, then seek out similar events, and then develop their own exclusive take on the trigger event or aspects of it. In the cases of both Jennifer Livingston and Whitney Kropp, an initial report on one network led to coverage on multiple networks the following day.

Another example of a positive feedback loop between media outlets is when media personalities who normally appear on one outlet appear on other outlets. For instance, after Tyler Clementi's suicide, talk show host Ellen DeGeneres became an outspoken anti-bullying proponent. Her commentary on several of her programs and in a video she posted on her website was picked up by other media outlets, including news, lifestyle, and tabloid programs. On October 1, 2010, CNN's *Showbiz Tonight* preceded its airing of a video clip with the following introduction: "An emotional Ellen DeGeneres appeared to choke up today on her talk show sharing her heartbreak over the shocking suicide of a Rutgers University student." Her comments were discussed or aired the same day on CBS's *Early Show* and *CBS Evening News* and on CNN's *Newsroom*. CNN tabloid-type shows (e.g., *Issues with Jane Velez-Mitchell* also aired the same video clip on October 1). The following day, ABC's *Good Morning America* and *NBC Nightly News* also ran parts of the clip, and CNN's *Newsroom* re-aired it. On October 4, journalists were still talking about DeGeneres's comments (e.g., CNN's *American Morning*), and the next day DeGeneres was a guest on CNN's *Anderson Cooper 360*. (The latter program was a collaboration with *People Magazine* called "Bullying: No Escape," illustrating that "partner journalism" exists alongside "pack journalism.") The original video clip from October 1 continued to be aired days and weeks later (e.g., ABC's *Good Morning America*, October 7; NBC's *Today*, October 16 and 18). The media also aired subsequent clips from DeGeneres's talk show, such as when CNN's *Showbiz Tonight* (October 6) reported that she had "ramped up her war on bullying on her show today revealing a texting campaign to benefit the Trevor Project." Thus DeGeneres's comments on her talk show in response to media reporting were themselves treated as (media-generated) events that resulted in their own "wavelets" of coverage, including her appearances on other programs.

There were also loops that involved responses to individual news stories. One dramatic example concerns the suicide of 14-year-old Kenneth Weishuhn in Iowa on April 17, 2012. After Weishuhn "came out" to friends, he was bullied and harassed, which included death threats by phone. After his suicide, the *Sioux City Journal* made the unusual decision to run an anti-bullying editorial on its front page. The editorial became the subject of coverage by other outlets. CNN's Randi Kaye said: "The paper makes a powerful argument, saying schools, parents, and the community must take a stand against bullying" (*Saturday Morning News,* April 28, 2012). Feedback loops can also be more complex than this, particularly in the competitive, fragmented, and around-the-clock contemporary news media landscape. We found examples of a "hall of mirrors" effect whereby news media produced coverage in response to other coverage, and then treated that coverage as a new story.

One example involved the bullycide of Carl Walker-Hoover Jr., the 11-year-old boy from Springfield, Massachusetts. Only a few news media outlets initially reported his suicide. Later, some media linked his death to that of Phoebe Prince, who died by suicide nine months later and in a town thirty miles from Walker-Hoover Jr.'s. His mother, Sirdeaner Walker, became an anti-bullying crusader and her efforts led to more stories. The pattern thus far was that of the positive feedback loop typical of much bullycide reporting. However, the news media attention took an unusual turn when the ABC program *Extreme Makeover: Home Edition* remodeled Ms. Walker's home. The program was aired on December 2, 2011. That same day, the *New York Times* noted in its television-programming section how the home had been made over, "including the third floor, where Carl took his own life," and noted that *Extreme Makeover*'s producers had flown the Walker family to Los Angeles for an anti-bullying rally attended by the Kardashian sisters (Kim, Kourtney, and Khloe) and the teen singers Demi Lovato and Cody Simpson. Two days later, on December 4, the *New York Times* ran a sports column describing how Ray Allen of the Boston Celtics had made a "surprise appearance" at the unveiling of the makeover, "lighting up the face of 8-year-old Charles Walker." Thus in this case we saw a newspaper cover a television program's response to media coverage of a bullycide. (And of course the discussion in this book adds another link to the media chain.)

With the addition of entertainment media, complex relationships developed that sometimes blurred fantasy and reality. For instance, fictional depictions of bullying sometimes developed more referential power than did actual cases. Several examples involve the Fox television program *Glee,* which depicts a high school singing group whose members are routinely bullied. A segment on NBC's *Today* (May 24, 2011) about cosmetic surgery for teens who have been bullied opened with the following: "On a recent episode of the TV show 'Glee,' Rachel considered plastic surgery to fit in. In real life, 13-year-old Aubrey Woodward is considering plastic surgery as a way to avoid bullying at school." A more extensive example is when Drew Pinsky had Max Adler as a guest on his CNN show (February 22, 2012). Adler is an actor who plays the character Dave Karnofsky, a closeted homosexual and homophobic football player on *Glee.* Adler was joined by Zac Toomay, a high school swim team captain who "struggled with coming out of the closet in high school." Pinsky introduced the show by saying that Adler's character had attempted suicide on an episode of *Glee* that week and that "viewer reaction has been intense." (Adler was quick to assure viewers that "thankfully, [Karnofsky] does survive.") Pinsky added: "We're going to address that topic and talk to somebody who's actually lived this," referring to Toomay, the swim captain. However, Pinsky did not devote much attention to Toomay; rather, the bulk of the show was a profile of Adler that included at least four excerpts from the *Glee* episode that Pinsky found "very powerful, intense, and reflective of something that goes on in high school." Adler agreed, saying: "Yes, it really does mirror what's happening now." Pinsky also noted that Chris Colfer (another *Glee* actor) had been bullied in school and so "this must be a very powerful thing for him to represent." Adler went on to give his opinion about school policy and bullying prevention. Pinsky then turned to Toomay and said: "Well speaking of stories, Zac, *I don't know your story.* Can you tell us to what extent you've had to deal with these sorts of things?" After Toomay responded briefly, Pinsky asked whether Toomay had any ideas about helping young people dealing with bullying "other than people like Max raising awareness." Drew Pinsky's elevation of fiction over lived experience in his interview of Adler and Toomay reinforces the news value of the primacy of the visual and is more broadly emblematic of the late modern condition. In an age when even "reality" television can be scripted and events are turned into television movies seemingly almost overnight, fantasy and reality have become blurred, and the media have the power to simultaneously capture and fracture experience as never before.

The news media's fixation with itself created a paradox when journalists occasionally questioned how much or whether their outlet (or the news media in general) should be reporting a story. By definition, this "meta" discussion is itself more coverage of the story. One notable example is Erin Burnett's interview of criminologist Jack Levin of Northeastern University on CNN's *Newsroom* (February 19, 2013). The two were discussing Adam Lanza, the man who committed the Sandy Hook Elementary School massacre. Burnett mentioned reports that Lanza had collected articles about Anders Breivik, who committed a mass murder in Norway. She asked Levin: "Is it possible that had Anders Breivik not done what he did, that Adam Lanza wouldn't have done what he did?" Levin responded: "I doubt that very much," but he continued by saying that "the copycat phenomenon does indeed thrive and prosper on excessive publicity." Driving his point further while also perhaps contradicting himself, he added that "we send a terrible message to all of those bullied youngsters out there" that they will become famous if they "kill a lot of people." Based on our reading of the transcript, Burnett seemed flustered, responding: "Jack, are you saying—I mean, we're talking here. You're talking about CNN. You're talking about the media. I mean, should we not cover the story as we've covered it or what do you think the answer is?" Levin replied: "Oh, not at all. You know, reporters have not only a right but a responsibility to inform the public, especially about these horrible tragedies *that are so newsworthy.*" He added that the question was how much coverage is appropriate, and said that "reporters ought to show restraint, *just like the rest of us.*" Otherwise the media are "playing right into the hands and the guns of these bullied youngsters who want to get even." He believed that Lanza had been "brutally bullied" and "wanted desperately to be famous and important, and we gave him that chance." Levin's call for restraint is obviously futile. An event such as Sandy Hook produces a news wave that is akin to a tsunami, but that eventually subsides until the next mass tragedy occurs. His plea is clearly also selective. We probably do not need to comment any further than noting the following: a Google search in late October 2013 combining the search terms "Jack Levin" and "Adam Lanza" resulted in 129,000 hits. Creation of copycat killers represents one kind of *interactive momentum* whereby the media shape a response to an incident by reporting on it, and then report on the response. This is similar in concept to the positive feedback loop, but in this case the interaction is between events and reporting rather than about reporting influencing other reporting.

Interactive Momentum

News media do not just interact among themselves, of course: events influence coverage, and coverage influences events. This cycle does not have a clear beginning, making it very difficult to separate cause from effect (Vasterman, 2005). As a social problem begins to receive widespread coverage, this interactive momentum increases in speed and intensity. Interest groups, academics, and politicians are affected by coverage and respond to it, thus joining "in the slipstream of all this media attention" (Vasterman, 2005, p. 519). We found many instances, large and small, illustrating interactive momentum. Some involved reaction to trigger events, particularly bullycides. After the suicide of Jamey Rodemeyer, the singer Lady Gaga dedicated a song to him at a concert and said she would meet with President Obama about ways to end school bullying (CNN's *Anderson Cooper 360,* September 27, 2011). (Rodemeyer had been a fan and was buried in a "Born This Way" t-shirt [CBS's *Early Show,* September 22, 2011]). Zachary Quinto (an actor on the television show *Heroes* and in *Star Trek* films) "came out" in an article in *New York Magazine* and also on his blog, crediting Rodemeyer's suicide as the impetus. In turn, ABC journalist Dan Kloeffler "came out" on air when he reported the story about Quinto, joking he would "drop my rule about not dating actors." He wrote on his blog that he also was motivated by "too many tragic endings" involving LGBT youth (October 17, 2011).

There were also more dramatic instances where coverage of trigger events caused individuals to take action that led to more coverage. One case involved a married "megachurch" leader, Bishop Jim Swilley, who "came out" to his congregation. He said he had initially thought that he would never publicly acknowledge that he was gay, but that the "four, five, six suicides in just a matter of days," including that of Tyler Clementi, represented "kind of the tipping point" for him (CNN's *Newsroom,* November 13, 2010). Another example is that of Joel Burns, a Fort Worth, Texas, city councilman who gave a lengthy and emotional speech at a council meeting in response to news coverage about "the numerous suicides in recent days [that] have upset me so much and have just torn at my heart," including Asher Brown's in Houston. Video of parts of the speech was broadcast on many news programs, and Burns was also widely interviewed, including on ABC's *World News Tonight* and *Nightline* (October 15, 2010).

In the surge of coverage, media outlets sought out an exclusive take on the Burns story. Ali Veshi of CNN's *Newsroom* offered one such approach, airing the entire speech and offering what he called an exclusive interview with Burns (October 15, 2010). Although most media outlets did not air Burns's speech in full, it was the subject of dozens of news reports and as of early 2013 had collected more than 2.8 million hits and 32,000 comments on YouTube. Burns was also profiled on the TED website.

The Burns story was only one of many that brought out the "anti-bullying industry" in full force. Other events, from the mundane to the tragic, also called forth numerous industry claimsmakers who presented an increasingly uniform construction of bullying and its dangers. The media also commonly referred to anonymous experts ("experts say") as well as to invisible consensus (e.g., "parents are increasingly concerned") to suggest authoritativeness and unanimity of opinion, respectively; both helped to secure the proposed frame. We now turn to a discussion of this industry, and then conclude the chapter by chronicling some of the backlash to the way that it has constructed the bullying threat.

Combining Commerce and Concern

In 2002, an article in the *New York Times* (February 24) read: "For many school principals and counselors across the country, relational aggression is becoming a certified social problem and the need to curb it an accepted mandate. A small industry of interveners has grown up to meet the demand." By 2013, this "small industry" had become a behemoth, consisting of a complex amalgam of individuals and nonprofit and commercial enterprises including academic researchers, consultants, school officials, politicians, journalists, authors, celebrities, victims, advocacy groups, multinational corporations, and major league sports teams. The US public had become awash in anti-bullying messages, and it appeared the people were listening; a national poll showed that more than three-quarters of Americans "believed that bullying is a 'serious problem that adults should try and stop whenever possible'" (*NYT,* May 12, 2012). Bullying prevention had achieved its own month (October), and October 7 had been designated the "World Day of Bullying Prevention" or "Blue Shirt Day" (see NBC's *Today,* September 12, 2012). Anti-bullying had also gained its own ribbon color—teal. Adding to the calendar and the color, the Gay and Lesbian Alliance Against Defamation (GLAAD) created an annual "Spirit Day" and asked the public to take a stand against anti-gay bullying and encouraged supporters to wear purple on October 17. The media responded. On CNN's *Dr. Drew,* the host and his guest (R. J. Mitte, supporting actor on the television show *Breaking Bad*) wore purple and discussed Spirit Day (October 18, 2012). Lisa Sylvester wore a "lovely purple sweater" and Wolf Blitzer a purple tie on CNN's *Situation Room,* and they reported that the US secretary of education, Arne Duncan, had also donned purple attire (October 19, 2012). Such support of various anti-bullying efforts was one small way that news media enhanced the growing anti-bullying industry.

Advocacy Groups

A number of advocacy groups and campaigns were created during the bullycide era, adding to the plethora of those already existing. Some were grassroots organizations or campaigns started by concerned high school or college students, while others were big-ticket foundations established by celebrities. The first category included an effort titled "Seven Million Acts of Love" started by Max Sidorov, the man who initiated the online fundraising campaign for bullied bus monitor Karen Klein (CBS's *Morning News,* September 12, 2012). Two Barnard College students started a movement called "We Stop Hate" that produced anti-bullying videos that caught the attention of the performer Lady Gaga (*NYT,* May 17, 2012; NBC's *Today,* April 22, 2013). Lady Gaga herself earned a great deal of media attention when she and her mother, Cynthia Germanotta, launched her "Born This Way" foundation partly to combat bullying. She made a number of appearances around the country, and her foundation created a custom-made tour bus that provided an "interactive experience, where kids can . . . find resources for behavioral and mental health services, bullying and suicide prevention" (ABC's *Good Morning America,* January 16, 2013). Her mother also spoke at some of these events (CNN's *Early Start,* August 6, 2012). Perhaps the most prominent and sustained advocacy involved the "It Gets Better" project (discussed in Chapter 6), cofounded by the writer Dan Savage and his husband, Terry Miller. Thousands of videos were created and uploaded, and the project published the book *It Gets Better: Coming Out, Overcoming Bullying, and Creating a Life Worth Living* (*NYT,* June 30, 2013). An off-Broadway play about Savage's childhood was produced (*NYT,* May 10, 2013), and Savage made numerous speaking appearances.

Savage and Lady Gaga were hardly the only famous advocates. Marlo Thomas and Alan Alda were involved in the "Free to Be" foundation, which promoted the message "Don't be a bystander" (*NYT,* October 24, 2012). Thomas threw her support behind the "Great American No Bull Challenge" (NBC's *Today,* October 18, 2012). The bullied bus monitor Karen Klein started a self-named foundation of her own and pledged to fund it with some of the proceeds from the donations she received. She made an appearance on NBC's *Today* during which she handed out shirts; giving one to journalist David Gregory, she said without irony: "You're lucky you didn't get a pink one" (October 4, 2012).

There were also extensive and coordinated advertising efforts. The *New York Times* described a campaign supported by the Ad Council (October 24, 2012). Its cost—up to $1 million—was covered in part by Johnson & Johnson, and it received pro bono help from New York's leading ad agency, Doyle Dane Bernbach (DDB). The campaign was supported by extensive research and testing. The Ad Council also helped expand the US Department of Education's anti-bullying website, StopBullying.gov. Major league sports teams and players also joined in anti-bullying efforts. Baltimore Ravens linebacker Brendon Ayanbadejo was an outspoken proponent of gay marriage and endorsed efforts to reduce anti-gay bullying (*NYT,* April 14, 2013). World Wrestling Entertainment launched a project called "Be a Star" involving "WWE superstars . . . telling personal stories of being bullied as a kid" (CNN's *Newsroom,* March 31, 2012).

Experts and Consultants

By 2013, even a seemingly straightforward bullying event required expert opinion. For instance, one broadcast of *The O'Reilly Factor* involved discussion of a "vicious brawl in upstate New York" in which a mother cursed and screamed at her daughter in an effort to get her to attack her alleged bully (Fox, March 21, 2013). O'Reilly brought in two experts, attorney and psychologist Dr. Bonny Forrest and psychologist Dr. Wendy Walsh; the latter was identified in the transcript as a "human behavior expert." Forrest said that the brawl was a very unusual incident, but nonetheless linked it to concerns about overly stressed parents. Walsh echoed the "stress" narrative and added that this stress tends to create guilt. The result, Walsh claimed, was the creation of two types of parents: "jellyfish parents," who fail to set boundaries, and at the other extreme, "brick wall parents," who are overly harsh. (Walsh is treading familiar ground here but using flashier terms than the ones normally employed: permissive parents and authoritarian parents, respectively.) Walsh then suggested that the brawl incident was a symbol of parents being "pushed to the wall" by unresponsive school systems. Forrest appeared to concur, pointing out that the mother "was trying to defend her kid." Adding one more cause to the mix, Forrest said that the problem was intergenerational, in that "violence was probably used against the mother when she was young." O'Reilly replied that he would rather not speculate; instead, his narrative was that the woman who encouraged the brawl was "an idiot" and "an ignoramus" who should have taken her complaints to the authorities. O'Reilly's pithy comment illustrates that he thought the "expert" portion of the program could have been bypassed.

The anti-bullying advocacy went beyond just talking heads on television. The news media featured stories on a number of consultants and speakers who were profiting handsomely from anti-bullying work. One school speaker, called "Mr. Mojo," was said to do 200 talks per year (CNN's *Saturday Morning News,* July 14, 2012). Football player Leroy Butler was to be paid $8,000 to speak at a church about his anti-bullying book (the event was canceled because Butler had publicly supported Jason Collins, the NBA player who had publicly "come out" [CNN's *Sunday Morning News,* May 2, 2013]). Certain experts appeared to rush to the scene of major incidents; CNN reported that cyberbullying speaker, author, and consultant Parry Aftab had traveled to Vancouver Island, "where we did programs on Amanda Todd," in response to her bullycide (*Newsroom,* November 30, 2012). The *New York Times* ran a story about consultant Casey Truffo, titled "What Brand Is Your Therapy?" (November 25, 2012). Truffo described her work with a therapist, Sandra Bryson, whose practice was failing to thrive. Truffo found that Bryson, a generalist, had "a blah-sounding message and no angle," so Truffo suggested she find a specialty that "captured the zeitgeist but didn't feel played out." When Bryson told Truffo she had an interest in helping parents and was facile with technology, Bryson was rebranded as "an expert who helps modern families navigate digital media," after which she "became a sought-after speaker on so-called hot issues like screen time, cyberbullying and sexting." The *New York Times* article said that as a result of this rebranding effort, Bryson's annual income increased 15 percent.

Academics are an important component of the bullying industry, although during our study period they were not featured in news media as much as were other claimsmakers—and when they were featured, their financial interests were not a point of discussion. However, entire academic careers have been made through bullying research. Many researchers have copyrighted their bullying assessment tools, with some charging for their use. For instance, the Hazeldon Foundation, according to its website, charges $39.95 per thirty students to provide and analyze the Olweus Bullying Questionnaire. Schools are charged $1.00 per student for the online version. Hazeldon also offers for sale a multitude of materials for schools, teachers, and students. Many anti-bullying activists and writers are listed with the major speakers' bureaus. Notwithstanding this somewhat uncomfortable mix of money and advocacy/education, we did not find any significant critical coverage of the consultant/academic side of the bullying industry in our media sample.

Nonnews Media Output

In this category we witnessed the positive feedback loops inherent in news media coverage of other media products. Controversy over the "R" rating of the documentary *Bully* produced a media wave, as discussed earlier. In fact, nowhere were art, commerce, and social interests so inextricably linked than in this controversy. A petition protesting the restrictive rating was started on Change.org by Katy Butler, a lesbian who had been bullied in school. By April 2012, there were 600,000 signatures, including those of members of Congress and many celebrities (*NYT*, April 7). Piers Morgan interviewed Harvey Weinstein, head of the company distributing *Bully,* on his CNN program and commended him for having "rallied the celebrity troops" with a "stunning list" that included Mariah Carey, Jimmy Fallon, Chelsea Handler, Hugh Jackman, Katy Perry, Ryan Seacrest, Jessica Simpson, and Justin Timberlake (*Piers Morgan Tonight,* March 30, 2012). Morgan added: "The list is endless, all Tweeting, as I have done this week and others at CNN, #BullyMovie, urging the MPAA to see sense [*sic*] and give this—what are you after? A PG-13." Those in the music industry also got involved, such as producer Kevin Mackie, who in 2012 won the Grammy Award for Best Children's Album for *All About Bullies* (CNN's *Erin Burnett Outfront,* March 2). The *New York Times* detailed the new "gay anthems" released by singers Ke$ha, Katy Perry, and Lady Gaga, all of which contained implicit or explicit anti-bullying messages (November 7, 2010). Justin Bieber released a song, "Born to Be Somebody," that played in an ad for the documentary *Bully* (CNN's *Newsroom,* April 10, 2012). Later, Bieber agreed to record an anti-bullying video as part of the settlement of charges against him relating to injuries suffered by some fans at a concert (*NYT*, October 10, 2012). Taylor Swift's song "Mean" became "a sort of anti-bullying, anti-meanness anthem," according to Lesley Stahl of CBS's *60 Minutes* (December 23, 2012). Stahl told viewers that Swift was a "cultural leader" and told Swift:

"You are a role model and you know it." Swift responded: "I think it's my responsibility to know it, and to be conscious of it."

Book publishers are a significant component of the anti-bullying industry. The *New York Times* reported in early 2013 that publishing houses were "flooding the market with titles that tackle bullying" and that the number of books with the word "bullying" in the title had increased by 26 percent over the preceding decade (March 27). The article, titled "Publishers Revel in Youthful Cruelty," noted that the books were aimed at all age groups, from elementary school through adulthood. Elizabeth Bird of the New York Public Library said: "There is no end in sight" to the increase. Others also chimed in, with both social good and profit in mind, in efforts spanning the entire range of culture, from high to low. A high-end endeavor was the artist Virgil Marti's "Bully Wallpaper," which the *New York Times* described as setting "grainy photos of 70's era boys from his junior high school yearbook" against a traditional wallpaper background (January 24, 1999). The newspaper reviewed or mentioned the "Bully Wallpaper" artwork at least three more times (April 29, 2001, June 29, 2003, January 13, 2011). Of course, it might be argued that this very book of our own, *Confronting School Bullying,* is yet another example of this trend.

Corporate Marketing

Hyundai was one of several corporations that included bullying as a theme in an advertisement (see CNN's *Early Start,* February 4, 2013). Office Depot mounted a much broader marketing scheme by uniting with the boy band One Direction in a back-to-school campaign that had an estimated $10 million budget (*NYT,* May 30, 2013). (The prior year, the retailer had teamed with Lady Gaga's foundation.) An executive said the company wanted "to take it to the next level," an effort that in addition to back-to-school paraphernalia included multimedia tie-ins and sponsorship of the band's North American summer tour. Similarly, several publishing houses "started anti-bullying campaigns built around their books" (*NYT,* March 27, 2013). Michelle Fadlalla of Simon and Schuster said that while "the intention is service . . . at the same time it is definitely an opportunity for us to gather sales because it is such a hot topic." Mattel introduced "Chrissa," an American Girl doll profiled as having moved to a new neighborhood and been met by a group of bullying girls (*NYT,* September 27, 2009). Over time, Mattel's efforts became more elaborate. The *New York Times* (October 5, 2011) described how Mattel teamed up with Lauren Parsekian and Molly Thompson, who had started "The Kind Campaign" and produced the documentary *Finding Kind*. This led to a tie-in with Mattel's Monster High line of dolls. Lori Pantel, Mattel's vice president of marketing for girls, said of these efforts that "we balance profit with a sense of social responsibility [and] I don't see any reason why we can't reach both goals simultaneously." One company created a $90 "iSafe BagsUrban Crew" backpack; while the backpack apparently was not created as an anti-bullying device, the *New York Times* said it contained an alarm that could be used to "ward off school bullies or parking lot attackers" (July 26, 2012).

Anti-bullying clothing was easy to find as well. The much-maligned children's pageant performer and reality show star Honey Boo-Boo and her mother, Shannon, teamed with the UR brand to produce a line of shirts bearing the Honey Boo-Boo label (see CNN's *Dr. Drew*, October 23, 2012). (UR produces what it describes on its website as "anti-bullying apparel and accessories.") A more upscale example involved clothing designer Rachel Roy's t-shirts, which were featured in a "Bobbie's Style Buzz" segment on NBC's *Today* (October 31, 2012). Bobbie Thomas told hosts Kathie Lee Gifford and Hoda Kotb that she had "just [come] across so many fun things that had a fun message to really kind of put your personality out there." She started with "one that I really love" that was "a cool way to support the bullying sort of efforts." The "fun things" in this case were t-shirts that read "I Don't Date Bullies" and "Bullying Is Never Fashionable." The immediate reaction from Gifford was tactile: "so soft." Kotb agreed and Thomas repeated "so soft," and then: "Really fun way to kind of support the cause."

This exchange illustrates that by 2012, anti-bullying had become both a commodity and a cause, and distinguishing between self-interest and social concern became increasingly difficult. Bullying was a cause célèbre—an easy social issue to take a stand on—but it also retained some of its immediacy and grassroots appeal. Joining the anti-bullying movement, then, was strongly alluring to those who wished to make a buck or make a point (or just as commonly, both). The hall-of-mirrors media effect served to further confuse motives as facets of the bullying industry were juxtaposed, packaged, and cross-promoted. Bullying was a social problem that could provide a pithy t-shirt slogan or serve as metaphor for the gravest evil.

In fact, school bullying came to be compared to many unrelated phenomena, a process we identified in Chapter 1 as "defining across." For example, a student who was denied entry to a school because the school district claimed he would face health risks said: "It feels like I'm being bullied in a way that is not right" (NBC's *Today*, October 17,

2012). Bullying claims were frequently defined across nonschool incidents, and sometimes by those who had reason to know better. For instance, one of CNN anchor Randi Kaye's "Weekly Focus on Bullying" stories involved a teenager with Down's syndrome who was removed from an airplane because according to American Airlines the boy had become a safety risk due to his behavior (*Saturday Morning News*, September 8, 2012). The father, Robert Vanderhorst, told Kaye that he and his wife first complained to the airline and then, when they were not satisfied with the response, "lawyered up." Vanderhorst said that his attorney told him that the airline may have violated federal and state laws, including the Americans with Disabilities Act. However, Kaye posed the question as to whether the boy and his family had been "bullied" by the airline. "Bullying" was also the word used to describe a host of other behaviors that seemed unfair or just rude.

Backlash

As the bullying industry gained in size and power, and as signs of domain expansion became obvious, some raised claims of opportunity or hypocrisy while others attempted to stem bullying's expansion. Some even stepped back and challenged the construction of bullying as a social problem. For instance, Mike Males wrote an op-ed in the *New York Times* (January 29, 2011) decrying how "news media continue to press alarming claims of new epidemics of bullying, 'cyberbullying,' 'hooking up,' 'sexting,' dating violence, violence by girls, gay suicide, depression, narcissism, materialism, dumbness and other vaguely defined trends." Males felt that the "hyping of fake trends and anecdotal patterns"—including through the manipulation of statistics—was taking attention away from more serious problems facing young people. Similarly, a letter to the editor in the *New York Times* decried how basic mental health programs are unfunded while "newly minted mental health issues like bullying are showered with dollars" (February 3, 2013).

However, such broad claims were relatively uncommon. Katie Couric demonstrated some skepticism when she asked Lee Hirsch, the director of *Bully*, whether bullying had actually gotten worse or whether it had "become sort of the *cause du jour* for celebrities" (ABC's *Good Morning America*, April 5, 2012). But often, commentators impugned the motives of individuals or organizations rather than questioning the entire industry or movement. We saw examples of the former when some news media questioned Harvey Weinstein's anti-MPAA lobbying efforts. While many in the media supported Weinstein, others asked whether his company had in fact orchestrated this apparently grassroots effort. The head of the National Association of Theater Owners, John Fithian, sent a memo to his membership saying that the Weinstein Company had "chosen to generate public outcry about the 'R' rating in the successful effort to secure significant free media for the movie." In turn, Weinstein acknowledged that his company had lobbied for support and endorsements, but insisted that "the groundswell came to us" (*NYT*, April 7, 2012). Whatever the case, Fithian was correct—the controversy over the rating appeared to be driving much of the media coverage of the film; we found twenty-five stories about this controversy in 2012, making it one of the most-reported bullying-related stories of that year.

We mentioned earlier the release of "gay anthems"; the *New York Times* reported that while these were mostly well-received, "for some . . . there is a whiff of opportunism behind the artists' good intentions" (November 7, 2010). Greg Gutfeld of Fox's *The Five* was much more pointed about celebrities' efforts. On one program, he seemed to begin on a positive note, saying: "I think it's incredibly cool for celebrities to love free animals [*sic*] and to join anti-bullying crusades" (March 27, 2013). Nevertheless, he claimed that Hollywood celebrities lack the "moral spine" to oppose abortion, because taking a moral stand "involves judgment and there is nothing more uncool among celebrities than making judgment [*sic*]." He raised a similar point when he discussed a documentary on Angela Davis that was produced by the actress Jada Pinkett-Smith. He said: "Hooray for Hollywood, a place where terrorists get tribute." He added, apparently ironically: "Thankfully, though, Jada strongly condemns bullying" (Fox's *The Five*, April 5, 2013).

Others decried bullying's domain expansion across a range of unrelated phenomena. The *New York Times* reported in several stories (e.g., February 25, 2008, April 23, 2011) that schools were incorporating the lessons of the Holocaust into anti-bullying curricula. A similar effort by two museums was detailed and then denounced by Edward Rothstein, the newspaper's arts and culture critic. Rothstein first reported (April 23, 2011) that the Illinois Holocaust Museum and Education Center had mounted a special children's exhibit that "provides a safe space where they can brainstorm strategies on how to speak up for those experiencing hatred, prejudice and discrimination through bullying and acts of intolerance within their local and global communities." In a subsequent article (April 30, 2011), Rothstein described several displays at the

Museum of Tolerance in Los Angeles, including a "Tolerancenter" that "strains to tie together slavery, genocides, prejudice, discrimination and hate crimes, while showing even elementary school students (as the museum literature says) 'the connection between these large-scale events and the epidemic of bullying in today's schools.'" Rothstein wrote that this approach of "sweeping moralizing" suggests that "the differences between hate crimes and the Holocaust—between bullying and Buchenwald—are just a matter of degree" and, "far from making genocide unthinkable, have helped make it seem as commonplace a possibility as schoolyard bullying" (April 30, 2011).[1] Rothstein dramatically illustrates both the opportunities and the dangers inherent in the expansion of social problems. As they expand in scope, depth, and application, social problems can motivate action, attract resources, and be applied in new environments and situations. However, they can also create confusion, opposition, resentment, and scorn, and consensus can be fractured to the point of collapse.

While the anti-bullying movement is far from collapsing, we did see other strong objections to this defining across in our sample. Greg Gutfeld of Fox's *The Five* objected to the process on numerous occasions. On one program, he reported that some parents in Missoula, Montana, claimed that their school district was bullying their children by having them sing Christmas carols in school (December 19, 2012). He said that bullying's "definition is stretched to imply any activity that implies exclusion." He continued: "If everyone isn't having fun, then it's discrimination and therefore mean." The result, he said, was that "all fun activities" were being banned and then replaced "with a dreary socialism." On a later show he said that "bullying is a catch phrase now. People are taking the word bully and attaching it to everything" (Fox's *The Five,* March 5, 2013). He continued: "There's going to be a plane bully. There's going to be [a] school bully. . . . Bully is now the phrase that you attach to everything."

It is thus worth noting that subsequent to these comments, Gutfeld himself got caught in bullying's domain expansion, defining bullying across to situations that were even more extreme than those he had called problematic. For instance, he said: "The real [bully] is coercive government that tries to take money out of your pocket" (Fox's *The Five,* March 5, 2013). In discussing the Pinkett-Smith documentary about Angela Davis mentioned earlier, he said: "I just want [to know] what Jay-Z and Jada Pinkett and Will Smith think about communism, because communism is bullying. It's taking people's civil liberties away from them, [it's] stripping them of their rights" (Fox's *The Five,* April 5,

2013). Two weeks later, Gutfeld was discussing the murder trial of Dr. Kermit Gosnell, a Philadelphia physician who performed late-term abortions. Gosnell was accused of killing "seven viable fetuses by plunging scissors into their necks and 'snipping' their spinal cords" (*NYT,* March 18, 2013). Gutfeld said of the alleged homicides: "I mean, it does qualify as bullying. . . . I think this qualifies as bullying a baby, when a baby is born and you kill it" (Fox's *The Five,* April 22, 2013). He said he wished that Hollywood celebrities would comment on this case the same way they object to bullying, adding: "A child can't grow up to be bullied if they are murdered on a table." Four days later, in his broadest "meta" claim, he called the anti-bullying movement itself bullying: "Bullying is bad. But the new anti-bullying movement is basically an early onset course of political correctness to brainwash kids. It's almost a new kind of bullying" (Fox's *The Five,* April 26, 2013).

Media critic Eric Deggans offered a more sophisticated, extended, and comprehensible cultural critique of bullying and the entertainment industry on NPR's *All Things Considered* (June 20, 2012). Deggans first said that "sometimes it seems like bullying is everywhere in the news," but he added that "we've heard of bullying in so many Public Service Announcements and TV shows, that the words have less meaning." Deggans played a clip from the Food Network's *Cupcake Wars* in which a contestant had created an anti-bullying cupcake. He asked rhetorically: "Really? Will a sign dipped in raspberry glaze stop a kid [from] getting shoved in a locker?" Deggans went on to point out that the media present bullying "as something only terrible people do [that is] so disconnected from its reality that people don't even realize when they're doing it." He provided several examples from reality television programs such as *Dance Moms, Masterchef,* and *American Idol.* He said: "Their bullying is rewarded with fame and fat paychecks. . . . Small wonder we're all a bit confused when an earnest celebrity faces the camera and tells us bullying kills, because, too often in Hollywood, it's just a really good career move."

However, some in "Hollywood" were also taking critical notice of bullying's ubiquity and industry status. It was an indication of bullying's "arrival" as a media phenomenon that it became the subject of parody. One notable example is a *South Park* episode that originally aired April 11, 2012. (As of this writing, all *South Park* episodes can be viewed at no cost on the producers' website, http://www.southpark studios.com/full-episodes.) This episode involves a student production of an anti-bullying documentary at the behest of Bucky Bailey, the founder of an organization that is repeatedly referred to as "Bully Buckers—

Trademark." (The reference may be a parody of "Bully Busters," a moniker that has been trademarked.) The episode includes a character who is bullied out of his lunch money by his grandmother, as well as several characters who bully others in the name of anti-bullying. It also parodies the media's fetish for decontextualized statistics by having several characters ask: "Do you realize that in America, ohohoh, over 200,000 students are afraid to go to school because of bullying?!" (This is clearly a version of the oft-repeated statistic of 160,000 students who miss school daily, discussed in Chapter 3.) At the center of the episode is a musical number in which students are exhorted to "all get together and make bullying kill itself." One verse goes: "We can make [bullying] stop. We can stomp it out. We can beat its ass until it starts to cry. Let's gang up on it and tell it that it smells. And beat its ass worse if it ever tells." The episode also satirizes the battle to change the MPAA's "R" rating of the documentary *Bully*. At one point in the episode an issue arises with the distribution of a documentary made by *South Park*'s student characters, with one of the characters asking the student producer: "If it needs to be seen by everybody, then why don't you put it out on the Internet for free?!" The producer responds: "What—what was the question?"

Leaving aside questions of sensitivity and taste, this episode of *South Park* can be interpreted in several ways: as an indication of bullying's maturation as a social problem, as a reflection of cynicism about anti-bullying efforts, and as pointed commentary on the rise of the anti-bullying industry. The episode also points to the mechanisms of informal social control utilized by those who wish to make bullying a deviant practice and expose (and exploit) its ills. We now turn to how the news media engaged in their own program of informal social control that sometimes acted in concert with formal methods, amplifying their effect.

Media Moral Outrage

The highly politically polarized nature of US culture, combined with an around-the-clock news cycle and other factors, has led to moral outrage becoming the new normal. Once news media had constructed bullying as an epidemic with lethal consequences, they were able to wield their power of informal social control through construction of a moral narrative. Anger became particularly amplified when the news media were reporting on the responses of formal social control, such as the filing of criminal charges. Here the news media exacted what Altheide (1992) calls "gonzo justice," whereby they "folded" themselves into other systems of public punishment through "a combination of public spectacle, moral authority and news legitimacy." However, "outrage journalism" was not limited to gonzo justice alone. There were several events that resulted in "pack journalism," through which news media excoriated (we could say scapegoated) a target who had offended the anti-bullying moral order. Also, in a self-reinforcing cycle, news media reported on the public's generalized outrage, such as that directed at school officials who failed to stem the bullying epidemic. That reporting created fear and then further outrage, which news media also reported. The celebrification of the journalist served to heighten the spectacle through the expression of strong emotion sometimes grounded in experience. Some commentators also expressed outrage over others' outrage, such as the backlash to anti-bullying efforts discussed previously.[2]

We begin with two minor outrage skirmishes that had ironic overtones. In the first, Lady Gaga accused Kelly Osbourne of bullying celebrities over their weight and clothing choices on her "e-show" *Fashion Police* (reported on CNN's *Showbiz Tonight,* January 15, 2013). In turn, Sharon Osbourne, Kelly's mother and wife of Black Sabbath singer Ozzie Osbourne, shot back, "calling the pop star a bully, defending her daughter Kelly from Gaga's controversial comments" (ABC's *Good Morning America,* January 11, 2013). An analogous situation occurred when actor Jon Lovitz appeared on CNN's *Dr. Drew* (April 30, 2012). Pinsky told his audience that Lovitz had used Twitter "to expose and shame three high school students who allegedly put a swastika [and] feces on a teen's doorstep." Lovitz labeled the girls' behavior as "bullying." Pinsky said that the girls were expelled as a result of Lovitz's exposure of the incident and asked whether Lovitz had himself bullied the girls. The actor responded: "Well, then, I guess, if standing up to abuse is bullying—" and Pinsky finished the thought: "Then, so be it." Lovitz added, referring to the girls' accusation: "That's just an abusive comment back." Thus, to be clear: we have a bullying-allegation chain wherein Lovitz accused the girls of bullying *him* by saying he was bullying *them* because he had reported their original bullying.

Other events created more sustained media waves that afforded opportunities for "teachable moments" but instead sometimes spiraled into moralizing and scapegoating. After video was posted of Rutgers University's basketball coach Mike Rice directing "gay slurs" at his players, Rice was constructed as the epitome of the homophobic jock/jerk. His behavior was also cast in the preexisting frame of the anti-gay bullying of Tyler Clementi at Rutgers (CNN's *Newsroom,* April 3, 2013). News media also expressed outrage through widely reported coverage of "jokes" that comedian and actor Tracy Morgan had made in a stand-up routine. Morgan said that gay kids should "get over it" (bullying) and that if he had a gay son he would stab him to death (e.g., CNN's *Saturday Morning News,* June 11, 2011). LGBT activists and others demanded that Morgan issue an apology. When Morgan's subsequent apology wasn't sufficient, more angry coverage ensued. That coverage was magnified by interactive momentum and positive feedback loops. Faith Ford, who was promoting a television movie about bullying in which she starred, was asked to comment about Morgan (CNN's *Showbiz Tonight,* June 10, 2011). Also, the rapper T.I. discussed Morgan's routine in an interview with *Vibe,* and then CNN interviewed T.I. about the *Vibe* interview (*Showbiz Tonight,* December 1, 2011).

Another incident that received even more attention was the Facebook post of Clint McCance, a school board official in the Midland School District in Arkansas. McCance, who later resigned his position, was reacting to a call for students and staff to wear purple in recognition of the widely reported bullycides of LGBT youth in late 2010. His post read in part: "Seriously, they want me to wear purple because five queers committed suicide. The only way I'm wearing it for them is if they all commit suicide." He also wrote: "I like that fags can't procreate. I also enjoy the fact that they often give each other AIDS and die." McCance concluded by saying he would "disown my kids if they were gay." His comments were condemned by many, including Arne Duncan, the US secretary of education, who said: "I can't tell you how shocked and, frankly, how angry I am by those statements" (CNN's *Anderson Cooper 360,* October 28, 2010). Anderson Cooper conducted perhaps the only media interview of McCance, in which Cooper appeared quite measured (CNN, October 28, 2010). However, most other coverage was marked by outrage. Wendy Murphy, a former prosecutor, told CNN's Jane Velez-Mitchell: "I tell you what, I'm thinking maybe tonight while he's asleep we should all get a bucket of purple paint and write the word [expletive deleted] on his house. I know you probably had to bleep me but I had to say it" (October 28, 2010). It is indicative of the shift in public consciousness over anti-gay bullying—and the depth of the reservoir of moral outrage—that a national story resulted from the comments of a school board member in rural Arkansas. This story, relatively minor in consequence although dramatic in content, created a forum in which to continue the narratives of LGBT victimization and to reinforce the message of unresponsive or even hostile school systems: *No wonder kids are killing themselves with people like that in charge.*

Outrage journalism not only can scapegoat the perpetrators but also has the danger of re-victimizing the victims. In Chapter 4 we discussed the *Dr. Drew* program about the alleged sexual abuse of boys by their soccer teammates (CNN, September 24, 2012). Pinsky interviewed two of the boys whom he called "John" and "Billy" along with psychologist Michelle Golland, who said that the boys "are in trauma." Pinsky agreed, saying "it's post-traumatic stress," and Golland added: "Absolutely. And they are showing signs of depression and anxiety." Pinsky said that John was "the one that's so deeply affected now." Pinsky told the boys they were "heroes for stepping up" and added: "The people that try to go alone and quiet and they're ashamed and don't tell anybody . . . are the people who have long-term consequences from these kinds of experience." There is empirical support for Pinsky's broad claim that speaking about and getting help for one's abuse is beneficial. At the same time, we question whether a nationally televised news program is the best forum for advancing children's healing from traumatic sexual abuse. In addition, Pinsky claimed that the boys' identities were being protected. However, they were identified as soccer players at a particular school, thus letting viewers know the school they attended and that they were on the soccer team, so it appears that the anonymity assurance was rather thin. This point appears particularly relevant given the "relentless bullying" that one of Pennsylvania football coach Jerry Sandusky's sexual abuse victims suffered at the hands of his classmates after the abuse and the victim's identity were revealed, as reported by ABC's *20/20* (October 19, 2012).

Outrage culminated in coverage of the criminal charges against the alleged bulliers of Phoebe Prince and Tyler Clementi. As previously discussed, the charges in each of those cases appeared out-of-balance with the behaviors; thus prosecutors effectively laid the full blame of the suicides onto the defendants, although none of them was charged with actually causing the deaths. The facts in each case, and the path followed by prosecutors, satisfy the seven elements of "gonzo justice" proposed by Altheide (1992). These include an extraordinary response by the formal justice system, presentation of the case as an exemplar, and audience familiarity with other reports about the problem. This allowed the news media, hungry for viewers and retribution, to whip up public outrage and demonize the perpetrators. In some cases the public spectacle turned quite ugly, such as in the case of Dharun Ravi (Clementi's dorm mate), who was pilloried on the basis of his immigration status.

Members of the public demanded he be deported, although the crimes he was eventually convicted of did not make him eligible (see *NYT,* September 12, 2012). A blogger for the *New York Post* called it "bullshit" that Rhavi, whom he termed the "spy cam creep," wasn't deported (June 9, 2012). A public spectacle that focuses on the defendants serves to expiate the public's collective guilt by focusing on the bad people who did the bad thing, and thus the media again sometimes miss the opportunity for "teachable moments."[3]

This is not to say that individuals should be let off the hook for the damage they cause. School board member Clint McCance's comments and Tracy Morgan's "jokes" were shockingly insensitive, but these are hardly isolated incidents. The news media's focus on McCance alone allowed them to construct him as the stereotypical bigoted Southerner while leaving the rest of us untouched. The extraction of justice from individual bullies also represents a return to the focus we detailed in Chapter 2, with the media once again putting forward the dichotomous construction of the evil bully and the innocent (if flawed) victim and de-emphasizing the role of institutions and cultures.

Notes

1. A later *New York Times* article by a different writer about similar efforts was uncritical. That article detailed efforts by the Museum of Jewish Heritage to post personal Holocaust stories on its website so that "the stories resonate with young people on a personal level, challenging them to reflect on larger themes of intolerance, bullying and injustice" (*NYT,* March 21, 2013).

2. Greg Gutfeld of Fox's *The Five,* whose outrage is chronicled in some detail in this chapter, decries the condition in his 2012 book *The Joy of Hate: How to Triumph over Whiners in the Age of Phony Outrage.* The book is a rather humorous, paradoxical, and mostly stream-of-consciousness rant against what he sees as related evils: the excessive tolerance, entitlement, and victimhood that the political left uses to demonize and clobber into silence those who hold opposing viewpoints. He writes: "I see our country under attack—not by offensive people like me, but by people who claim to be offended. By people like me. See, nothing offends me more than people who are always offended" (p. xv). We assume that Gutfeld feels that his outrage against phony outrage is genuine.

The book includes a chapter on bullying called "Wooly Bullies" in which he acknowledges at the outset that "bullying sucks" and at the end that bullying is wrong "when it's real" (p. 216). In between, he makes some of the points about which we have quoted him (and sometimes in almost exactly the same language): that bullying "is an easy thing to get earnest about" (p. 214), that the term "bullying" is applied too easily, and that people never claim to have been bullies themselves (although he does make this claim of himself). He also decries how being labeled a bully "makes you a cash cow for experts who make money off this sudden bullying epidemic" (p. 212).

While some of the issues we raise are similar to those that Gutfeld raises, we think that his anti-anti-bullying discussion is overly politicized and too facile, because, among other things, it ignores the full range of discursive resources—and thus the reserves of power and the imbalances of resources and power—that can be employed in bullying. Also, what he says about school bullying is brief and overly dismissive, considering the considerable empirical evidence of bullying's harms; he concludes the chapter by saying: "But it'll only 'get better' if we admit most of it dissipates like memories of the flu. And that we gave as good as we got" (p. 216).

3. We can observe similar processes even in cases where charges are proportionate to the harm, and where outrage is warranted. The case of Matthew Shepard, the gay college student in Wyoming who was murdered, provides one such example. The hate crime itself, rather than the social processes that feed into such crimes, became the focus of coverage (Ott and Aoki, 2002).

8

Finding Comfort in Complexity

> I feel that it takes everyone to be committed to this problem. It's not the parent's problem alone. It's not the teacher's problem alone. It's not the community's problem alone. It's everyone's problem.
> —Author and consultant Theresa Bey
> (*CNN News*, January 25, 1996)

Throughout this book we have detailed how the construction of school bullying as a social problem has expanded in several ways. We noted that the early discourse of school bullying focused on individual pathology and later moved on to broader explanations, including familial, institutional, and sociocultural failure, buttressed by an epidemic narrative that worked to foment domain expansion. Through a process of defining down, school bullying was expanded to include mutually consensual behaviors such as friendly teasing and conflicts between youth that did not necessarily embody the power imbalance associated with the conventional definition of bullying. In defining out, school bullying was expanded to include a wider range of individuals, making it seem as though every child was a potential bully, victim, or both. Finally, in defining across, school bullying came to be used as a metaphor for every social ill. While we have presented these shifts in chronological order, the construction of school bullying unfolded in a more wavelike pattern of expansion and contraction in ways that moved the narrative forward, drew the narrative back, and always left open paths for the reemergence of earlier frames. In other words, early causal explanations grounded in individual pathology were never fully abandoned, even as families, institutions, and the broader sociocultural milieu were brought into the fold. In the broadcast media in particular,

189

the overall expansion from individualized causes to shared cultural and social responsibility that began in the 1990s took a turn around 2010, when bullying was once again defined up in ways that returned the focus to the individual level.[1]

In this final chapter, we explore how this return to the individual was expressed in news media discourse, starting with additional examples of domain expansion. We then turn to implications for the construction of school bullying as a social problem. In particular, we discuss how the constant wavelike fluctuations in explanatory frames and their corresponding calls to action work to confuse the construction of school bullying as a social problem by sending conflicting and contradictory messages. We conclude with a discussion of how a more holistic perspective that recognizes and is comfortable with complexity may serve to stem the tide and offer an appropriately nuanced approach to dealing with school bullying.

A Return to the Individual

In the process of defining bullying up, news media traveled two parallel and paradoxical tracks. On the one hand, news media focused on victims' psychological states and their risk of self-harm, thus separating bullying from other forms of peer-on-peer violence; bullying's main harm was said to be psychic and thus bullying was significantly de-physicalized. News media frequently featured commentators and victims saying they would actually prefer physical bullying. "Dr. Phil" McGraw's comments in this regard were typical: "We know . . . that psychological injuries, verbal abuse, mental/emotional abuse, can have a much more devastating effect on someone than physical abuse. I mean, you can get hit; you get a fat lip. That's not OK . . . but that heals, and you get over it" (CNN's *Anderson Cooper 360,* April 9, 2010). This distinction between physical injuries and other forms of harm also reflects the media's ongoing construction of bullying as a middle-class concern. Bullying came to be constructed as different *in kind,* not just in seriousness, from the physical threats posed in urban schools, where weapons and gangs were said to be more prevalent. Cyberbullying in particular emerged as a dominant frame through which school bullying was de-physicalized.

An important element of this "psychic harm" construction of bullying is that the verbal and emotional abuse are repeated and the damage accumulates over time—"verbal bullying sticks with you" (CNN's

Newsroom, October 5, 2010). The media commonly depicted victims as being "tormented" or "terrorized" over a span of weeks, months, and even years. Repetition is a part of many academic definitions of bullying and also undergirds most lay understandings of the term. In order to recapture the harm of this de-physicalized bullying, some commentators attempted to make tangible the intangible, such as when psychologist Susan Lipkins claimed: "Research shows that if you have been bullied significantly for two weeks, the chemicals in your brain are actually changing" (CNN's *The Joy Behar Show,* November 4, 2010). And Dr. Phil McGraw employed a bodily metaphor when he said that due to emotional and verbal abuse, the victim's *"psychological skin* gets burned" (speaking on CNN's *Anderson Cooper 360,* March 20, 2010).

Paradoxically, the media also began to conflate most examples of peer aggression as constituting bullying, including extreme violence that sometimes occurred between youth who had shared no prior aggressive behavior or even any prior contact. Even as the psychic harm construction was taking hold, the media began to expand its construction of bullying by rendering more and more interpersonal *physical* violence of youth "at issue" (see Jenness, 1995, p. 233). Here, not only did we witness the news media returning to their prior focus on bullying as physical violence, but we also witnessed them doing away with the requirement of repetition. Thus the news media returned to the undifferentiation and conflation of some of its 1990s coverage, but no longer was this construction applied mostly to "dangerous" schools. As "Judge Judy" Scheindlin claimed: "Bullying has become more intense. It's no longer giving somebody a bloody nose" (CNN's *Larry King Live,* November 10, 2010).

There are many examples of the broadcast news media defining school bullying up by conflating it with very serious, even onetime, violence, although the practice was nearly absent from the *New York Times* articles in our sample. It sometimes occurred in subtle ways, such as with bullying being lumped together with all forms of peer aggression. For instance, in a report about a fistfight melee involving several girls, Jeff Gardere of CBS's *Early Show* (September 24, 2010) stated: "Statistics show that . . . thirty percent of kids in our schools, if not more, are involved in these *fights and bullying, and so on."* Another subtle form of defining bullying up included attempts to explain acts of extreme violence by looking for a bullying relationship, much as journalists had come to assume that a time bomb was to blame for a school shooting. This was demonstrated by an exchange between a host and a caller on CNN's *Nancy Grace* (July 23, 2010). Jane Velez-Mitchell, who was sitting in for Grace, reported on the hunt for the killer of a 17-year old girl. The caller wondered whether the girl had experienced problems with anyone in school and continued: "There's so much bullying going on anymore [now] via Internet and cell phones. If anything like that has happened to her, say in the past year, that might link somebody to this happening to this poor young lady?" Velez-Mitchell responded: "Excellent question." The fact that Velez-Mitchell believed the question to be an "excellent" one demonstrates how even homicide had become linked to bullying in a taken-for-granted fashion. Bullies were now being constructed as potential killers, morphing the classic murder mystery question from "Did the *butler* do it?" to "Did the *bully* do it"?

Conflation also occurred more explicitly, such as in many stories about Michael Brewer, a 15-year-old whom classmates doused with alcohol, set on fire, and left for dead. Terry Moran on ABC's *Nightline* (August 23, 2010) called the attack on Brewer "the *bullying story* that transfixed and horrified parents across the nation." A psychologist at Emory University, Nadine Kaslow, said about the attack: "I don't think this is new. To some extent this is an extreme form of bullying" (ABC's *Good Morning America,* October 10, 2009). Other instances of serious assault were also conflated with bullying. Chris Cuomo on ABC's *20/20* (October 15, 2010) reported on a vicious attack on a girl that was not "typical teenage drama" but rather "a beating so brutal, she woke up in the hospital." The victim said of her assailant: "I think she was trying to kill me," and the victim's mother asked rhetorically: "What would make somebody so angry as to take her face and repeatedly bash it into [paving stones] till her face was falling off and leave her unconscious?" Cuomo reported that the school where the attack occurred refused to expel the "bully." A similar story, in which a young woman had her skull fractured by another girl who was then arrested for aggravated assault, was described on *CBS Evening News* as "a case study in violent bullying at school" (May 12, 2013). CNN reported that a high school student, Kardin Ulysee, was "bullied, beaten, and left blind in one eye" by "a group of boys [who] jumped him in the school cafeteria" (*Saturday Morning News,* June 23, 2012). Another incident in Chicago was videoed and posted on YouTube. Several correspondents on ABC's *Good Morning America* (January 24, 2010) described the incident. One said it was "vicious," another said it depicted seven teenagers "stomping, punching and slamming another boy to the ground," and another said that after the boy was on the ground and being kicked, one of the assailants pulled a shoe out of his bag and started hitting the boy in the face with it. One of the assailants had been arrested, and Robin Roberts introduced the story by saying the arrestee was caught "bullying and beating another kid." Don Lemon, reporting on the same story, said that "the typical bullying has gone to a whole different level" (CNN's *Newsroom,* January 28, 2012).

This narrative was even extended to homicide. Monique Rivarde, the mother of Bobby Tillman, who was beaten to death at a party for allegedly "looking at someone the wrong way," said on CNN's *Newsroom:* "My son died from bullying" (November 10, 2010). There was no indication from this story that Tillman knew any of his attackers, and reports in other media claimed that he had not. For example, an online report from *ABC News* (November 12, 2010) claimed that Tillman "was picked for the assault at random as he passed a group of teenagers who said they intended to attack the next male they saw." Ironically, Tillman was said to have attended a performance of a play the night of his attack called *Being Bullied* that was produced by his grandmother. This may explain his mother's just-quoted comment, as well as a similar comment quoted in the online ABC report: "He had never been bullied until he was bullied when he passed away. When they killed him, that was bullying." Lamenting the inability of children to defend themselves more generally, security consultant Dwayne Stanton conflated the tragic 2012 fatal shooting of twenty children and six adults at Sandy Hook Elementary School with bullying, noting: "And, unfortunately, you have bullies, and people like this kid [Adam Lanza], who go out here and take full advantage of that" (Fox's *Your World with Neil Cavuto,* December 14, 2012).

This tendency to define bullying in ways that conflated it with all forms of youth violence was neither universal nor uniform among media sources. However, it occurred frequently enough to appear to be an important additional piece of the bullying narrative. Moreover, it serves as another example of how news media and other claimsmakers often oversimplify the school bullying discourse in ways that confuse the problem. Once a particular frame is constructed, it is employed with increasing regularity, even when describing dissimilar situations (e.g., both minor forms of teasing and serious forms of violence). Rather than debasing serious forms of violence to "mere bullying," this process of conflation worked to elevate or define bullying up. This form of defining up also further perpetuated the idea that peer-on-peer violence is all the same and is solely driven by bad kids attacking good kids.

A Perfect Storm

As we have detailed throughout this book, by the time this return to the individual began, around 2010, the news media landscape had been dramatically altered in several ways. First, attention to school bullying had become commonplace, as illustrated by consistent and dramatic increases in coverage of bullying-related stories in our news media sample. Second, the news media and other claimsmakers had been articulating a series of often-conflicting and oversimplified constructions. School bullying had been defined up, down, and out in ways that made almost every child a potential bully-victim and almost any problematic behavior a form of bullying. Third, school bullying had come to be viewed as a public health crisis of epidemic proportions, bolstered by oft-repeated fears of bullycides and time bombs. Finally, it was clear to many involved in the news media discourse that schools were either unwilling or unable to protect the nation's children due to widespread institutional failure. And news media and other claimsmakers were more than willing to ensure that parents and the rest of us knew it. School bullying had become an ever-growing problem with increasingly severe consequences with little or no effective institutional responses in place to help stem the tide. The confluence of all of these processes served as a perfect storm through which the construction of school bullying swirled to a frenzy, eliciting calls for increased informal social control of youth. Unfortunately, the discourse of informal social control worked to further confuse the already frantic news media landscape. Like the frenetic construction of the causes of school bullying described throughout this book, contradictory and confusing messages about what exactly kids, parents, and schools should be doing were more the rule than the exception.

Vigilantism

One call for the imposition of informal social control among children was for victims to fight back. In many instances, these messages came directly from parents: "My son and I have Asperger's, and what I've learned early is that if you will fight, then bullies will leave you alone" (NPR's *Talk of the Nation,* March 23, 2010). Some parents were quite active in support of their child's vigilantism. One mother gave her son a stun gun to take to school in order to protect against bullies (CNN's *Newsroom,* May 6, 2012; ABC's *Good Morning America,* May 6, 2012). In other instances, parents were caught on video encouraging their children to fight alleged bullies. NBC's Peter Alexander reported that "two men [were] ordered to appear in court suspected of encouraging and recording a fight between two young boys" (*Today,* July 1, 2012). According to reporter Ron Allen, one of the dads indicated "he regrets some things he's heard saying [in the video] but said he too was helping his son fight back against months of harassment." Similar videos were replayed and discussed on other broadcast shows (see CNN's *Issues with Jane Velez-Mitchell,* December 26, 2011; CNN's *Newsroom,* December 9, 2012; Fox's *The O'Reilly Factor,* March 21, 2013). Other parents were even more direct. In September 2010, James Jones boarded his daughter's school bus and threatened to kill the boys who were allegedly bullying her. NBC's Matt Lauer described the incident as "a father's temper used to protect the daughter he loves" (*Today,* October 4, 2010). In May 2012, a Florida woman was arrested and charged with child abuse for choking a boy who was allegedly cyberbullying her daughter. Later that same year, another Florida mom was charged with child abuse and trespassing on school property after boarding a school bus and physically attacking a 17-year-old boy whom she accused of bullying her son (CNN's *Situation Room,* September 20, 2012).

Parents weren't the only ones encouraging or engaging in vigilante justice. For instance, Fox's Bob Beckel proclaimed, "The fact is that these punks don't know anything else but physical retribution" (*The Five,* April 3, 2012). He went on to describe his own experience as part of a high school "bully group that went around picking on bullies. . . . And as far as I'm concerned, they're terrorists and they ought to be terrorized." He also told stories of his own exploits in vigilante justice as a parent, recalling an incident in which he threw the father of an alleged bully "down the steps" and "cracked his head open." Psychologist and bullying expert Susan Lipkins appeared on both NBC (*Today,* September 18, 2010) and CNN (*The Joy Behar Show,* November 4, 2010) suggesting that children should be taught that "they have the right to protect themselves and that they have to defend themselves" (quoted from the *Today* appearance). CNN's Soledad O'Brien had a similar take: "I have to tell you, if my kid was being bullied and couldn't get any help on it, I would tell them to go smack that other kid. . . . I'm sure that's exactly the wrong thing to do" (*Starting Point,* October 1, 2012). In response to one of the aforementioned Florida women being charged with child abuse, O'Brien stated: "Obviously, going on a bus and trying to pound a 17-year-old kid if you're a grown woman is wrong. But . . . I understand the frustration of feeling like your kid has been mercilessly tortured by somebody" (*Starting Point,* September 20, 2012).

In some instances, these kinds of responses were officially sanctioned. In Florida, a 15-year-old boy fatally stabbed a 16-year-old classmate during an altercation at a bus stop. The 15-year-old allegedly had been the victim of prolonged bullying by the classmate. Charges were not filed in the case because of Florida's now controversial "Stand Your

Ground" law (*Newsroom,* January 5, 2012). Of course, stabbing a bully to death is an extreme form of self-defense that few in the news media were willing to advocate. In the lead-in to the story about this 15-year-old, CNN's Randi Kaye noted that "the story I'm about to tell you raises troubling questions about how far is too far when it comes to self-defense against bullies." But when juxtaposed with the potential for bullycides, reluctance sometimes faded. In March 2011, for instance, a video was posted to YouTube showing 16-year-old Australian teen Casey Heynes slamming a bully, 12-year-old Richard Gale, to the ground after enduring taunts and punches to the face, and the video went viral, catching the attention of numerous broadcast shows. As reported on NBC's *Today* (March 20, 2011), "Casey has become a hero to many for fighting back from what he described as repeated bully attacks." Fox's Sean Hannity seemed to agree: "I was like, good boy. If he's [my] son, I'd pat him on the back" (March 30, 2011). On NBC, anchor Jenna Wolfe, after discussing the video, asked psychologist Charles Sophy: "Isn't it healthy to do that as opposed to him internalizing all his emotions and perhaps leading to something he could do to [hurt] himself?" To which Sophy replied: "Yes, absolutely. It is very good for him to have vented his emotions." Sophy went on to explain that this may not have been the most "responsible and safe" thing to do and added: "But yes, he does need to get it out, otherwise it does become an internalized issue."

However, even as victims were being encouraged to fight back against bullies, they were also being told more broadly not to engage in physical violence. Speaking on NPR's *Morning Edition,* Johns Hopkins University professor Catherine Bradshaw noted the contradictory message many kids were receiving: "We've done research on this issue, and quite often, parents will tell their kids: No, don't get into fights. Don't do that. But if somebody hits you, you better hit back" (March 25, 2010). These were not the only mixed messages conveyed to children or parents in the news media.

Many news media and expert claimsmakers were adamant that in order to fight bullying, those who were not necessarily bullies or victims (i.e., bystanders) would need to step up and take a more active role in controlling the behavior of their peers, placing the onus of control on the backs of students. Kirk Smalley, father of a bullycide victim, noted: "The kids are the ones that can stop the bullying. . . . They are the only ones that can stop it" (CNN's *Newsroom,* March 10, 2011). Both bystanders and victims were encouraged to report bullying to an adult authority. Speaking on CNN, Barbara Coloroso wanted kids to "stand up and speak out" (*Anderson Cooper 360,* April 1, 2010). Recognizing the contradiction between telling on a bully and the cultural norms against "tattling," Coloroso urged children to understand that "there's a difference between telling and tattling, reporting and ratting." Fox's Bill O'Reilly took a similar tack, telling children who were victims of bullying to "go to your parents" (May 18, 2010). Similarly, he let victims know that they were "not a snitch" or "a squealer," but an "American." However, news media and other claimsmakers were also making it clear that this strategy was often unlikely to help in any significant way. After being asked what to tell kids who were being bullied, author Brigitte Berman told CNN's Jane Velez-Mitchell: "Well, the one thing I always encourage is talk to a trusted adult" (April 2, 2010). She then lamented: "The problem right now is there are no trusted adults in the schools." These contradictory messages were placing children in a precarious position, one that parents were becoming more and more familiar with as well.

Even with claimsmakers urging kids to come forward, news media stories typically pointed out that the real tragedy was that children most likely wouldn't go to their parents for help, although estimates of the likelihood varied widely if provided at all. Frequent media guest Parry Aftab said that "85 percent of the middle schoolers we polled have been cyberbullied and only 5 percent will tell parents. So they're hiding it from you" (NBC's *Today,* May 16, 2008). Clinical psychologist David Swanson said on CNN, "66 percent [of bully victims] don't say anything to their parents. So they hold this stuff inside" (*Dr. Drew,* October 11, 2012). Swanson urged parents to be proactive: "If you're a parent at home and you're watching this, I think more than anything what you want to do is be talking every night to your kids. Wait until that sun goes down. Wait until they're vulnerable. Get rid of the text messages and sit down and talk to them. Because this is an epidemic." Swanson's position seems to support the increased imposition of parental social control, whether in the service of preventing the creation of a bully or victim. Speaking on CNN, "digital lifestyle expert" Mario Armstrong made a similar suggestion: "We need to become online hall monitors if you will. We need to become friends with our kids online and let them know that we're watching what they're doing in their best interest" (*Saturday Morning News,* October 16, 2010).

This suggestion, however, was contradicted by other expert claimsmakers. Psychologist and attorney Bonny Forrest took a different approach when she said: "I think that so many parents want to be friends with their kids these days, too. They are Facebook friends. . . .

So now we are all on a first name basis with kids and they think they can mouth back to us. It's our own fault" (Fox's *The O'Reilly Factor,* March 21, 2013). Similarly, as media claimsmakers exhorted parents to be highly proactive and interventionist, they also regularly cautioned them not to overreact; if they suspected their child was being victimized, they were to keep an open mind and proceed with prudence. For example, the author Rosalind Wiseman, cautioning parents that their behavior served as a model to their children, said that if parents suspected their child had been bullied, they didn't have the right to "go after that person . . . [or have] the right to bully that person back" (NPR's *Tell Me More*, February 26, 2013). She wondered why a parent "immediately goes from a small problem to an enormous problem and reacts so strongly and disproportionately," asking: "How did we get to this place?"

That we have arrived at this place is indeed unfortunate, but also unsurprising. By early 2013, when Wiseman was interviewed, parents had been subjected for years to a barrage of news reports featuring alarming horror stories and uncaring or incapable schools. A consistent media message directed at parents was that they should partner with schools in order to prevent or respond to bullying. A letter to the editor in the *New York Times* noted: "Starting early, parents and schools, in partnership, need to make it a priority to quit blaming the victim, and to teach lessons of empathy, every day. It's the only way to make school safe for every child" (March 26, 2008). Some commentators went even further, suggesting that schools were unlikely to respond at all if parents were not proactive. On NBC's *Later Today,* clinical psychologist Dr. Ruth Peters lamented the lack of attention schools were paying to bullying: "There is . . . implicit tolerance. A lot of schools feel that either, A, they can do nothing about the bully, or, B, that it's a part of growing up, and you just gotta let it happen" (February 16, 2000). She went on to implore: "If parents get involved . . . they will do something. But the parent has to be assertive and firm." On the other hand, claimsmakers also pointed out the potential inability of parents to be proactive, since schools were failing to let them know what was happening with their children: "People . . . blame the parents so often but many parents aren't actually informed by the school that their kids are engaged in bullying behavior so they don't even have the opportunity to parent" (CNN's *Starting Point,* March 29, 2012).

The message of this onslaught of contradictions was that parents were consistently contributing to the problem of school bullying. Whether producing bullies or failing to protect their children from those bullies, parents were positioned as doing too much or too little, knowing too much or too little, and caring too much or too little. This alone could help explain the fear and anxiety expressed by so many parents in the news media discourse. Parental fears were further heightened through an additional media narrative: the reason that bullies were running amok in our schools was that the people running those schools were (at best) asleep at the switch.

School-Based Interventions

Although many in the news media discourse situate schools as uncaring and ineffective, school personnel have long attempted to deal with the so-called culture of bullying within educational institutions. The problem, however, is that these attempts have most consistently aligned with individual-level solutions. During our study period, calls for schools to do more were quite common and typically fit within three categories: (1) schools should provide better training and reporting, and have better recordkeeping; (2) they should do more to change the behavior and attitudes of individual school kids; and (3) they should adopt zero-tolerance policies aimed at punishing bullies to the greatest extent possible. All of these programs are based on Dan Olweus's conception of bullying as an individual-level phenomenon. Walton characterized Olweus's approach: "Bullying is tacitly posited as perpetrated by 'bad' children against 'good' children, where the overall purpose of intervention is that 'bad' children will be exiled or rehabilitated for the sake of the 'good' children, as well as for the school as a whole" (2005, p. 94).

This individual focus is true of even many so-called whole-school programs. In our research we encountered many academic articles that purported to address school "cultures" that fostered bullying. Before we reviewed them, we supposed that their authors might address such factors as the belittling of teachers, hyper-competitiveness, and institutional racism and homophobia. Some did. For instance, MacDonald and Swart (2004) identified autocratic and authoritarian power structures at a school as contributing to its bullying problem; and Moon, Hwang, and McCluskey, in their study of bullying in Korean schools, found that "school-generated strains have significant effects" (2011, p. 869). However, we were more often disappointed. For instance, Unnever and Cornell wrote a seemingly promising article titled "The Culture of Bullying in Middle School" in which they cited other research undertaken to "describe the basic components of the culture of bullying" taking into account "the wider system of the school" (2003, p. 7, citing Charach, Pepler, and Ziegler, 1995). So far, so good. However, Unnever and Cornell went on to quote from Charach, Pepler, and Ziegler (1995), who asserted that this "culture" and "wide system" involved "the aggression of bullies [that] is inextricably linked to the passivity of victims in a context where adults are generally unaware of the extent of the problem, and other children are unsure about whether or how to get involved" (2003, p. 7). Unnever and Cornell also cited Salmivalli (1999), who, they wrote, considers bullying "a group phenomenon that is facilitated by students taking on different class roles, including students who assist or reinforce the bully and students who are passive bystanders" (2003, p. 7). In these models, then, "the overwhelming focus is placed on the behavior of the players in each bullying drama," namely the bully, victim, and bystanders (Walton, 2005, p. 96), and the only way that the school itself is implicated is that staff may be "unaware of the extent of the problem" (Unnever and Cornell, 2003, p. 7).

Thus there is no room for considering that teachers and staff may be willfully blind or actually enabling of bullying; that institutional violence creates imbalances of power; or even that certain groups of students tend to be bullying targets. The last of these three oversights possibly reflects a factor that is underexplored in much bullying research—the actual content of the bullying. Unless research is specifically focused on particular attributes of victims (sexual orientation, race, disability), discussion of the bullying problem at a particular school is strangely devoid of what students are bullying each other *about*. This is a consequence of an absence of such questions from standardized questionnaires and insufficient qualitative research that attempts to understand school bullying from the perspective of students themselves, something we pick up later in the chapter. All of this is not to say that there is a complete absence of attention to school cultures in academic research—in fact, we also pick this up at the end of this chapter as one promising approach. We find it surprising, however, given the widespread narrative of institutional failure, that in our study period the news media rarely implicated schools' fundamental structures or practices in the etiology or enabling of bullying.

This focus on individual pathology in the design of school-based interventions was expressed perhaps most clearly by *New York Times* reader Helen Wintrob, who faulted the "current pervasiveness of unrecognized and unattended-to bullying in schools" (September 5, 2006). Wintrob's letter to the editor came in response to a "Personal Health" column written by Jane E. Brody that provided advice to parents on dealing with children who did not want to go to school. To illustrate the appropriate response, Brody featured the story of "James," described as "a tall, bright, personable 12-year-old" for whom "everything fell apart" when he advanced on to a large middle school and started showing up to class late, which Brody attributed to, among other reasons, his "being bullied and hit by several older boys." His teachers simply marked him late and gave him detention. His grades began to plummet and he started missing school, and eventually became unable to attend at all. He was evaluated and was diagnosed with "a serious anxiety disorder set off by the abrupt change in school environment." Brody provided a happy ending: "Medication and 18 months at a therapeutic school, where James made steady progress, turned the situation around," although she added rather darkly: "Had James not gone willingly to the therapeutic school, the courts would have forced him to attend a school for delinquent children." Brody then explained why "school refusal behavior" is so common at James's age: students "are thrust into the chaos of middle school and the confusion of dealing with so many teachers," a challenge that is compounded by "hormonal upheaval." Brody then briefly stated that the most common cause of school refusal is bullying.

Wintrob responded: "I found it surprising that you glossed over the social conditions related to school refusal and focused instead on psychotropic and psychotherapeutic treatments for the victim." She concluded: "Wouldn't it be better and less costly to help schools to find ways to minimize the environmental factors leading to school refusal?" Wintrob's letter did not specify what conditions or factors were overlooked; however, several are apparent from a review of Brody's column. Brody mentioned once that James had been "bullied and hit," but she did not return to that fact. This is notable for its own sake but also because Brody identified bullying as the leading cause of school refusal. Other factors we might question are why James's teachers were incurious and punitive about his chronic tardiness, and why middle schools must be "large and centralized" and "chaotic." We could also ask why a child who felt he could not go to school because of anxiety or bullying (or both) should run the risk of being labeled delinquent.

Brody's article and Wintrob's critique help illustrate the tendency to pathologize victims' responses rather than problematizing the institutional settings in which they are shaped. School and mental health professionals in the United States tend to construct school avoidance as a problem located in the individual (see Salemi, 2006) or at best in mother-child attachment. Also, "school refusal behavior" is akin to a psychiatric diagnosis and thus reflects a tendency toward medicalizing deviance. It almost goes without saying that in order for behavior to be medicalized, it must first be defined as deviant, which is also a label attached to the individual. Perhaps a diagnosis of "school refusal behavior" is thought to be less stigmatizing than "chronic truancy," but it still delimits the problem at the level of the student.

A similar pattern emerged with the adoption of zero-tolerance policies. Such policies include the automatic suspension or expulsion of students who engage in bullying behaviors on school grounds. In the *New York Times,* this was most often articulated through letters to the editor. For instance, in response to a story about the filing of charges in the Phoebe Prince case, one reader who identified himself as a "classroom teacher for 41 years" noted: "If any good can come out of this nightmare of a student's suicide it would be to remove chronic bullies from the school until we can be sure that they will stop their intimidating behavior" (April 4, 2010). Another reader suggested that "laws should be changed so that schools would have the ability to suspend students for their behavior and have the students' permanent records reflect their heinous acts, allowing colleges to take this facet of one's character into consideration" (April 7, 2010). The branding of students as bullies for the remainder of their lives, a modern-day scarlet letter of sorts, is reminiscent of the continued stigmatization of those who find themselves caught up in criminal justice systems, paralleling the ongoing "tough on crime" discourse that has led to the United States having the world's highest incarceration rate.

One problem with these kinds of approaches, however, is the difficulty in determining what constitutes bullying. This problem is illustrated by a passage from the guide for one of the most widely discussed "whole-school" approaches to bullying prevention: "It can be difficult to determine if a situation is rough-and-tumble play, real fighting, or bullying," because a fight may be caused by a victim finally fighting back against prolonged bullying, "or an episode that both parties claim is 'fun' or 'innocent play' may actually be bullying." The guide goes on to suggest: "For these and other reasons, you may want to prohibit any of these behaviors in your school or on school grounds, whether they are actually rough-and-tumble play, fighting, or bullying. It is also very important that you and other staff intervene immediately to stop any inappropriate or suspicious behavior, even though it sometimes may not be aggressive in nature but rather a somewhat noisy but basically friendly interaction" (Olweus Bullying Prevention Program, 2007, p. 7).

Here we see an example of defining bullying down to include rough-and-tumble play and noisy but basically friendly interaction. However, calls for zero-tolerance policies were also couched in the language of conflation, or defining bullying up.

For example, when asked by NBC's Ann Curry, "So what is it that you think . . . that a school should do when they have evidence of bullying?" Janis Mohat, mother of bullycide victim Eric, responded: "A school should have a true zero tolerance. If a staff member sees or hears it, they need to confront it. . . .You cannot turn your back on even one instance of this kind of terrorism" (*Today,* October 11, 2010). While it may seem as though these kinds of responses are limited to laypersons and those most directly impacted by tragedies such as bullycides, the reality is that some in positions of official power also situated zero-tolerance policies as a necessary and effective response to school bullying. In response to a videoed assault in Florida, a judge ordered that the assaulter, a 14-year-old eighth-grade girl, be banned from all public schools in the county (*CBS Evening News,* May 12, 2013; CNN's *Newsroom,* May 14, 2013). We can certainly sympathize with the anguish experienced by any parent who must endure their child being seriously harmed or even killed. It is also not surprising, given the strength of collective notions of retributive justice in the United States, that a judge would ban a child from an entire public school system. However, as a society, basing our response to bullying in the language of conflation and in the context of relatively rare horror stories may actually work to generate a kind of backlash that, in the long run, limits our ability to address the problem effectively.

Speaking on NPR's *Morning Edition,* for example, Emily Bazelon noted: "The punishment route takes us toward long-term suspension and expulsion. And neither of those punishments has been shown to deter bad conduct. And they also cause academic problems for kids who usually need to be in school learning" (April 17, 2013). Echoing this concern, a *New York Times* feature article posed the question: "How about helping the bullies, who are, after all, also pediatric patients?" (June 9, 2009). The article went on to note: "Some experts worry that schools simply suspend or expel the offenders without paying attention to helping them and their families learn to function in a different way." The newspaper also reported that "studies have not found that zero tolerance has created safer schools or better learning environments" (March 19, 2010).

Others argued that the use of zero-tolerance policies actually made it more difficult for victims to defend themselves. Rener Gracie, founder of the Gracie Bullyproof Program in California, noted: "The problem is [that] the bullies violate the rules, and the kids who are the victims now of the abuse, the violation of the rules, are too scared of the policy to stand up for themselves" (CNN's *Newsroom,* October 6, 2010). That victims might be scared to stand up to bullies is perhaps of little surprise considering that those who do, risk not only additional bullying, but also suspension, expulsion, or even arrest. In one instance, "a twelve-year-old Texas girl . . . was arrested for applying perfume in class" after classmates "told her that she smelled bad" (CBS's *This Morning,* May 5, 2012). Another bullying victim, a 10-year-old boy in Cincinnati, was "charged with inducing panic" after bringing "a BB gun to school . . . to fight off bullies who teased him about his small size and for wearing ankle braces" (CNN's *Saturday Morning News,* April 21, 2012). In Columbus, Ohio, a child was suspended for three days for holding his finger up to another boy's head and pretending to shoot him "kind of execution style," as a district spokesman put it (*Boston Globe,* March 5, 2014). According to this same *Boston Globe* article, "a Maryland school suspended a 7-year-old boy who had chewed a Pop-Tart into a gun shape."

But this is not the only problem with the adoption of zero-tolerance policies aimed at reducing bullying. This "get tough" rhetoric has led to a more vocal backlash against school-based responses that some might deem appropriate. For instance, in 2000, an 11-year-old boy was suspended for sexual harassment for reading a crude poem to several girls. As the *New York Times* (April 16, 2000) pointed out: "The decision was portrayed in the news media as political correctness run amok." However, as the newspaper also pointed out, this boy had used obscene language, bullied boys, and caused trouble in "numerous incidents." Our point here is not to come down one way or the other regarding this particular punishment for this particular young man. Instead, we suggest that a reliance on standardized mechanisms of social control, such as zero-tolerance policies and the criminalization of bullying, work to the detriment of all involved. These mechanisms call for the imposition of a preset punishment for all rule infractions, regardless of intent or extenuating circumstances. When applied to youth in ways that are perceived as unjust, news media and other claimsmakers push back and the distinction between what is actually troublesome, repeated behavior, and what is not, becomes distorted.

It is not surprising to us, however, that schools took such a hard line on bullying, considering that the consequences of doing nothing (or being perceived to have done nothing) were continuously worsening.

News media coverage of civil lawsuits filed against schools underscored these consequences. The media often referred to lawsuits in conjunction with or in response to the failure of school-based interventions and illustrated a "new normal" based in outrage and overreaction related to the purported epidemic of school bullying. For example, in New Jersey, a school district was ordered to "pay $4.2 million to a student who was paralyzed after being attacked by a bully" (CNN's *Newsroom,* April 19, 2012; also reported on CNN's *Saturday Morning News,* April 21, 2012). In describing the incident that led to the lawsuit, CNN reported that the victim "was punched in the stomach by another student," triggering "a blood clot which caused paralysis." We did not find any coverage of the initial incident that resulted in this lawsuit. It wasn't until the settlement was reached that news media found this particular bullying story worthy of coverage. In other instances, news of civil-legal settlements reignited coverage of previously reported incidents as well. In response to Phoebe Prince's suicide, the school district settled with Prince's family, paying out $220,000 (reported on Fox's *The O'Reilly Factor,* January 12, 2012). Parents of Jon Carmichael, a 13-year-old bullycide victim in Texas, "filed a $20 million federal lawsuit" alleging "officials at his former school ignored the relentless bullying" (CNN's *Anderson Cooper 360,* March 29, 2011). The combination of defining bullying up, horror stories, and institutional failure worked to frame lawsuits targeted at schools as the only hope.

In addition to reporting on these lawsuits, news media and other claimsmakers offered explicit support for their use. In response to one young man's bullying experience, CNN's Soledad O'Brien suggested: "That was a giant bully, a scary bully. Get a lawyer, Preston. Call me. Will Cain [an attorney guest on her show] will represent you" (October 9, 2012). Here, not only is a news media claimsmaker calling for the filing of a lawsuit, but she is also actually offering to support that effort through direct intervention. Jane Velez-Mitchell offered a similar suggestion: "First thing I say, because there's so many bullying problems in this country is, get a lawyer. Don't—don't try to solve this yourself" (CNN, December 26, 2011). Calls such as this were neither uncommon nor surprising, especially considering the kinds of domain expansion described throughout this book. As bullying was defined up to include serious forms of violence, it was also defined down to include less problematic behavior such as consensual teasing, resulting in an elevation of the latter to the former. Simultaneously, the construction of school bullying and bullycide as epidemics flooding the nation combined with an institutional failure frame in ways that heightened anxiety among news media and other claimsmakers. If schools weren't willing or able to do anything, they would be held accountable. But schools weren't the only ones feeling the brunt of this anxiety. Soon kids would find themselves at the losing end of a trend toward the criminalization of school bullying.

Criminalizing and Legislating Bullying

For some, the imposition of school-based mechanisms of social control was not enough. In response to the bullying of bus monitor Karen Klein, four students were suspended from school for a year and required to attend a reengagement school and participate in anti-bullying classes and community service. Seemingly ignoring many aspects of the kids' punishment, Fox's Bob Beckel suggested: "They gave them a year off? That encourages bullying. If I [knew] I'd get a year off, I'd bully" (*The Five,* July 2, 2012). Considering some of Beckel's earlier-described comments, it is likely that Beckel the bully would have had a tough time dealing with Beckel the anti-bullying vigilante during that year off. Nonetheless, as an alternative to suspension, Beckel mused: "How about sending them to prison?" Calls for drastic measures such as the imprisonment of 14-year-old children engaged in verbal bullying were relatively rare, but notable in terms of their illustration of the kinds of knee-jerk reactions often espoused in response to horror stories, bully-cides, and unique yet truly disturbing incidents like kids bullying a bus monitor.

In his 2007 book *Governing Through Crime,* Jonathan Simon notes that "crime in and around schools is playing . . . a role as the problem that must be confronted and documented by a reinforcing spiral of political will and the production of new knowledge about school crime." The result, Simon argues, has been a "tilting [of the] administration of schools toward a highly authoritarian and mechanistic model" (pp. 207, 209). The adoption of zero-tolerance policies as discussed earlier is one illustration of this type of model. So too are the continued calls for the criminalization of bullying and legislative action at the state and federal levels. In this sense, we might argue that schools are being *governed through bullying.*

As discussed previously, criminal charges were filed and took a central role in the news media discourse surrounding the suicides of Phoebe Prince and Tyler Clementi. In these cases, prosecutors applied existing criminal sanctions in contexts where laws against bullying had not yet been enacted or were not applicable. For instance, Prince's bullies were charged with crimes including "statutory rape, violation of civil rights with bodily injury, harassment, stalking and disturbing a school assembly" (*NYT,* March 30, 2010). In the Clementi case, Dharun Ravi was charged with and eventually convicted of crimes including invasion of privacy and bias intimidation (a type of hate crime). In response to the cyberbullying-related suicide of 13-year-old Megan Meier in Missouri, federal prosecutors filed charges against 49-year-old Lori Drew, not for culpability in Meier's suicide, but for violating the Computer Fraud and Abuse Act after "posing as a teenaged boy on a MySpace page" (*Fox News,* November 18, 2008). Similarly, in response to the bullying-related suicide of Audrie Pott in California, CNN legal analyst Sunny Hostin noted that "the law doesn't really provide for these bullies then being charged . . . in connection with the deaths of these victims" (*Newsroom,* April 12, 2013). She went on to suggest that this would change: "I suspect there will be some crafty prosecutors, some creative prosecutors that will start looking at these cases like this, because something needs to be done." The changes that Hostin predicted, however, had already begun to occur, as she herself had noted a year earlier in response to a father who filed for a restraining order against his child's 14-year-old bully: "I say bravo to the father. I think it's using a tool to protect your child, and I like it" (*Newsroom,* January 27, 2012). In another instance, a restraining order was filed against a 9-year-old. When asked why he was bringing an attorney into the situation, the bullying victim's father noted: "I contacted the school and tried to go through the school to handle these measures. Nothing was being done. My daughter was still being bullied" (CNN's *Starting Point with Soledad O'Brien,* April 24, 2012).

The trend toward the criminalization of bullying is bolstered by the passage of anti-bullying legislation that calls for criminal-legal controls. The institutional failure frame, painfully illustrated by bullycides, accelerated a wave of anti-bullying legislation that had begun in 2007, which saw fourteen laws enacted. There were twenty more in 2008, fifteen in 2009, and twenty-one in 2010 (see Stuart-Cassel, Bell, and Springer, 2011). As of July 2013, there was only one state (Montana) without an anti-bullying statute, and nearly every state prohibited cyberbullying or "electronic harassment" in some form (Hinduja and Patchin, 2013). Thus the reach of the school system's control now in many cases extends beyond a school's physical boundaries. Florida is just one state that now allows (but does not require) schools to monitor and discipline students for electronic bullying even if students use a non-school-provided device at a non-school-related location, so long as the bullying

"substantially interferes with or limits the victim's ability to participate in or benefit from the services, activities, or opportunities offered
by a school or substantially disrupts the education process or orderly
operation of a school" (Fla. Stat. § 1006.147 [2013]). This statute was
enacted in 2008 and called the Jeffrey Johnston Stand Up for All Students Act; Johnston was a 15-year-old who died by suicide in 2005,
after being "worn out by a perpetual assault that made him question
his sexuality and cost him his wide circle of friends," according to the
Orlando Sun-Sentinel (September 18, 2011). Many other media
reports credited publicity of specific bullycides as being a leading
impetus for additional legislation, including those of Jaheem Herrera
in Georgia (CNN's *Newsroom,* October 15, 2010), Phoebe Prince in
Massachusetts, and Tyler Clementi in New Jersey. In other cases, the
media reported that activist action after a bullycide led to legislation;
for example, CNN reported that after the suicide of Kenneth Weishuhn
Jr., "advocacy groups are upping their anti-bullying efforts in Iowa"
(*Saturday Morning News,* April 21, 2012). The media also reported on
parents of bullycide victims lobbying legislators for stronger laws; for
example, Kirk Smalley in Oklahoma (CNN's *Newsroom,* October 4,
2010), Sirdeaner Walker in Massachusetts (NBC's *Today,* September
7, 2011), and Cynthia Logan in Ohio (CBS's *48 Hours,* September 16,
2011).

In some instances, these new laws worked to further criminalize
bullying. As reported on CNN's *Saturday Morning News* (December 1,
2012), in response to the bullycide of Canadian teen Amanda Todd,
"her hometown has launched a new anti-bullying campaign called 'Be
Someone' that will allow police to issue fines to those caught bullying
in public or online." A town in Wisconsin passed an ordinance author-
izing police "to ticket parents of bullies, which could mean hefty
[fines] that increase for chronic offender[s]" (CBS's *This Morning,*
June 8, 2013). At least partly in response to concerns over cyberbullying, the Missouri legislature updated its harassment law to include
electronic communications. A teacher in North Carolina threatened to
call the police when he realized that students had created a fake Twitter
account under his name. In reporting this story, NPR's Lisa Miller
noted that "under the new North Carolina law, the student behind the
tweets could spend a month in jail and pay a $1,000 fine" (*Morning
Edition,* February 19, 2013).

More commonly, however, these laws were aimed at establishing
mechanisms for the mandatory reporting of bullying incidents. For
instance, CBS's Charles Osgood informed viewers that "New Jersey

enacted a law . . . that some are calling the toughest anti-bullying law in the country" (*Sunday Morning News,* January 9, 2011). Before moving on, Osgood noted that the New Jersey law "requires schools there to appoint anti-bullying experts and make regular public reports on bullying incidents." The move toward mandatory reporting might actually do more to support the continued growth of the anti-bullying industry than it does to fix the problem of bullying. The statistics that are the product of mandatory reporting will undoubtedly show consistent increases in bullying over time, as long as an ever-widening range of behaviors are included within its definition, as schools become more adept at recordkeeping, and perhaps as victims feel more secure in reporting. These statistics will in turn provide the basis of arguments for the further treatment of school bullying as an epidemic and further reinforce the need for mechanisms of formal social control such as additional school safety officers, which in turn will feed the narrative of dangerous schools and the need for additional reporting of bullying incidents. Instead of directly dealing with the problem of school bullying, these laws contribute to the heightened anxiety surrounding school bullying and further dilute the already problematic discourse. Of course, this kind of nuanced understanding of legislative action was not articulated in news media accounts during our study period. For the most part, reporting on anti-bullying legislation was almost always brief. In the vast majority of cases, the specific content of such laws was not analyzed or even reported on. It was also very rare to find a story that investigated how a law was being implemented. Thus the media "black boxed" (see Latour, 1999) the processes of both legislation and administrative implementation. The fact that a state has enacted legislation does not mean that the law is sensible, clear, comprehensive, well-funded, or well-implemented. Thus it seems odd to us that so little media attention was paid either to the specific provisions of legislation or to an evaluation of their effectiveness. Perhaps for most, the idea that something, anything, was being done to stem the tide of the epidemic of school bullying was sufficient.

Yet another indication of the move toward governing through bullying is the involvement, although limited, of the federal government in anti-bullying efforts. For instance, the US Congress has held some hearings and introduced the Safe Schools Improvement Act, which later died in committee. In 2009, President Obama appointed Kevin Jennings, a well-known anti-bullying advocate, to be the assistant deputy secretary for the Office of Safe and Drug-Free Schools, the so-called Safe Schools Czar. Then, in 2010, President Obama held an anti-bullying conference at the White House (CNN's *Newsroom*, March 10, 2011) and later he recorded a video as part of the "It Gets Better" project (CNN's *Newsroom*, October 22, 2012). Federal officials made the rounds of talk shows and did print interviews. Russlynn H. Ali, assistant secretary in the US Department of Education, said: "Folks need to wake up. . . . We have a crisis in our schools in which bullying and harassment seems to be a rite of passage, and it doesn't need to be that way" (*NYT*, October 26, 2010). The Obama administration's proposals included providing $120 million in grants to states, requiring states to keep and report bullying statistics, and coordinating anti-bullying efforts. While limited, the imposition of mandatory reporting and the allocation of federal funds would serve as additional incentives to maintain the discourse of formal social control. In perhaps the most widely reported federal move, the US Department of Education issued a ten-page letter to school systems notifying them that acts of bullying could be prosecuted under various federal laws; the letter asserted that anti-gay bullying could violate Title IX, a federal law directed at gender discrimination in education. The justification was that much anti-gay bullying is based on traits of gender nonconformity (NPR's *Tell Me More*, October 28, 2010), as we discussed in Chapter 6.

Considering all the rhetoric surrounding the epidemic of school bullying, it is hardly surprising that schools and parents started to seek out formal mechanisms of social control like those described here. This, of course, created a bit of a paradox. On the one hand, schools are admonished for not doing enough to prevent the bullying of innocent young victims under their care. And parents and others are willing and able to engage civil-legal remedies in the face of perceived institutional failure. This exacerbates a climate of fear among school personnel in ways that increase reactionary responses such as zero-tolerance policies and criminal-legal sanctions. On the other hand, the imposition of such policies and sanctions also triggers a backlash of sorts. Like kids, parents, and schools, those responsible for the imposition of formal mechanisms of social control are also placed in a precarious position.

In Chapter 6 we discussed claims that anti-bullying programs and legislation were just another form of political correctness or a Trojan horse aimed at promoting various causes (e.g., LGBT rights) through the idea of tolerance. Systematic solutions, such as governmental intervention, were sometimes mocked. For example, Fox's Greg Gutfeld responded to US representative Barbara Lee's call "to create [a] federal 'Department of Peace-Building' to reduce the military and also to end bullying" by stating: "Anything that sounds like a bunch of third graders could have come up with it, will kill you. Department of Peace-Building? What's next? Association of soft hugs and pudding? Organization of forgiveness and lunchables? Sorry, peace-building equals death" (*The Five,* February 27, 2013).

There were a host of more specific objections to state and federal anti-bullying efforts. Even with the very limited federal response, there were some questions raised in the media as to whether bullying was a proper policy domain for the federal government. Michel Martin asked Melody Barnes, director of the Domestic Policy Council at the White House, whether bullying is "something that rises to the level of federal concerns" (NPR's *Tell Me More,* March 15, 2011). Barnes responded carefully: "I think people often confuse the fact that we are calling attention to something with the idea that we are dive-bombing in and saying we're the federal government. We're here to singularly fix this. And that's not what we're saying." She later added: "We're just shining a light on [bullying], saying this is important. Here's what we can do, while we're also asking others to hear the call and take action in their communities."

Federal policy was objected to in stronger terms on at least two *Fox News* programs. Here the long-standing tensions between the roles of the federal and state governments were in dramatic relief. Republican strategist Karen Hanretty objected strongly both to Kevin Jennings's writings and his appointment as Safe Schools Czar. Hanretty said: "I think [Jennings] would like to mandate tolerance from people at the federal level [as] opposed to letting school boards and local legislators and local attorneys general deal with bullying issues at a local level. He wants to mandate it at a federal level and he wants to push a *certain agenda* that is far outside of mainstream America" (*Hannity,* June 20, 2011). Hanretty went on to define Jennings's "agenda" as including "forcing sexuality on kindergartners or elementary children." This tendency to conflate sexual or affectional identity with sexual behavior was a common rhetorical maneuver, as explored earlier in this book.

Glenn Beck had a different set of objections, taking issue with the federal Department of Education letter regarding Title IX and bullying mentioned earlier. Beck felt that the letter was a "weird" reinterpretation of civil rights law that had "taken big brother to a whole new level" (Fox's *Beck,* March 16, 2011). He quoted from the letter's provision that schools need to "curb harassment" even if it "occurs outside the school grounds" and said: "So, now, the school has to listen in to regular conversations at lunch time. And then they also have to watch the Internet. . . . So, if your kid is posting something on Facebook at 7:00 at night, your principal better know about it." The provision of the letter that Beck most objected to was the suggestion that schools may "need to provide training or other interventions not only for the perpetrators but also for the larger school community." Beck continued: "Wow! . . . I can't wait for them to come knocking at my door for a conversation [about] what one of my kids' schoolmates . . . said on Facebook on his own time and they knock on my door and they say, hey, you got to go to harassment training and I'm going to teach them something called property lines and trespassing, get the hell off my property. What do you think? Is that harassing? I hope not." Such hyperbole from the media was not uncommon. However, we did not find state legislators objecting to federal encroachment, probably because the federal proposals involved "shining a light" more than crafting definitive policies and also provided for additional funding opportunities.

This backlash was sometimes also aimed at the criminalization of bullying. For instance, the arrest of a 7-year-old in New York for stealing $5 of lunch money from a classmate was met with shock. The boy's lawyer, Jack Yankowitz, stated that the treatment of this young man was "unconscionable. This is such a travesty what occurred here. Heartbreaking." To which CNN's Ashleigh Banfield responded, "I think you could say travesty is an understatement" (*Newsroom,* January 31, 2013). It is hard to imagine anyone who would argue that the handcuffing and arrest of a 7-year-old boy for stealing lunch money is anything less than shocking and appalling. But perhaps we shouldn't be all that surprised. As CNN legal contributor Paul Callan noted on the same show: "I think it's part of the criminalization of childhood that's taking place where all of these matters that were handled by parents and teachers are getting referred to the cops." Similar stories of young people being arrested for what seemed like minor instances of bullying littered the news media landscape, leading some to question the practice. ABC's Chris Cuomo articulated these kinds of concerns: "Imagine going into the post office and seeing these crimes on those 10 most wanted flyers, classroom edition, burping, doodling, throwing a tantrum. Bad behavior to be sure, but worthy of arrest at 5 years old? Everything I listed are crimes that got kids handcuffed by police. Of course, we want law and order in our classrooms, but at what cost?" (*20/20,* September 28, 2012).

CBS's Jeff Glor asked a similar question: "Are we criminalizing kids? . . . According to the *New York Daily News,* from October to December of last year, police here in New York arrested on average five school kids a day, and it's happening all over the country" (*This Morning,* May 5, 2012). When CNN's Joy Behar mused: "Maybe schools need security guards everywhere," author and anti-bullying advocate Rachel Simmons responded: "We don't need security guards and we don't need courts. I don't think that is the issue. I think that we need education. I think schools need to spend real time teaching kids nonviolent conflict resolutions" (April 6, 2010). Like Rachel Simmons, many of those who questioned the adoption of formal mechanisms of social control in response to bullying pointed to the need for a more measured approach. We agree. However, the articulation of a more measured approach hardly meets the criteria of newsworthiness. As long as the construction of school bullying is grounded in a news media discourse that perpetuates domain expansion, focuses on horror stories, and oversimplifies social problems, we will not be able to fully address the complexity of school bullying. There are, however, promising theoretical approaches that have emerged in the academic literature, but their translation into actual programs remains spotty.

A Social-Ecological Approach

In order to address school bullying effectively and comprehensively, we must acknowledge that school bullying operates across multiple levels—individual, familial, institutional, communal, and sociocultural. Instead of a zero-sum game in which school bullying is constructed as a problem with causes and solutions at only one of these levels at a time, we must learn to be comfortable with complexity. For sure, there were some in the news media who attempted to swim upstream. Even as early as 1993 (*NYT,* August 11), experts in the field were articulating the need for "efforts aimed at the family, the classroom, the community, and the media." The fact that similar kinds of claims continued to be articulated in 2013 suggests that these voices tend to get lost in the cacophony of domain expansion and reactionary policy debates. Moreover, the academic literature has yet to identify a consistently effective approach to bullying prevention.

Recent meta-analyses have provided varied evidence. In one such analysis, Ttofi and Farrington concluded that "more intensive programs were more effective, as were programs including parent meetings, firm disciplinary methods, and improved playground supervision" (2011, p. 43). In another, Barbaro and colleagues found that "the most efficient interventions are those that are developed from a multidisciplinary perspective or global focus and that are directed at improving social and interpersonal skills and at modifying attitudes and beliefs" (2012, p.

1650). Thornberg's review of qualitative research "highlights the importance of not reducing anti-bullying practices to just focus upon deficits within bullies and victims but considering and dealing with the school and peer cultures as well as the social psychology of everyday school life" (2011, pp. 264–265). Adding to the confusion, Hong and Espelage suggest that there is a "lack of efficacy data in the bullying literature" and that this is the result of a "disconnect between the empirical support for the social-ecological model of bullying and the current prevention efforts" (2012, p. 318).

In support of this claim, Mishna suggests that "there is now virtually unanimous agreement that an ecological systems theoretical framework . . . is most suitable for understanding and addressing bullying" (2012, p. 25). While we agree that such an approach is "most suitable," we are not exactly clear among whom this agreement is unanimous. Nor do we find that the approach has been adopted to the extent that Mishna claims (as Hong and Espelage note). The closest that schools have come to a social-ecological framework is through adoption of the "whole-school" approaches advocated by Dan Olweus and others. While these approaches are promising, their effectiveness has yet to be fully supported by rigorous social scientific study (see, for instance, Hong and Espelage, 2012). In addition, these approaches do not seem to fully address the macro-systemic issues (e.g., broader sociocultural influences), which are an important aspect of the social-ecological frame.

We agree with the suggestion of Carrera, DePalma, and Lameiras that "the social-ecological model has expanded a narrow focus on the individual to include his or her immediate social contexts, such as family, school, and neighborhood" (2011, p. 488). Henry (2009) articulates a similarly complex approach to understanding school violence more broadly. He suggests an analysis that considers sources of violence at five levels, ranging from individual to societal/cultural. Kochenderfer-Ladd and Troop-Gordon suggest that this focus on context marks a "second generation of peer victimization research" and broadly defines context "to encompass not only physical location and space, but also developmental periods, social environs, and individual characteristics" (2010, p. 221). Similarly, Hong and Espelage expand the notion of context within the perspective of an ecological system theory and suggest that "bullying victims and perpetrators are part of the complex, interrelated system levels that place them at the center and move out from the center to the various systems that shape the individual" (2012, p. 313). Given this more nuanced understanding of bullying, it is actually not surprising to find conflicting evidence of the efficacy of bullying prevention programs. Like attempts to standardize curricula across multiple kinds of learners and educational contexts, the standardization of anti-bullying approaches is doomed to fail. No single, universal model for bullying prevention is likely to emerge when we understand that manifestations of school bullying will vary across time, space, and place.

In order to fully understand the complexity of bullying (as a behavior as well as a set of human interactions and experiences), we must address not only individuals but also the various relationships and contexts within which they operate, their experiences of those relationships and contexts, and the broader sociocultural milieu. While studies of bullying that employ a social-ecological frame suffer from methodological limitations (as do any social scientific studies), they do challenge us to think more holistically about bullying prevention. We suggest that the social-ecological approach serves as a countercurrent to the trend toward simplification that has been discussed throughout this book. In particular, it challenges our attempts to solve the problem of bullying through increased criminalization and a continued emphasis on the individuals involved (i.e., bullies and victims) without attending to the social and cultural contexts through which those individuals experience their sense of self and interact with others. By realizing that bullying is extremely complex and nuanced, we allow educators and others to adopt a wider range of solutions, thus pulling back from automatic, draconian responses. By realizing that bullying has contributing causes at various social levels simultaneously, we allow space for prevention to be targeted at the "right" level, as particular contexts dictate. Moreover, by realizing that bullying should be carefully considered as a complex process, we resist the temptation of domain expansion and thus target the behavior we intend to target, and leave other solutions to those other conditions. In other words, the adoption of a social-ecological framework opens the space for us to define bullying right.

Defining Bullying Right

Perhaps the most important starting point for defining bullying right would be to address the social life of children in more comprehensive ways. In a review of Swedish educational and medical texts, Larsson notes that "aspects or values linked with children and childhood have been discovered, invented, or re-valued at different points" and concludes that "the social life of schoolchildren was discovered around 1970" (2012, p. 121), at the same time that an interest in bullying arose.

In the United States, this "discovery" was delayed a couple of decades, perhaps because interest in bullying in this country did not take hold until the middle to late 1990s, as pointed out at the beginning of this book. We would argue that attention to the social life of schoolchildren is important, but that this attention must be grounded in the lived experiences of those children, from their own perspectives. This means we must take greater account of how children actually experience and construct bullying in their roles as bullies, victims, bully-victims, and bystanders.

School officials seem obsessed with control through one-size-fits-all responses and don't seem very interested in the messiness of children's relationships. Anti-bullying programs frequently miss their mark because they are addressing a problem that isn't quite understood, as bullying is pre-defined and then mathematically assessed from a distance. In measuring the extent of bullying, academic researchers "tell students (and teachers) what bullying is, and what it is not, before they fill in the form" (Duncan and Owens, 2011, p. 306). This is part of an understandable quest for valid and reliable measures, and for generalizability; however, it does not capture children's conceptions of what bullying means to them, what causes it, and what to do about it. Doing better means we have to take kids' points of view seriously (see Oliver and Candappa, 2003, for a sustained discussion). This is admittedly hard to do when zero-tolerance policies are widespread while at the same time claimsmakers suggest that we coddle children too much. As to the latter, the metaphor of the "helicopter parent" is an apt one, because from the seat of a helicopter it's hard to hear children through the noise or see them clearly through the dust being stirred up. Being overly protective and overly punitive takes agency away from children and thus weakens and silences them. Though it may sound trite, the first challenge is to meet children where they actually are, while also trusting in their significant capacity for development.

Listening to children can sometimes expose us to uncomfortable cruelty. That some girls use "slut shaming" as a method to bully other girls who have been sexually assaulted is shocking and disturbing to most adults. And, rightly so, the video of bus monitor Karen Klein being bullied by kids shocked and alarmed us too. However, these incidents are likely less surprising to young people who understand one another's capacity for brutality. Adult claimsmakers sometimes lose touch with—or don't want to believe—the everyday language and behaviors of children. Given the media coverage of bullying, journalist Tai Hernandez's claim that a school bus is "supposed to be a safe haven" for students appears rather naive (ABC's *Good Morning America,* March 30, 2013). Likewise, the Motion Picture Association of America's decision to give the documentary *Bully* an "R" rating due to use of profanity seems to assume that the students' language in the documentary was a bizarre aberration from what children hear every day.

The paucity of deference to the child's viewpoint is felt even in academic research. In recent years, the study of childhood has emerged as a significant research field, with a wide variety of focal areas. Martens, Southerton, and Scott review the extensive literature on childhood consumption and conclude that researchers have focused on documentary and pictorial evidence "rather than investigating children themselves, whether by talking with them [or] through observation" (2008, p. 159). Pascoe echoes the suggestions of youth sociologists to take young people more seriously "as actors in their own social worlds." Specifically, she suggests that use of the term "bullying" infantilizes youth and makes adults blind to the way that bullying reflects "inequalities in larger social structures," and recommends that researchers view the bullying interaction, rather than the individuals involved, as the unit of analysis (2013, p. 95).

An analogous point can be made with regard to research on school bullying. Most research is quantitative and describes the extent of bullying, the correlates of bullying (e.g., age and gender effects), or evaluates the impact of anti-bullying interventions. Qualitative approaches are less common, but can open a door into social lives of children and illustrate their complexity. Thornberg (2011) reviews a number of such studies that employ ethnography, observation, interviews, and focus groups. He notes that besides providing a richness of method, these studies adopt a number of different theoretical perspectives and also help to frame bullying as more than just a psychological phenomenon. Some qualitative studies have also shown that, on the one hand, bullying is sometimes a very subtle phenomenon that might not be obvious or even observable to the uninvolved, such as teachers and administrators, but that, on the other hand, the behavior that school staff might interpret as bullying may be viewed by students as everyday "drama," as researchers Danah Boyd and Alice Marwick point out (see *NYT,* September 23, 2011). These findings could explain, at least in part, why school staff sometimes underrespond or overrespond to bullying incidents. Qualitative studies also tell us that students get rewards from bullying, both social and emotional. Bullying can be a way to achieve status or can even be a method of forming friendships. We would add that students have revealed in interviews that bullying can be exciting and "fun," as Kerbs and Jolley (2007) report in their article "The Joy of Violence." The idea that violence can be pleasurable is in line with both psychoanalytic theory (see Goldwater [2007], an article that is also titled "The Joy of Violence") and cultural criminological theory regarding the "seductions of crime" (Katz, 1988). Importantly, qualitative research reveals that bullies and victims have "careers" that develop in phases over time (see the discussion in Thornberg, 2011). Seeing bullying as a developmental process offers insight into why patterns of bullying—and also why labeling of students as bullies or victims—can become quite entrenched. Last, qualitative methods allow researchers to expose the ways that institutional-level (and larger) structures and processes support or enhance bullying. MacDonald and Swart (2004) conducted an ethnographic study of a primary school and document how a culture of bullying arose from an authoritarian power structure at the school. Similarly, Twemlow and Sacco (2013) suggest that bullying be framed as an indication of dysfunctional school leadership rather than a sign of individual psychopathology. Other research explores the "normative cruelties" at schools and claims that current anti-bullying programs do nothing to address boys' and girls' (sometimes violent) policing of hetero-normativity (Ringrose and Renold, 2010). In short, we should "listen to the children," as one research article is subtitled (Cowie, 2011).

Of course, if we are arguing for a shift toward actively and attentively listening to kids about their experiences with school bullying, we might also suggest seriously considering their ideas when it comes to responding to bullying. Stories of young people challenging bullying in their schools were not uncommon in our news media sample. Young people across the United States are developing and actively engaging in the very kinds of prevention strategies that experts and news media claimsmakers have been calling for. If Maisie Kate Miller is any indication, we may be surprised by the capacity of young people to recognize the complexity of bullying and offer more nuanced and productive responses. Maisie responded to her own victimization by starting an anti-bullying campaign she called "Pigtails for Peace" (NPR's *Tell Me More,* November 30, 2012). After being teased by another girl at school about her looks, Maisie asked her friends via Facebook to support her by wearing pigtails to school. The response was overwhelming and her campaign became "more than a stand against one nasty comment. It's a stand against bullying everywhere."

The fact that she responded to her bullying victimization by rallying the support of friends is not unique. Even the wider response in the school and beyond was not uncommon as bullying garnered ever-greater attention in the news media. However, Maisie didn't stop there. As NPR's Michel Martin pointed out in her interview with Maisie, she "posted a second message at some point in the course of the day, reminding people not to bully the bully." Maisie noted that "people would start to be rude, mean, even some of them were, like, asking me if they wanted me to beat her [the bully] up." Instead of responding through vigilantism, however, this young woman reached out to help protect the very person who had harmed her. As Maisie told Michel Martin, "I immediately felt some kind of remorse because I knew that . . . the next day was going to be a hard day for her." Maisie later found out that the girl had been "going through a really rough time lately," noting "everyone has excuses and I think excuses are fair and I definitely—if I had known what she had been going through, I don't know what I would have done differently, but I'm just glad the bullying had stopped."

Maisie was not the only young person interviewed in the news media who expressed such a clear recognition of the complexity of bullying and its impact. All of us could learn quite a bit from these young people, if only we took the time to listen to their stories and understand their lives more fully. While we don't want to lay the problem and solution at the feet of kids, they clearly lack agency in the current discourse of school bullying. It would be a mistake not to partner with them or free them to creatively engage the problem of school bullying. We would also caution against placing too much of the burden on individual children, due to the risk of engaging in the very same kinds of individualizing we lament throughout this book. Indeed, if our reconsideration of school bullying were to end here, we would be engaging in the same kinds of reductionism we have attempted to bring to light in this book. As we have discussed in some detail here, bullying behavior does not exist in a vacuum. In line with our contextual constructionist theoretical orientation, a social-ecological approach to bullying would also require that we address interpersonal, institutional, and sociocultural contexts. Based on our analysis, we suggest that a more holistic understanding of school bullying would require a focus on several of these contexts.

First, we have little doubt that bullying serves as a mechanism through which cultural ideologies regarding gender and sexuality are enforced. For young girls, bullying serves as a mechanism through which violations of beauty and chastity are policed. Similarly, for young boys, bullying serves as a mechanism through which violations of hetero-masculinity are policed. We cannot expect to fully address school bullying without also reflecting on how parents, schools, news media, and the rest of us contribute to the notion that there is a limited range of ways to do "girl" or "boy."

Second, school bullying must be viewed as connected to, if not a direct reflection of, the kinds of social control employed within schools and elsewhere. If we want children to treat one another with greater compassion and respect, it would follow that we need to model such treatment in the ways we respond to them. Zero-tolerance policies and the criminalization of bullying have the opposite effect. Policies grounded in retributive justice, while seemingly effective in placating parental and public concerns, work to reinforce the notion that those who violate norms (e.g., bullies) deserve to be punished and labeled as outcasts. Is it any surprise, then, that youth who view their peers as violating gender and sexual norms use bullying as a form of punishment?

Finally, we cannot ignore the influence of news media and the expanding anti-bullying industry. The nuance called for by a social-ecological understanding of the complexity of bullying is not very newsworthy. Focusing on individual perpetrators and victims fits more closely with the ways that social problems are constructed by news media, allowing claimsmakers to use language that connects to individual and collective emotionality. For instance, anger targeted at evildoers who victimize vulnerable peers taps into existing emotion cultures surrounding threats from and to children. A focus on the individual also allows claimsmakers to mobilize others in their fight against bullying without having to own up to the notion that everyone (even those they are attempting to mobilize) contributes to the institutional, cultural, and social contexts through which bullying takes place. Constructing bullies as out-of-control villains bolsters calls for expanded social control and an anti-bullying industry grounded in fighting a war on bullying. Not unlike the damaging wars on drugs, poverty, and crime, the war on bullying is supported by a self-perpetuating system of surveillance and control.

Even as of this writing, school bullying continues to be constructed as an increasingly serious social problem—an epidemic. If the current trends in news media discourse continue, we may all find ourselves adrift while experts, academics, and political leaders at all levels struggle to get a handle on the "ever-increasing" dangers of school bullying. As domain expansion continues to occur, prevention efforts take on the form of a Sisyphean feat. As one works to get a handle on current constructions of school bullying, prevention strategies are articulated and build momentum. The problem of school bullying, however, continues to expand and is rebuilt and renovated in ways that challenge the newly established prevention strategies. So, we begin to push the boulder back up the hill, adopting the new problem construction and articulating new prevention strategies. Up and down we go, continuously expanding, retreating, and rebuilding as school bullying is maintained as a serious social problem in need of serious responses. Our argument, however, is not that these claimsmakers are wrong. Quite to the contrary, our point is that everyone is right to some degree. Much academic research shows that bullying can lead to long-lasting negative effects. Adults can be and are burdened by the harms experienced at the hands of those who bullied them as children (see, for instance, Ttofi et al., 2011). However, the causes of bullying exist at every level; therefore, prevention strategies must be implemented at every level. And while we need to partner with children, no longer can we place the full weight of responsibility on the shoulders of children alone.

Note

1. Stories in the *New York Times* did not seem to follow the same progression as in the broadcast media. While the same kinds of explanations were articulated in both, stories in the *New York Times* adopted a variety of explanations earlier and more fluidly. One reason for this difference may be the greater reliance on academic researchers as claimsmakers and more frequent incorporation of research studies as evidence in the *New York Times* stories as compared to in the stories of the broadcast media. In addition, the greater inclusion of scholarly experts led to increased counterclaims regarding the causes of bullying. It seems as though the *New York Times* wrestled with the complexity of explaining bullying to a greater degree than did the broadcast media.

APPENDIX

Methodology

Within this book we apply a social constructionist lens to the development of school bullying as a social problem. From both an interpretivist and realist standpoint, reflexivity is essential. Reflexivity refers to an acknowledgment and meaningful treatment of the researchers' own influence on the research process, from selection of the research topic all the way through the presentation of their findings and discussion of implications for future research and policy. We begin, therefore, with a brief overview of how this project took form. From there, we discuss the specific methods used to collect and analyze the data.

Origins of the Project

This project began as a more focused exploration of media coverage of two bullying-related suicides in Massachusetts. On April 6, 2009, 11-year-old Carl Walker-Hoover Jr. hanged himself in an apparent response to bullying at school. Less than a year later, on January 14, 2010, and fewer than thirty miles away, 15-year-old Phoebe Prince hanged herself, similarly in an apparent response to bullying at school and on the Internet. Two suicides, occurring in relatively close proximity (geographically and temporally), resulted in significantly distinct reactions in media and public discourse.

Media attention surrounding Carl Walker-Hoover's suicide was relatively brief. While his mother, Sirdeaner Walker, worked to turn this tragedy into a force for change, appearing on several national news and popular television outlets (e.g., *Anderson Cooper 360* and

The Oprah Winfrey Show), coverage in the local news media quickly dissipated. Carl Walker-Hoover's case was, however, later returned to when bullying-related suicides came to be linked to one another and to broader concerns regarding bullying as a serious social problem. However, even then, his suicide was sometimes mentioned in passing and with an anonymous reference such as "the 11-year-old boy" (e.g., CNN's *Campbell Brown* and CNN's *Rick's List,* March 30, 2010; NPR's *Morning Edition,* April 10, 2010); in some other cases, facts about him and his suicide were stated incorrectly.

The media narrative around Prince's suicide was quite different. Our original analysis suggests that the local newspapers worked to construct a narrative that fit with the broader frame of ideal innocent victim versus evil perpetrators. The coverage of the circumstances surrounding Prince's suicide was protracted and detailed in comparison to the coverage of Walker-Hoover's as well as other suicides. Over time, the media escalated the language used to describe the bullying, the breadth and depth of harm, and the vitriolic response from community members. Specific bullies were eventually identified and named, and later charged with criminal offenses ranging from harassment to statutory rape. Prince's suicide emerged as a *signal crime* (Innes, 2003), sparking the passage of long-stalled anti-bullying legislation in Massachusetts, and serving as a continuing reminder of the perils of bullying, both at school and online.

While we explore the Prince case and its role as a signal crime in more detail in Chapter 5, we mention it here to help situate the analysis presented in this book. Perhaps most relevant is that our original analysis suggested that news media constructions of incidents weigh as heavily on their evolution as potential signal crimes as do the specific characteristics of the incidents themselves. Moreover, news media constructions of particular incidents can be used as evidence of a growing, worsening social problem. As frames are constructed and then take hold, specific incidents are presented in ways that conform to and reinforce existing narratives. When confronted with discrepant information, those engaged in the discourse can filter out such information, adapt the information in ways that maintain the accepted frame and narrative, or introduce the information as a new or expanding version of what has already been established as a social problem. In this sense, claimsmakers continuously renovate and rebuild social problems in order to maintain relevance in what seems to be a constant stream of competition for public and news media attention. This book presents the results of our attempt to explore these processes by focusing on the construction of school bullying as a social problem by and through news media in the United States.

Data Collection

The data sources in the current analysis were selected through a purposive sampling of national television, radio, and print news outlets in the United States. We focused on national news outlets because our original analysis suggested that bullying had gained momentum as a large-scale social problem requiring national-level policy responses (e.g., the introduction of federal anti-bullying legislation and the convening of hearings by Congress). We also included multiple media in order to capture the influence that a particular medium may have on the construction of the social problem. From television, we focused on the news divisions of ABC, CBS, CNN, Fox, and NBC. From radio we selected *National Public Radio*. And from the print media we selected the *New York Times*. While these are certainly not the only national news media outlets available, we hold that they capture a wide range of perspectives regarding bullying and other topics. We also feel that the national news outlets provided similar kinds of coverage compared to local outlets. This belief was bolstered by a comparison of the coverage of the Prince and Walker-Hoover suicides from our original analysis of the local Boston print news and the coverage in the news media outlets included in the current analysis.

A search of each media outlet was conducted using the Lexis-Nexis database, which provides textual transcripts for newspaper articles and television and radio shows. On Lexis-Nexis, *New York Times* articles are usually "more complete" versions of the story that appeared in print. Also, especially in later years, the broadcast transcripts usually indicated that they were "rush transcripts" and may not be completely accurate. Our timeframe ranged from January 1, 1992, to June 30, 2013. This timeframe was selected after an initial perusal of results from the *New York Times*. We assessed ebbs and flows in coverage and came to the conclusion that prior to 1992 there was relatively little attention given to school bullying in the national media. This starting point also allowed us to capture the influence of major school-related events (e.g., school shootings) on the construction of bullying as a social problem. Once our timeframe was selected, we conducted a search using the following sequence of terms: (bullying) OR (bully) OR (bullies) OR (bullied) OR (cyberbullied) OR (cyberbullying) OR (cyberbullies) AND (school) AND NOT (pulpit).

Articles from the *New York Times* included features, columns, editorials, and letters to the editor, all of which were included in the final sample. For the television and radio outlets, transcripts not associated with what are marketed as "news programs" and those not originally distributed via the corresponding medium were removed. For instance, transcripts from CNN.com were removed, as were transcripts from daytime television shows such as *The Oprah Winfrey Show*. We did, however, include "tabloid news" shows that were originally broadcast on CNN's offshoot network HLN. We refer to HLN shows as CNN because the transcripts did not distinguish between the networks, identifying both as CNN. While we considered eliminating such shows because they do not fit the strict definition of a news program, we decided to include them in the final sample because they help to capture a wider range of media and tend to include a broader range of claimsmakers.

Data Analysis

Our analysis was informed by applications of critical realism to qualitative research. In particular, Maxwell distinguishes between two analytic strategies—categorizing and connecting—relating them to "the distinction between similarity and contiguity." These two concepts

> refer to two fundamentally different kinds of relationships between things, neither of which can be assimilated to the other. Similarity relationships are based on resemblances or commonalities independent of proximity in time or space. Ontologically, similarity relationships are virtual relationships, based on comparison rather than actual connection or influence. Relationships of contiguity, on the other hand, presume, explicitly or implicitly, a real connection or association that is not a matter of similarity. (2012, p. 109)

Categorizing strategies involve traditional approaches to coding in which researchers pull apart their data, apply labels, and categorize those labels in order to draw comparisons between and within categories. We engaged in a categorizing strategy via a thematic content analysis of the textual transcripts. We employed an etic approach, applying a predetermined set of coding categories. The categories were actually an outcome of the original research that led to this larger project, in essence serving as a pilot study. In that research, we employed a more open-ended emic approach to data analysis, through which a distinct set of codes, categories, and themes emerged. We then used those to structure the current analysis. We remained open to additions to or modification of the original categories throughout the analytic process. In this way, we think we were able to balance structure with fluidity in ways that maintained the recursive patterns of qualitative textual analysis. The results of this categorizing strategy form the foundation for Chapters 2 through 5, in which we describe news media constructions of bullies and victims as well as various explanations for school bullying.

Connecting strategies, on the other hand, are focused on "identifying key relationships that tie the data together into a narrative or sequence, and eliminating information that is not germane to these relationships" (Maxwell, 2012, p. 115). Maxwell goes on to contrast these strategies with categorizing strategies: "Instead of segmenting events and then *categorizing* these segments to create a structure of similarities and differences among these, this approach segments the data and then *connects* these segments into a relational order within an actual context" (p. 116, emphasis in original). We employed a connecting strategy by analyzing two specific cases of bullying-related suicide: Phoebe Prince and Tyler Clementi. In each case, we attempted to maintain the structure of the narrative (as constructed in the news media) as well as understand how the narrative connected to broader cultural and social contexts (i.e., gender and sexuality, respectively). We also employed a connecting strategy in analyzing the process through which news media and other claimsmakers went about the construction of school bullying as a social problem. This is the focus of Chapter 7.

Initially, to bolster reliability, each of us separately coded a subset of five transcripts from 1992 and five from 2011. We then compared coding in order to clarify our understanding of the codes and identify any discrepancies. Upon completing our comparison, we recoded these transcripts in order to bolster consistency across coders. We then coded an additional ten transcripts and again compared for consistency. Once we were both comfortable with the application of the coding scheme, the remaining transcripts were distributed between the two of us. Throughout the coding process, when additions and modifications to the original list of codes were warranted, we mutually decided on their inclusion in the analysis.

References

Adorno, T. (1998). *Critical models: Interventions and catchwords*. New York: Columbia University Press.

Altheide, D. L. (1992). Gonzo justice. *Symbolic Interaction* 15 (1): 69–86.

Anderson, E., Adams, A., and Rivers, I. (2010). "I kiss them because I love them": The emergence of heterosexual men kissing in British Institutes of Education. *Archives of Sexual Behavior* 41 (2): 421–430.

Athens, L. H. (1989). *The creation of dangerous violent criminals*. New York: Routledge.

Barbaro, J. A. J., Hernández, J. A. R., Esteban, B. L., and García, M. P. (2012). Effectiveness of antibullying school programmes: A systematic review by evidence levels. *Children and Youth Services Review* 34: 1646–1658.

Bart, M. (1998). Creating a safer school for gay students. *Counseling Today* 26 (September): 36–39.

Bauman, S., and Newman, M. L. (2013). Testing assumptions about cyberbullying: Perceived distress associated with acts of conventional and cyberbullying. *Psychology of Violence* 3 (1): 27.

Beasley, C. (2005). *Gender and sexuality: Critical theories, critical thinkers*. Thousand Oaks, CA: Sage.

Beaty, L. A., and Alexeyev, E. B. (2008). The problem of school bullies: What the research tells us. *Adolescence* 43 (169): 1–11.

Becker, H. (1963). *Outsiders: Studies in the sociology of deviance*. New York: Free Press.

Belknap, J. (2007). *The invisible woman: Gender, crime, and justice*. 3rd ed. Belmont, CA: Thomson Wadsworth.

Berger, P., and Luckmann, T. (1966). *The social construction of reality: A treatise in the sociology of knowledge*. Garden City, NY: Doubleday.

Berkey, B. R., Perelman-Hall, T., and Kurdek, L. A. (1990). The multidimensional scale of sexuality. *Journal of Homosexuality* 19 (4): 67–87.

Best, J. (1987). Rhetoric in claims-making: Constructing the missing children problem. *Social Problems* 34 (2): 101–121.

———— (1990). *Threatened children: Rhetoric and concern about child-victims*. Chicago: University of Chicago Press.

229

———— (2005). Lies, calculations, and constructions: Beyond *How to Lie with Statistics*. *Statistical Science* 20 (3): 210–214.

———— (2012). *Damned lies and statistics: Untangling numbers from the media, politicians, and activists*. Berkeley: University of California Press.

Blumer, H. (1971). Social problems as collective behavior. *Social Problems* 18 (3): 298–306.

Bogard, C. (2003). Explaining social problems: Addressing the whys of social constructionism. In J. A. Holstein and G. Miller (eds.), *Challenges and choices: Constructionist perspectives on social problems* (pp. 187–208). New York: Guilford.

Boydstun, A. E., Hardy, A., and Walgrave, S. (n.d.). Two faces of media attention: Media storms vs. general coverage. Media, movements, and politics working paper. University of Antwerp. http://uahost.uantwerpen.be/m2p /publications/1353093661.pdf.

Buchwald, E., Fletcher, P. R., and Roth, M. (2005). *Transforming a rape culture*. Rev. ed. Minneapolis: Milkweed.

Buckingham, D., and Jensen, H. S. (2012). Beyond "media panics": Reconceptualising public debates about children and media. *Journal of Children and Media* 6 (4): 413–429.

Butler, J. (1990). *Gender trouble: Feminism and the submersion of identity*. New York: Routledge.

———— (2009). Performativity, precarity, and sexual politics. *AIBR: Revista de Antropologia Iberoamericana [Journal of Latin American Anthropology]* 4 (3): i–xiii.

Campbell, M., Spears, B., Slee, P., Butler, D., and Kift, S. (2012). Victims' perceptions of traditional and cyberbullying, and the psychosocial correlates of their victimisation. *Emotional and Behavioural Difficulties* 17 (3–4): 389–401.

Carrera, M. V., DePalma, R., and Lameiras, M. (2011). Toward a more comprehensive understanding of bullying in school settings. *Educational Psychology Review* 23: 479–499.

Casella, R. (2001). *At zero tolerance: Punishment, prevention, and school violence*. New York: Lang.

Centers for Disease Control and Prevention. (1995). Youth risk behavior surveillance—United States, 1993. *MMWR: Morbidity and Mortality Weekly Report* 44 (SS-4): 1–55.

———— (2012). Youth risk behavior surveillance—United States, 2011. *MMWR: Morbidity and Mortality Weekly Report* 61 (SS-4): 1–168.

Charach, A. G., Pepler, D., and Ziegler, S. (1995). Bullying at school: A Canadian perspective. *Education Canada* 35: 12–18.

Chen, L. M., Cheng, W., and Ho, H. C. (2013). Perceived severity of school bullying in elementary schools based on participants' roles. *Educational Psychology*: 1–13. http://dx.doi.org/10.1080/01443410.2013.860220.

Christie, N. (1986). The ideal victim. In E. Fattah (ed.), *From crime policy to victim policy* (pp. 17–30). London: Macmillan.

Cohen, J. W. (2008). Coding gender: Using IMP to construct a content analysis of gender definitions in scientific research. *Journal of Integral Theory and Practice* 3 (2): 129–154.

Cohen, J. W., and Martin, R. (2012). The four dimensions of gender. In D. McDonald and A. Miller (eds.), *Race, gender, and criminal justice: Equality and justice for all?* (pp. 17–34). San Diego: Cognella.

Conrad, P., and Angell, A. (2004). Homosexuality and remedicalization. *Society* 41 (5): 32–39.

Cover, R. (2012a). *Queer youth suicide, culture, and identity: Unlivable lives?* Burlington, VT: Ashgate.

——— (2012b). Mediating suicide: Print journalism and the categorization of queer youth suicide discourses. *Archives of Sexual Behavior* 41: 1173–1183.

Cowie, H. (2011). Peer support as an intervention to counteract school bullying: Listen to the children. *Children and Society* 25: 287–292.

Cullen, D. (2010). *Columbine.* New York: Twelve.

Curtis, L. A. (1973). Victim precipitation and violent crime. *Social Problems* 21: 594–605.

DeJong, W., Schneider, S. K., Towvim, L. G., Murphy, M. J., Doerr, E. E., Simonsen, N. R., Mason, K. E., and Scribner, R. A. (2006). A multisite randomized trial of social norms marketing campaigns to reduce college student drinking. *Journal of Studies on Alcohol and Drugs* 67 (6): 868–879.

Demaray, M. K., Malecki, C. K., Secord, S. M., and Lyell, K. M. (2013). Agreement among students', teachers', and parents' perceptions of victimization by bullying. *Children and Youth Services Review* 35 (12): 2091–2100.

Diamond, L. M. (2003). Was it a phase? Young women's relinquishment of lesbian/bisexual identities over a 5-year period. *Journal of Personality and Social Psychology* 84 (2): 352–364.

Díaz, R. M., Ayala, G., and Bein, E. (2004). Sexual risk as an outcome of social oppression: Data from a probability sample of Latino gay men in three U.S. cities. *Cultural Diversity and Ethnic Minority Psychology* 10 (3): 255–267.

Duncan, N., and Owens, L. (2011). Bullying, social power, and heteronormativity: Girls' constructions of popularity. *Children and Society* 25 (4): 306–316.

Dunn, J. L. (2010). *Judging victims: Why we stigmatize survivors, and how they reclaim respect.* Boulder: Lynne Rienner.

Ellis, L., Robb, B., and Burke, D. (2005). Sexual orientation in United States and Canadian college students. *Archives of Sexual Behavior* 34 (5): 569–581.

Entman, R. M. (1994). Representation and reality in the portrayal of blacks on network television news. *Journalism and Mass Communication Quarterly* 71 (3): 509–520.

Epting, F. R., Raskin, J. D., and Burke, T. B. (1994). Who is a homosexual? A critique of the heterosexual-homosexual distinction. *Journal of Humanist Psychology* 22 (3): 353–370.

Faris, R., and Felmlee, D. (2011). Social networks and aggression at the Wheatley School. University of California–Davis. http://i2.cdn.turner.com/cnn/2011/images/10/10/findings.from.the.wheatley.school.pdf.

Fishman, M. (1997 [1982]). News and nonevents: Making the visible invisible. In D. Berkowitz (ed.), *Social meanings of news* (pp. 210–229). Thousand Oaks, CA: Sage.

Foucault, M. (1977). *Discipline and punish: The birth of the prison*. New York: Vintage.
——— (1978). *The history of sexuality*. Vol. 1. New York: Pantheon.
Fuentes, A. (2011). *Lockdown High: When the schoolhouse becomes a jailhouse*. London: Verso.
Fuss, D. (1989). *Essentially speaking: Feminism, nature, and difference*. London: Routledge.
Gagnon, J. H., and Simon, W. S. (1973). *Sexual conduct: The social sources of human sexuality*. Chicago: Aldine.
Garofalo, R., Wolf, R. C., Wissow, L. S., Woods, E. R., and Goodman, E. (1999). Sexual orientation and risk of suicide attempts among a representative sample of youth. *Archives of Pediatrics and Adolescent Medicine* 153: 487–493.
Ghaziani, A. (2011). Post-gay collective identity construction. *Social Problems* 58 (1): 99–125.
Gibson, P. (1989). Gay and lesbian youth suicide. In M. R. Feinleib (ed.), *Report of the Secretary's Task Force Report on Youth Suicide*, vol. 3 (pp. 110–142). Washington, DC: US Department of Health and Human Services.
Goldwater, E. (2007). The joy of violence. *Modern Psychoanalysis* 32 (1): 20–42.
Gonzalez, F. J., and Espin, O. M. (1996). Latino men, Latina women, and homosexuality. In R. P. Cabaj and T. S. Stein (eds.), *Textbook of homosexuality and mental health* (pp. 583–601). Washington, DC: American Psychiatric Press.
Grattet, R., Jenness, V., and Curry, T. R. (1998). The homogenization and differentiation of hate crime law in the United States, 1978 to 1995: Innovation and diffusion in the criminalization of bigotry. *American Sociological Review* 63 (2): 286–307.
Greenberg, D. F. (1988). *The construction of homosexuality*. Chicago: University of Chicago Press.
Greene, M. B. (2000). Bullying and harassment in schools. In R. S. Moser and C. E. Franz (eds.), *Shocking violence: Youth perpetrators and victims—A multidisciplinary perspective* (pp. 72–101). Springfield, IL: Charles C. Thomas.
Greer, C. (2007). News media, victims, and crime. In P. Davies, P. Francis, and C. Greer (eds.), *Victims, crime, and society* (pp. 20–49). London: Sage.
Griffin, R. S., and Gross, A. M. (2004). Childhood bullying: Current empirical findings and future directions for research. *Aggression and Violent Behavior* 9: 379–400.
Gubrium, J. F., and Holstein, J. A., (2008). The constructionist mosaic. In J. A. Holstein and G. Miller (eds.), *Challenges and choices: Constructionist perspectives on social problems* (pp. 3–10). New York: Guilford.
Gutfeld, G. (2012). *The joy of hate: How to triumph over whiners in the age of phony outrage*. New York: Random.
Haas, A. P., Eliason, M., Mays, V. M., Mathy, R. M., Cochran, S. D., D'Augelli, A. R., Silverman, M. M., et al. (2011). Suicide and suicide risk in lesbian, gay, bisexual, and transgender populations: Review and recommendations. *Journal of Homosexuality* 58: 10–51.

Hacking, I. (1999). *The social construction of what?* Cambridge: Harvard University Press.

———— (2004). *Historical ontology.* Cambridge: Harvard University Press.

Hamburger, M. E., Basile, K. C., and Vivolo, A. M. (2011). *Measuring bullying victimization, perpetration, and bystander experiences: A compendium of assessment tools.* Atlanta: Centers for Disease Control and Prevention, National Center for Injury Prevention and Control.

Hatzenbuehler, M. L. (2011). The social environment and suicide attempts in lesbian, gay, and bisexual youth. *Pediatrics* 127: 896–903.

Heckert, A., and Heckert, D. M. (2002). A new typology of deviance: Integrating normative and reactivist definitions of deviance. *Deviant Behavior: An Interdisciplinary Journal* 23: 449–479.

Henry, S. (2009). School violence beyond Columbine: A complex problem in need of an interdisciplinary analysis. *American Behavioral Scientist* 52 (9): 1246–1265.

Hinduja, S., and Patchin, J. W. (2013). State cyberbullying laws: A brief review of state cyberbullying laws and policies. Cyberbullying Research Center. http://www.cyberbullying.us/Bullying_and_Cyberbullying_Laws.pdf.

Hirschman, A. O. (1991). *The rhetoric of reaction: Perversity, futility, jeopardy.* Cambridge: Harvard University Press.

Hong, J. S., and Espelage, D. L. (2012). A review of research on bullying and peer victimization in school: An ecological system analysis. *Aggression and Violent Behavior* 17: 311–322.

Hoover, J. H., and Stenhjem, P. (2003). Bullying and teasing of youth with disabilities: Creating positive school environments for effective inclusion. *Examining Current Challenges in Secondary Education and Transition* 2 (3): 1–7.

Horton, P. (2006). Bullies and the bullied: The construction of a discourse of blame. Paper presented at the ninth annual Nordic Youth Research Information Symposium (NYRIS) conference, Stockholm, January 12–14, 2006.

Ibarra, P. R., and Kitsuse, J. I. (1993). Vernacular constituents of moral discourse: An interactionist proposal for the study of social problems. In G. Miller and J. A. Holstein (eds.), *Constructionist controversies: Issues in social problems theory* (pp. 25–58). New York: Aldine de Gruyter.

Innes, M. (2003). "Signal crimes": Detective work, mass media, and constructing collective memory. In P. Mason (ed.), *Criminal visions: Media representations of crime and justice* (pp. 51–69). Cullompton, UK: Willan.

Jasanoff, S. (2004). The idiom of co-production. In S. Jasanoff (ed.), *States of knowledge: The co-production of science and social order* (pp. 1–12). New York: Routledge.

Jenness, V. (1995). Hate crimes in the United States: The transformation of injured persons into victims and the extension of victim status to multiple constituencies. In J. Best (ed.), *Images of issues: Typifying contemporary social problems,* 2nd ed. (pp. 213–237). New York: Aldine de Gruyter.

Jewkes, Y. (2011). *Media and crime.* London: Sage.

Justice Policy Institute. (2011). *Education under arrest: The case against police in public schools.* Washington, DC.

Katz, J. (1988). *Seductions of crime: Moral and sensual attractions of doing evil.* New York: Basic.

Kaufman, P., Chen, X., Choy, S. P., Ruddy, S. A., Miller, A. K., Fleury, J. K., et al. (2000). *Indicators of school crime and safety, 2000.* Washington, DC: US Departments of Education and Justice.

Kerbs, J. J., and Jolley, J. M. (2007). The joy of violence: What about violence is fun in middle-school? *American Journal of Criminal Justice* 32 (1–2): 12–29.

King, M., Semlyen, J., Tai, S. S., Killaspy, H., Osborn, D., Popelyuk, D., and Nazareth, I. (2008). A systematic review of mental disorder, suicide, and deliberate self harm in lesbian, gay and bisexual people. *BMC Psychiatry* 8 (1): 70.

Knauer, N. J. (2006). Homosexuality as contagion: From the well of loneliness to the Boy Scouts. *Hofstra Law Review* 29: 401–501.

Kochenderfer-Ladd, B., and Troop-Gordon, W. (2010). Introduction to the special issue: Contexts, causes, and consequences—New directions in peer victimization research. *Merrill-Palmer Quarterly* 56 (3): 221–230.

Kosciw, J. G., Diaz, E. M., and Greytak, E. A. (2008). *The 2007 National School Climate Survey: The experiences of lesbian, gay, bisexual, and transgender youth in our nation's schools.* New York: Gay, Lesbian, and Straight Education Network (GLSEN).

Kosciw, J. G., Greytak, E. A., Bartkiewicz, M. J., Boesen, M. J., and Palmer, N. A. (2012). *The 2011 National School Climate Survey.* New York: Gay, Lesbian, and Straight Education Network (GLSEN).

Kosciw, J. G., Greytak, E. A., Diaz, E. M., and Bartkiewicz, M. J. (2010). *The 2009 National School Climate Survey: The experiences of lesbian, gay, bisexual, and transgender youth in our nation's schools.* New York: Gay, Lesbian, and Straight Education Network (GLSEN).

Kunkel, K. R. (1999). Down on the farm: Rationale expansion as strategy in the anti-vivisection campaign. *Free Inquiry in Creative Sociology* 27(1): 47–55.

Larsson, A. (2012). The discovery of the social life of Swedish schoolchildren. *Pedagogica Historica* 48 (1): 121–135.

Latour, B. (1987). *Science in action: How to follow scientists and engineers through society.* Cambridge: Harvard University Press.

——— (1999). *Pandora's hope: Essays on the reality of science studies.* Cambridge: Harvard University Press.

Laumann, E. O., Gagnon, J. H., Michael, R. T., and Michaels, S. (1994). *The social organization of sexuality.* Chicago: University of Chicago Press.

Law, J. (2004). *After method: Mess in social science research.* New York: Routledge.

Liepe-Levinson, K., and Levinson, M. H. (2005). A general semantics approach to school-age bullying. *ETC: A Review of General Semantics* 62 (1): 4–16.

Lorber, J. (2000). Using gender to undo gender: A feminist degendering movement. *Feminist Theory* 1 (1): 79–95.

Lyons, W. B. T., and Drew, J. (2006). *Punishing schools: Fear and citizenship in American public education.* Ann Arbor: University of Michigan Press.

MacDonald, H., and Swart, E. (2004). The culture of bullying at a primary school. *Education as Change* 8: 33–55.

Magnusson, R. (1990). *Are gays right? Making sense of the controversy.* Colorado Springs: Multnomah.

Marr, N., and Field, T. (2001). *Bullycide: Death at playtime.* Oxfordshire: Success Unlimited.

Martens, L., Southerton, D., and Scott, S. (2008). Bringing children (and parents) into the sociology of consumption: Towards a theoretical and empirical agenda. *Journal of Consumer Culture* 4 (2): 155–182.

Maxwell, J. A. (2012). *A realist approach for qualitative research.* Los Angeles: Sage.

McCabe, P. C., Dragowski, E. A., and Rubinson, F. (2013). What is homophobic bias anyway? Defining and recognizing microaggressions and harassment of LGBTQ youth. *Journal of School Violence* 12 (1): 7–26.

McGregor, J. (2002). Restating news values: Contemporary criteria for selecting the news. Bond University. http://www.anzca.net/component/docman/cat_view/27-anzca-02/28-refereed-proceedings.html?start=5.

McMaster, L. E., Connolly, J., Pepler, D., and Craig, W. M. (2002). Peer to peer sexual harassment in early adolescence: A developmental perspective. *Development and Psychopathology* 14: 91–105.

Messerschmidt, J. W. (2006). Masculinities and crime: Beyond a dualistic criminology. In C. M. Renzetti, L. Goodstein, and S. L. Miller (eds.), *Rethinking gender, crime, and justice: Feminist readings* (pp. 29–43). Los Angeles: Roxbury.

Messner, M. (2002). *Taking the field: Women, men, and sports.* Minneapolis: University of Minnesota Press.

Mishna, F. (2012). *Bullying: A guide to research, intervention, and prevention.* Oxford: Oxford University Press.

Molotch, H., and Lester, M. (1974). News as purposive behaviour: On the strategic use of routine events, accidents, and scandals. *American Sociological Review* 39: 101–112.

Moon, B., Hwang, H.-W., and McCluskey, J. D. (2011). Causes of school bullying: Empirical test of a general theory of crime, differential association theory, and general strain theory. *Crime and Delinquency* 57 (6): 849–877.

Muhib, F. B., Lin, L. S., Stueve, A., Miller, R. L., Ford, W. L., Johnson, W. D., and Smith, P. J. (2001). A venue-based method for sampling hard-to-reach populations. *Public Health Reports* 116 (supp. 1): 216–222.

Muschert, G. W. (2009). Frame-changing in the media coverage of a school shooting: The rise of Columbine as a national concern. *Social Science Journal* 46 (1): 164–170.

Muschert, G. W., Henry, S., Bracy, N. L., and Peguero, A. A. (eds.). (2014). *Responding to school violence: Confronting the Columbine effect.* Boulder: Lynne Rienner.

Nadal, K. L., and Griffin, K. E. (2011). Microaggressions: A root of bullying, violence, and victimization toward lesbian, gay, bisexual, and transgender youths. In M. A. Paludi (ed.), *The psychology of teen violence and victimization,* vol. 1 (pp. 3–22). Santa Barbara, CA: ABC-CLIO.

Nansel, T. R., Overpeck, M. D., Pilla, R. S., Ruan, W. J., Simons-Morton, B., and Scheidt, P. (2001). Bullying behaviors among U.S. youth: Prevalence and association with psychosocial adjustment. *Journal of the American Medical Association* 285 (16): 2094–2100.

Nolan, K. (2011). *Police in the hallways: Discipline in an urban high school.* Minneapolis: University of Minnesota Press.

Norton, M. I., Sommers, S. R., Apfelbaum, E. P., Pura, N., and Ariely, D. (2006). Color blindness and interracial interaction: Playing the political correctness game. *Psychological Science* 17 (11): 949–953.

O'Grady, W., Parnaby, P. F., and Schikschneit, J. (2010). Guns, gangs, and the underclass: A constructionist analysis of gun violence in a Toronto high school. *Canadian Journal of Criminology and Criminal Justice [La Revue Canadienne de Criminologie et de Justice Pénale]* 52 (1): 55–77.

Oliver, C., and Candappa, M. (2003). *Tackling bullying: Listening to the views of children and young people.* Nottingham: Department for Education and Skills.

Olweus, D. (1992). Bullying among school children: Intervention and prevention. In R. D. Peters, R. J. McMahon, and V. L. Quinsey (eds.), *Aggression and violence through the life span* (pp. 100–125). London: Sage.

Olweus, D., and Limber, S. P. (2010). Bullying in school: Evaluation and dissemination of the Olweus Bullying Prevention Program. *American Journal of Orthopsychiatry* 80 (1): 124–134.

Olweus Bullying Prevention Program. (2007). *Recognizing the many faces of bullying.* Center City, MN: Hazeldon Foundation.

Ott, B. L., and Aoki, E. (2002). The politics of negotiating public tragedy: Media framing of the Matthew Shepard murder. *Rhetoric and Public Affairs* 5 (3): 483–505.

Paceley, M. S., and Flynn, K. (2012). Media representations of bullying toward queer youth: Gender, race, and age disparities. *Journal of LGBT Youth* 9: 340–356.

Paimre, M., and Harro-Loit, H. (2011). Media generated news waves: Catalysts for discursive change—The case study of drug issues in Estonian print media. *Journalism* 12 (4): 433–448.

Pascoe, C. J. (2013). Notes on a sociology of bullying: Young men's homophobia as gender socialization. *QED: A Journal in GLBTQ Worldmaking* (inaugural issue): 87–103.

Payne, E., and Smith, M. (2013). LGBTQ kids, school safety, and missing the big picture: How the dominant bullying discourse prevents school professionals from thinking about systemic marginalization, or Why we need to rethink LGBTQ bullying. *QED: A Journal in GLBTQ Worldmaking* (inaugural issue): 1–36.

Pritchard, D., and Hughes, K. D. (1997). Patterns of deviance in crime news. *Journal of Communication* 47: 49–67.

Pritchard, E. D. (2013). For colored kids who committed suicide, our outrage isn't enough: Queer youth of color, bullying, and the discursive limits of identity and safety. *Harvard Educational Review* (Summer): 320–345.

Renold, E. (2002). Presumed innocence: (Hetero)sexual, heterosexist, and homophobic harassment among primary school girls and boys. *Childhood* 9 (4): 415–434.

Reynolds, E. (2005). *Girls, boys, and junior sexualities.* New York: Routledge-Falmer.

Ringrose, J., and Renold, E. (2010). Normative cruelties and gender deviants: The performative effects of bully discourses for girls and boys in school. *British Educational Research Journal* 36 (4): 573–596.

Robbins, C. G. (2008). *Expelling hope: The assault on youth and the militarization of schooling.* Albany: State University of New York Press.

Rust, P. C. (2000). Bisexuality in HIV research. In P. C. Rodriguez Rust (ed.), *Bisexuality in the United States: A social science reader* (pp. 356–399). New York: Columbia University Press.

Salemi, A. M. T. (2006). The social construction of school refusal: An exploratory study of school personnel's perceptions. PhD dissertation, University of South Florida.

Salmivalli, C. (1999). Participant role approach to school bullying: Implications for interventions. *Journal of Adolescence* 22: 453–459.

Sasson, T. (1995). *Crime talk: How citizens construct a social problem.* New York: Walter de Gruyter.

Savin-Williams, R. (2001). Suicide attempts among sexual-minority youth: Population and measurement issues. *Journal of Consulting and Clinical Psychology* 69 (6): 983–991.

Schalet, A. (2006). *Not under my roof: Parents, teens, and the culture of sex.* Chicago: University of Chicago Press.

Schissel, B. (1997). *Blaming children: Youth crime, moral panics, and the policy of hate.* Halifax: Fernwood.

Schoen, S., and Schoen, A. (2010). Bullying and harassment in the United States. *The Clearing House* 83: 68–72.

Schwartz, P., and Rutter, V. (2000). *The gender of sexuality.* Walnut Creek, CA: AltaMira.

Seidman, S. (2005). From the polluted homosexual to the normal gay: Changing patterns of sexual regulation in America. In C. Ingraham (ed.), *Thinking straight: The power, the promise, and the paradox of heterosexuality* (pp. 39–61). New York: Routledge.

Simon, J. (2007). *Governing through crime: How the war on crime transformed American democracy and created a culture of fear.* New York: Oxford University Press.

Smith, P. K. (2004). Bullying: Recent developments. *Child and Adolescent Health* 9 (3): 98–103.

Spector, M., and Kitsuse, J. I. (1977). *Constructing social problems.* Menlo Park, CA: Cummings.

——— (2001). *Constructing social Problems.* Rev. ed. Hawthorne, NY: Aldine de Gruyter.

Spencer, J. W. (2011). *The paradox of youth violence.* Boulder: Lynne Rienner.

Spivak, H. (2003). Bullying: Why all the fuss? *Pediatrics* 112 (6): 1421–1422.

Springhall, J. (2008). The monsters next door: What made them do it? In C. Krinsky (ed.), *Moral panics over contemporary children and youth* (pp. 47–68). Burlington, VT: Ashgate.

Stassen Berger, K. (2007). Update on bullying at school: Science forgotten? *Developmental Review* 27: 90–126.

Sticca, F., and Perren, S. (2013). Is cyberbullying worse than traditional bullying? Examining the differential roles of medium, publicity, and anonymity for the perceived severity of bullying. *Journal of Youth and Adolescence* 42 (5): 739–750.

Stone, D. M., Luo, F., Ouyang, L., Lippy, C., Hertz, M. F., and Crosby, A. E. (2014). Sexual orientation and suicide ideation, plans, attempts, and medically serious attempts: Evidence from local Youth Risk Behavior Surveys, 2001–2009. *American Journal of Public Health* 104 (2): 262–271.

Stuart-Cassel, V., Bell, A., and Springer, J. F. (2011). Analysis of state bullying laws and practices. US Department of Education. http://www2.ed.gov /rschstat/eval/bullying/state-bullying-laws/state-bullying-laws.pdf.

Surette, R. (2007). *Media, crime, and criminal justice*. 3rd ed. Belmont, CA: Wadsworth.

Swearer, S. M., Turner, R. K., and Givens, J. E. (2008). "You're so gay!": Do different forms of bullying matter for adolescent males? *School Psychology Review* 37 (2): 160–173.

Taywaditep, K. J. (2002). Marginalization among the marginalized: Gay men's anti-effeminacy attitudes. *Journal of Homosexuality* 42 (1): 1–28.

Thomas, H. J., Connor, J. P., and Scott, J. G. (2014). Integrating traditional bullying and cyberbullying: Challenges of definition and measurement in adolescents—A review. *Educational Psychology Review* (March): 1–18.

Thornberg, R. (2011). "She's weird!": The social construction of bullying in school—A review of qualitative research. *Children and Society* 25: 258–267.

Timmerman, G. (2003). Sexual harassment of adolescents perpetrated by teachers and by peers: An exploration of the dynamics of power, culture, and gender in secondary schools. *Sex Roles* 48 (5–6): 231–244.

Ttofi, M. M., and Farrington, D. P. (2011). Effectiveness of school-based programs to reduce bullying: A systematic and meta-analytic review. *Journal of Experimental Criminology* 7: 27–56.

Ttofi, M. M., Farrington, D. P., Lösel, F., and Loeber, R. (2011). Do the victims of school bullies tend to become depressed later in life? A systematic review and meta-analysis of longitudinal studies. *Journal of Aggression, Conflict, and Peace Research* 3 (2): 63–73.

Twemlow, S. W., and Fonagy, P. (2005). The prevalence of teachers who bully students in schools with differing levels of behavioral problems. *American Journal of Psychiatry* 162 (12): 2387–2389.

Twemlow, S. W., Fonagy, P., Sacco, F. C., and Brethour, J. R. (2006). Teachers who bully students: A hidden trauma. *International Journal of Social Psychiatry* 52 (3): 187–198.

Twemlow, S. W., and Sacco, F. C. (2013). How and why does bystanding have such a startling impact on the architecture of school bullying and violence? *International Journal of Applied Psychoanalytic Studies* 10 (3): 289–306.

Unnever, J. D., and Cornell, D. G. (2003). The culture of bullying in middle school. *Journal of School Violence* 2 (2): 5–27.

van Dijk, J. J. M. (1999). Introducing victimology. In J. J. M. van Dijk, R. R. H. van Kaam, and J. Wemmers (eds.), *Caring for crime victims* (pp. 1–13). New York: Criminal Justice Press.

Vance, C. (1989). Social construction theory: Problems in the history of sexuality. In D. Altman, C. Vance, M. Vicinus, J. Weeks, et al. (eds.), *Homosexu-*

ality, which homosexuality? Essays from the international conference on lesbian and gay studies (pp. 13–34). London: Gay Men's Press.

Vasterman, P. L. M. (2005). Media-hype: Self-reinforcing news waves, journalistic standards, and the construction of social problems. *European Journal of Communication* 20 (4): 508–530.

Volk, A. A., Camilleri, J. A., Dane, A. V., and Marini, Z. A. (2012). Is adolescent bullying an evolutionary adaptation? *Aggressive Behavior* 38: 222–238.

Waidzunas, T. (2012). Young, gay, and suicidal: Dynamic nominalism and the process of defining a social problem with statistics. *Science, Technology, and Human Values* 37 (2): 199–225.

Walgrave, S., Boydstun, A. E., and Hardy, A. (2011). Testing and explaining the multi-media character of media storms. Paper presented at the annual meeting of the American Political Science Association. http://papers.ssrn .com/sol3/papers.cfm?abstract_id=1901798.

Walgrave, S., and Vliegenthart, R. (n.d.). Are agendas punctuated because of cascades? An empirical assessment of mass media's issue attention in Belgium. Paper presented at the annual meeting of the American Political Science Association. http://webh01.ua.ac.be/m2p/publications/1216814128.pdf.

Walton, G. (2005). "Bullying widespread": A critical analysis of research and public discourse on bullying. *Journal of School Violence* 4 (1): 91–118.

Weiss, A., and Chermak, S. (1998). The news value of African-American victims: An examination of the media's presentation of homicide. *Journal of Crime and Justice* 21: 71–88.

Weitzer, R. (2007). The social construction of sex trafficking: Ideology and institutionalization of a moral crusade. *Politics and Society* 35: 447–475.

White, R. A. (2012). Media reception theory: Emerging perspectives. *Brazilian Journal of Science Communication [Revista Brasileira de Ciências da Comunicação]* 16 (1): 8–21.

Wien, C., and Elmelund-Præstekær, C. (2009). An anatomy of media hypes: Developing a model for the dynamics and structure of intense media coverage of single issues. *European Journal of Communication* 24 (2): 183–201.

Wittman, C. (1970). *Refugees from America: A gay manifesto.* New York: Red Butterfly.

Wolfgang, M. (1958). *Patterns of criminal homicide.* Philadelphia: University of Philadelphia Press.

Woodford, M. R., Howell, M. L., Kulick, A., and Silverschanz, P. (2013). "That's so gay": Heterosexual male undergraduates and the perpetuation of sexual orientation microaggressions on campus. *Journal of Interpersonal Violence* 28 (2): 416–435.

Woodford, M. R., Howell, M. L., Silverschanz, P., and Yu, L. (2012). "That's so gay!": Examining the covariates of hearing this expression among gay, lesbian, and bisexual college students. *Journal of American College Health* 60 (6): 429–434.

Woolgar, S. (2002). Five rules of virtuality. In S. Woolgar (ed.), *Virtual society? Technology, cyberbole, reality* (pp. 1–22). Oxford: Oxford University Press.

Index

241

anti-bullying industry, 179. *See also* Rationale expansion; Substantive domain expansion
Drew, Lori, 207
Duke, Randy, 80
Duncan, Arne, 173, 185

Epidemic: bullying as, 2, 11, 53, 54–59, 71, 73–74, 194
Essentialism: and anti-gay bullying, 145–146; and gender, 21; and gendered bullying, 98, 118–119; and sex-gender dichotomy, 21; and sexuality, 24, 124
Expert claimsmakers: Aftab, Parry, 175, 197; Ali, Russlyn H., 210; Armstrong, Mario, 197; Bazelon, Emily, 6, 76, 203; Belsky, Jay, 76–77; Beresin, Eugene V., 98; Berman, Brigitte, 197; Besen, Wayne, 148–149; Blanco, Jodee, 41, 45, 47, 61; Bliss, Michelle, 153; Bradley, Michael, 88; Bradshaw, Catherine, 196; Brazelton, T. Barry, 40; Byard, Eliza, 148; Cairn, Robert, 76; Capaldi, Deborah, 42; Carlisle, Nicholas, 109; Cohen, Andy, 124; Coloroso, Barbara, 27, 40, 41, 90, 101, 196–197; Chesney-Lind, Meda, 105–106; Connor, Lorraine, 82, 83; Cushman, Candi, 151; Cullen, Kevin, 78; Dacus, Brad, 118; Davy, Lucille E., 58; Diamond, Lisa, 140; Epling, Kevin, 93; Eron, Leonard, 75; Faris, Robert, 13, 48–50; Felmlee, Diane, 13; Fischer, Brian, 159–160; Forrest, Bonny, 74, 174–175, 197–198; Finkelhor, David, 92;

Fowler, David, 152; Gardere, Jeff, 57; Golland, Michelle, 80, 186; Gordon, Karen, 112; Gracie, Rener, 203; Greene, Michael, 78, 94n1; Harmon, Mike, 152; Hartstein, Jennifer, 75, 102; Hess Olson, Laura, 41; Hicklin, Aaron, 134; Hughes, Jan N., 98; Jennings, Kevin, 61–62; Kaslow, Nadine, 192; Kennedy, Kerry, 94n1; Kilodavis, Cheryl, 107; Kilpatrick, Haley, 108; Kraus, Louis, 103; Krever, Thomas, 126; Lamont Hill, Mark, 47, 63, 64, 160; Lance Black, Dustin, 124, 126; Laursen, Finn, 151; Levin, Jack, 170; Lipkins, Susan, 41, 43, 46–47, 65–66, 85, 191, 195; Lowen, Cynthia, 36, 67; Males, Mike, 105–106; Murphy, Wendy, 185; Newman, Robert, 149; Oberschneider, Michael, 42, 85; O'Brien, Rob, 137; O'Donnell, Christine, 148–149; Overline, Jo, 86; Perkins, Tony, 138, 147–148, 151; Peters, Ruth, 198; Peterson, Penny, 98; Pollack, William, 55, 99, 137, 154n2; Prichard, Tom, 138; Prinstein, Mitchell J., 41; Romney, Ronna, 75; Rosenman, Debbie, 75; Saenz, Jonathan, 147; Savage, Dan, 173; Savin-Williams, Ritch, 140, 154; Scheinfield, Rachel, 76; Scheindlin, "Judge Judy," 191; Schlessinger, Laura, 85; Silver, Laura, 89; Simmons, Rachel, 99–100, 102–103, 108, 119n1, 213; Sophy, Charles, 42, 196; Stanton, Dwayne, 193;

About the Book

Is bullying an innocent part of growing up . . . or a serious problem requiring large-scale policy remedies? What is behind our rapidly changing perceptions of "acceptable" behavior? And when is the remedy worse than the problem? In their in-depth view of school bullying, Jeffrey W. Cohen and Robert A. Brooks navigate between empirical evidence and media accounts to make sense of ongoing debates and provide insights into the failure of punitive anti-bullying policies.

Jeffrey W. Cohen is assistant professor of criminal justice at the University of Washington, Tacoma. **Robert A. Brooks** is associate professor of criminal justice at Worcester State University.

Social Problems, Social Constructions

Joel Best and Scott R. Harris, series editors